LIBRARY RESEARCH MODELS

A Guide to
Classification, Cataloging,
and Computers

❧

THOMAS MANN

New York   Oxford
OXFORD UNIVERSITY PRESS
1993

Oxford University Press

Oxford   New York   Toronto
Delhi   Bombay   Calcutta   Madras   Karachi
Kuala Lumpur   Singapore   Hong Kong   Tokyo
Nairobi   Dar es Salaam   Cape Town
Melbourne   Auckland   Madrid

and associated companies in
Berlin   Ibadan

Copyright © 1993 by Thomas Mann

Published by Oxford University Press, Inc.
200 Madison Avenue, New York, NY 10016

Oxford is a registered trademark of Oxford University Press

Library of Congress Cataloging-in-Publication Data
Mann, Thomas, 1948–
Library research models : a guide to classification, cataloging,
and computers / Thomas Mann.
p. cm.   Includes bibliographical references and index.
ISBN 0-19-508190-0
1. Searching, Bibliographical.
2. Information retrieval.
3. Research—Methodology.
4. Research—United States—Methodology.
5. Least effort principle (Psychology)
6. Subject cataloging.
7. Subject cataloging—United States.
8. Subject headings, Library of Congress.
9. Classification, Library of Congress.
I. Title.   Z711.M36 1993
025.5'24—dc20   92-34311

Passages from Jerry Dupont, "De-Romancing the Book,"
Microform Review, vol. 19, no. 4, are reprinted with permission
by K. G. Saur, A Reed Reference Publishing Company.

1 3 5 7 9 8 6 4 2

Printed in the United States of America
on acid-free paper

This book is dedicated to three men
whose names are inscribed on
The Vietnam Veterans Memorial

Charles Mann (39W22)
James Mann (42W70)
Thomas Mann (35W72)

on behalf of my brothers, Charlie and Jim,
and myself

Preface

This book is aimed at two groups of readers. The first consists of those researchers who use large libraries—either university libraries or the larger private or government research facilities—with some frquency. I believe that my experience for the past fifteen years as a reference librarian at just such institutions will be very helpful to them in ways that they may not anticipate. I am convinced that most library users working on their own miss much more of what is actually available to them than they ever realize. This book will explain in some detail just why this is the case and what, specifically, readers need to know in order to avoid the same situation in the future.

In *A Guide to Library Research Methods* (Oxford, 1987) I outlined a basic model of procedures for using research libraries. In the present book I clarify and extend that model by comparing and contrasting it with several alternative models. All researchers work within the horizons of one or another of these mental constructs or frameworks. Each lays out and defines—and usually limits—the range of what users expect from libraries, what questions they permit themselves to ask in the first place, and what they judge to be satisfactory results, that is, results sufficiently acceptable to cause them to terminate their search. Yet few researchers are fully conscious of the limiting effects of the models they assume, or even of the fact that they are working within one model rather than another in the first place.

The second group consists of the professional staff who work in the research libraries. To the extent that librarians are aware they are utilizing one model or framework rather than another in the arrangement of research resources, the possibilities for improving service to users will

increase proportionately. It is sometimes difficult to look afresh at procedures laid out decades ago, and that have now assumed a life of their
own to the point that their original purpose has become obscured. This
book reexamines library systems in general from the standpoint of someone who actually *uses* them on a daily basis—in terms of their strengths
and of opportunities forgone whenever we select or emphasize one
avenue of access rather than another.

I have tried to avoid writing for academic specialists, and I hope that
anyone interested in the ways of organizing or arranging knowledge in
its broadest sense will find some interesting ideas to reflect on in this
discussion. (Fortunately, I have not found it difficult to write for a
general audience; the trick, I believe, is simply to avoid all use of the
terms "paradigm," "interface," "empowerment," and "information
society.")

Portions of this book have been cannibalized from internal papers and
memos written in my professional capacity as general reference librarian
in the Main Reading Room of the Library of Congress. One in particular
(*Cataloging Quality, LC Priorities, and Models of the Library's Future*
[Cataloging Forum, Library of Congress, 1991]) had limited distribution
externally, but since fewer than five hundred copies were actually
printed, I have shamelessly reworked and expanded it for this book.
Another entitled "Subject Searching in a Closed Stacks Library," is a
booklet I wrote four years ago for the Library of Congress, but at the
present writing it still has not been published, so I have used parts of it in
this book. Several other papers have, for the most part, simply vanished
into the black hole that resides at the center of any large federal bureau-
cracy. To the extent that I have borrowed from them, they are seeing the
light of day here for the first time.

I wish to thank Clifford Lynch, Jerry Dupont, and Theodore Roszak for
letting me quote unusually long sections from their very insightful writings; John Andelin, of the Office of Technology Assessment, for releas-
ing a semiburied contractor report; Lynn El-Hoshy for supplying a revised list of form subdivisions; and Cassy Ammen and Art Emerson for
technical help. I also wish to thank the Reverend Avery Dulles, whom I
have never met but whose wonderful book *Models of the Church* (Dou-
bleday, 1974) inspired me to attempt, in the field of library and information science, the kind of analysis he so successfully demonstrated in the
field of ecclesiology.

The opinions and judgments expressed in this book are, of course, my own; they should not be considered the official policy of any organization with which I am or have been affiliated. If they were to become so, I suspect I would die of a heart attack.

Washington, D.C. T.M.
October 1992

Contents

1. The Importance of Models in Concealing
   or Revealing Search Options   *3*

2. The Specific Subject or Discipline Model   *9*

3. The Traditional Library Science Model
   Part One: The Classification Scheme   *15*

4. The Traditional Library Science Model
   Part Two: The Vocabulary-Controlled Catalog   *25*

5. The Traditional Library Science Model
   Part Three: Published Bibliographies and Indexes   *45*

6. The Type-of-Literature Model   *57*

7. The Actual-Practice Model   *75*

8. The Principle of Least Effort   *91*

9. The Computer Workstation Model
   Part One: The Prospect   *103*

10. The Computer Workstation Model
    Part Two: Qualifications   *113*

11. The Methods-of-Searching Model   *151*

12. Implications of the Methods-of-Searching Model   *181*

Appendix 1
Class Z: Arrangement of Bibliographies   *193*

Appendix 2
Form Subdivisions Within the *Library of Congress
Subject Headings* System   *201*

Notes   *215*

Bibliography   *221*

Index   *243*

LIBRARY RESEARCH MODELS

1

The Importance of Models in Concealing or Revealing Search Options

Successful library research is to a large extent a function of the mental set that a researcher brings to the task. A number of different models are available by which one can attempt to understand and structure the avenues of access to the recorded knowledge of humanity. Furthermore, each of these models may be considered from two perspectives: (1) how well it serves as an intellectual framework (that is, as an internal mental road map) in revealing and clarifying the range of sources available; and (2) how well it serves as a principle of arrangement by which actual knowledge records themselves (including terminals for electronic sources) can be brought to a researcher's attention. (For example, does the model result in an arrangement that enables researchers to perceive related sources as a group? Further, which of the many possible relationships does it reveal and which does it blur, ignore, or conceal?)

The first of these two aspects of any research model is an element— often unconscious—of the mental set of the individual researcher; the second is primarily a matter of concern for librarians and other information professionals who must make conscious choices about how to arrange and present physical resources. I must emphasize, however, that it behooves researchers to understand the choices that librarians make, and especially to understand in the first place that they have indeed made choices, for each decision to present knowledge records in a certain way automatically entails several forgone opportunities for presenting the sources in other configurations, and in different relationships.

The mental sets or internal models of procedure that researchers adhere to are especially critical factors because they serve to limit the range of questions that will be asked in the first place. Those who perceive only general sources "out there" in libraries have a strong tendency to limit themselves to asking only general questions. Reference librarians see this all the time. For example, I once helped a woman who initially asked, simply, "Where are your books on English literature?" I had to explain to her that the library in which I work has closed stacks, and that the only books on English literature in open stacks were in the reference collection. "Where are the reference books on English literature?" she then asked. I showed her the volumes in the PR section (English literature) of the Library of Congress (LC) classification scheme, but then took her over to the Z7006 section and showed her the Modern Language Association's *MLA International Bibliography,* the largest index to literary criticism journals. I explained that this index covered over three thousand periodicals, and that it might be a better avenue of access to the scholarly literature if she had a particular author in mind— especially since the manual index was not very good for subject access (other than for an author as subject) prior to 1981. It turns out that she did not have a particular author in mind; and yet I had a strong sense that she was interested in a particular subject which for some reason she would not name, in spite of my attempts to elicit it.

I have learned that, in such cases, it is often useful to leave readers to their own devices for twenty minutes or so and then check back with them to see if they've discovered what they want. Usually, after they've experienced the frustration of browsing through only general sources with no luck, they are then more forthcoming about what they're really trying to find. This woman was not, however. When I again tried diplomatically to ask what she was ultimately trying to find, all she would respond—a bit more narrowly—was that perhaps sources in "nineteenth-century English literature" were what she wanted, but she wasn't sure.

I took a new tack at this point. I have found that most literary researchers have never used the *Arts & Humanities Citations Index* (*A&HCI*), which provides key word access to journal article titles from 1,300 periodicals; so I took the woman from the PR class to the AI3 class, where the *A&HCI* resides, to explain this particular option to her. I told her that this index had an advantage over the *MLA* set in that it would enable her to look for any two particular words to see if they appeared together in the title of some article. "For example," I said, "if you want articles on the Holy Grail, you can look for the exact words 'holy' and 'grail' to see if they appear together." "Oh," she blurted out, "what I really want is material on the image of the 'dark tower' in English literature. But can you really *do* that?"

Well, yes, librarians *can* do that. In this case, once I realized that her ultimate question was amenable to key word searching, I was immediately able to think of several sources that would allow access to relevant records through that method of approach. I made a printout for her from the online *MLA International Bibliography* (which, unlike the hardcopy version, is searchable by means of this approach); this gave us a list of twenty-nine articles. I also searched the *A&HCI* online, and found six articles there, plus four more in the hardcopy version that were not in the database version.

Now, at this point the woman asked me to stop, thinking she had more than enough material to work with. Later on, however, I tried a few other possibilities just to see how much further the subject could be easily pursued. (By "easily," in this case, I mean how large a number of additional likely citations I could find prior to actually reading any of the cited sources, and, from there, pursuing footnotes as an additional avenue of research.) The *Dissertations Abstracts* CD-ROM turned up three "hits" with the words "dark" and "tower" contiguous to each other; and twenty-five books showed up in the library's online catalog, including *The Dark Tower: Nineteenth Century Narrative Poems,* compiled by Dairine Coffey (Atheneum, 1967). I also found two published bibliographies of critical writings on Robert Browning, whose poem "Childe Roland to the Dark Tower Came" is probably the most famous work in English literature on the "dark tower" theme. Each of these two works—Leslie Broughton and others' *Robert Browning: A Bibliography, 1830–1950* (Burt Franklin, 1953) and William S. Peterson's *Robert and Elizabeth Barrett Browning: An Annotated Bibliography, 1951–1970* (Browning Institute, 1974)—has an index that pinpoints criticisms of the "Childe Roland" poem; together they listed sixty-eight sources, the large majority of which had not appeared on any of the computer printouts. (Some of these citations, too, concerned Browning's sources for the poem, which, presumably, would lead to other works, besides his own poem, on the dark tower.) A potential problem for the reader, had she wished to pursue the inquiry to this point, would have been that since each of these bibliographies has a Z8124.5 classification number, she would never have found them by browsing in the PR (English literature) area in general, or even in the PR4200–4248 section specifically on Browning, had she been allowed back in the stacks.

I must note one problem with the key word sources: they sometimes provide the right words in the wrong context. This proved to be the case with several of the items on the computer printouts, both those she actually saw and the ones I found later on my own. The important thing, however—regardless of such "false drops"—is that the woman, working with a reference librarian, quickly found herself in the position of having to cut a large set of potentially relevant sources down to size, rather than having none to look up in the first place.

The point here is simple: this researcher did not start with a conceptual model that afforded her the possibility of doing precise key word searching, and so she would not allow herself to ask the specific question: "Does the library have works on the 'dark tower' theme in English literature?" She perceived her only possible search strategy to be that of browsing through works in the very general category of English literature, and so she permitted herself only to ask for that portion of the stacks. (I suspect, too, that her adherence to this inadequate model was unfortunately cemented by some professor's admonition that she should not have to ask a librarian for help: "You're no scholar if you can't find what you need on your own" is the usual phrasing.) Since her mental set did not enable her to see that it is *possible* to ask an extremely specific question and expect an equally specific answer, she consequently did not *allow* herself to do so. As reference librarians will attest, a large number of people tend to ask not for what they want but for what they think they can get. This is a function of preconceived expectations of what a library can provide, which are usually grossly off target compared to the range and depth of sources that the library actually contains.

Furthermore, this researcher also assumed that the general sources which she expected to be of most help would be grouped together in one area (the PR section of the classification scheme, although she did not come in knowing the precise designation for it) rather than scattered among indexes and bibliographies in the AI3 and Z classes, and among computer terminals in three different rooms (an in-house online catalog, a CD-ROM machine, and a separate terminal for dial-up access to external databases). In other words, the physical arrangement of the library itself contributed to her problem by scattering the relevant sources in ways that were not perceptible to her.

In short, the researcher's conceptual model of how to carry out research—her expectations concerning both how best to search and what she was likely to find—effectively limited the range of questions she would allow herself to ask in the first place. Her expectations did not enable her to perceive the array of sources at her disposal (which, after all, could provide scores of relevant citations); nor did they enable her to perceive the weaknesses of the library's grouping of print sources by a classification scheme which, in this instance, effectively concealed almost all of the most relevant sources, both print and nonprint. As a reference librarian, however, I could perceive the relevant sources easily, once I knew her ultimate question, because I have a conceptual model that allows me to look for groups of sources other than those revealed by physical contiguity in the classification scheme. In this case I knew enough to seek out a collection of sources (both manual and computerized) that permits direct searching for key words, and another group of sources (published bibliographies) that makes possible indirect searching of a large list of potentially relevant citations through key word indexes at the back. I could thus mentally categorize—in advance of actually seeing them in front of me—a number of likely sources, even though the sources themselves were scattered throughout the library's classification scheme, or indeed weren't even *in* the classification scheme.

Since one's mental construct of what is possible has a direct influence in expanding or constricting the range of questions that a researcher allows herself to ask in the first place, librarians need to look more carefully at the strengths and weaknesses of the various available models. Furthermore, we need to consider how the actual arrangements of sources (including computer terminals) established by librarians succeed or fail in revealing to researchers relevant materials that they were not specifically looking for, or could not specify in advance. Finally, we need to consider an improved model that will reveal more options to library users.

2

The Specific Subject
or Discipline Model

Graduate courses on how to do library research are almost always taught along disciplinary lines: anthropologists learn the indexes, databases, and bibliographies appropriate to anthropology; prospective MBAs learn the sources specific to business and economics; psychologists learn the ones appropriate to their subject; and so on.

The advantage of any conceptual model that categorizes sources by subject or discipline is that of depth. An anthropology student, for example, will soon learn that she must go beyond the general sources such as *Readers' Guide to Periodical Literature* and *InfoTrac* which she consulted as an undergraduate to *Abstracts in Anthropology, Anthropological Literature,* and *Annual Review of Anthropology.* Similarly, a graduate student in psychology will learn to use *Psychological Abstracts* (in both hardcopy format and CD-ROM); and the business student will be taught to use *Business Periodicals Index, ABI/Inform, Predicasts F&S* indexes, and a host of other databases and manual sources appropriate to her subject area. Once she learns of these sources, the student, it is hoped, will allow herself to ask more penetrating questions that could never be successfully researched through general sources at the superficial level of *Readers' Guide* or *InfoTrac.*

As good as it is, however—and it is indeed necessary for advanced research—the Subject/Discipline model has major disadvantages in addition to its obvious strengths. The first difficulty is that it must be taught from a specific list of sources appropriate to the discipline. The problem here is that even students who become masters of that list are left helpless in other subject areas not covered by it. In other words, they have not learned how to use the library *as a whole.* In subjects outside

9

their area of specialization, they do not have a mental construct that will routinely allow them to ask questions as detailed, specific, or penetrating as those they would ask within their own discipline. And if they sometimes do have a specific question outside their own subject area, they know of no sources that will enable them to answer it, and so are often simply thrown back to the level of *Readers' Guide* and general browsing.

A related problem is that students taught according to this model also do not realize that works of interest to their own discipline frequently appear within many other disciplines. The anthropology student tends to learn primarily of those sources that have the word "anthropology" in their title, to the neglect of equally or even more useful sources whose application to the subject is not as obvious. My experience as a reference librarian is that students often do not know that the *MLA International Bibliography* provides the best coverage of the folklore journals; that *Psychological Abstracts, Sociological Abstracts, Historical Abstracts,* and *Biological Abstracts* (among many others) often provide better avenues of access to some anthropological topics than do the anthropology indexes; or that the multivolume *International Encyclopedia of the Social Sciences* and *Handbook of Indians of North America* can sometimes provide better introductory articles than the various one-volume encyclopedias specifically on anthropology. Nor do they know that the *Social Sciences Citation Index* (*SSCI*), which tells where any known anthropological (or other) source has been footnoted by subsequent journal articles, even exists—again, because it doesn't have the word "anthropology" in its title. (Other students—in education, business, psychology, urban studies, international relations, and so on—are also unaware of the *SSCI*, for similar reasons.)

It is sometimes amazing how much coverage of a particular subject is afforded by indexes outside the apparent boundaries of a specific discipline. Religion, for example, has its primary indexes in *Religion Index One, Religion Index Two, Religious and Theological Abstracts,* and a few other such titles; and yet articles on this subject can also routinely be found in scores of other indexes and catalogs covering tens of thousands of journals and other sources not indexed by the specifically "Religion"-oriented indexes. Indeed, one may regularly find material under the heading "Religion," or under related cross-references to which that heading refers, in *all* of the following:

Access (a supplement to *Readers' Guide*)
American Book Publishing Record
American Statistics Index
Applied Science and Technology Index
Art Index
Bibliographic Index
Biography Index
Biological and Agricultural Index
Business Index
Business Periodicals Index
CIS Congressional Index
Cumulative Book Index
Education Index
Essay & General Literature Index
Fiction Catalog
Fiction Index
General Science Index
Humanities Index
Index to Legal Periodicals
Index to U.S. Government Periodicals
Legal Resource Index
Library Literature
Magazine Index
Monthly Catalog of U.S. Government Publications
National Newspaper Index
Public Affairs Information Service
Readers' Guide to Periodical Literature
Short Story Index
Social Sciences Index
Statistical Reference Index
Subject Collections (a guide to special collections in libraries throughout North America)

Still more coverage, too, can be found in key word (rather than subject heading) indexes such as the *Arts & Humanities Citation Index, Social Sciences Citation Index, Index to Social Sciences and Humanities Proceedings*, and *Comprehensive Dissertation Index*.

Few of these titles (*Applied Science and Technology Index, Business Periodicals Index*) are such that one would think they pay much attention to religion. But to a surprising extent they do. And that is precisely my point: no subject of any amplitude is confined in coverage to only two or three indexes. Yet the Subject/Discipline model of library research creates the very strong subliminal impression that there *is* such limitation. I have used religion as one example, but I could equally well have used other whole disciplines such as art, business, literature, or psychology, or even more specific subjects such as "The Aged," "Blacks," "Computers," "Shipwrecks," "Developing countries," or "Women." There is always much more coverage of books and articles on a subject than any single list of discipline-specific sources can begin to suggest.

What is true of indexes to journal articles and books is also true of other types of library sources—encyclopedias, for example. I once helped a sociology graduate student who needed to find information about Ibn Khaldun, who had been described to her as "a fourteenth-century sociologist." She was familiar with various sources that are clustered in the HM17 area (Sociology dictionaries and encyclopedias) of the classification scheme; but they provided no information about him. I could see that she was right in trying to find an encyclopedia article; but I could also see that she was blind to the existence of encyclopedias in other subject areas that did not have the word "sociology" in their title. I therefore showed her the multivolume *Encyclopaedia of Islam*, which was of course not on her list of sociology sources, and it proved to have a seven-page article (in small print!) that was right on the button.

Some indication of the astonishing amount of cross-disciplinary coverage within specialized subject encyclopedias is available from a source entitled *First Stop: The Master Index to Subject Encyclopedias* (Oryx Press, 1989). As the title suggests, this single volume is a cumulative index to 430 different encyclopedias in all subject areas, and also to similar sources such as the *Oxford Companion* and *Cambridge Guide* series. One can look up any of forty thousand topics and easily see the range of cross-disciplinary coverage available on each. If one looks up

"Confucius" ("Confucian," "Confucianism"), for example, the references will point to articles in *Cassell's Encyclopedia of World Literature, Westminster Dictionary of Christian Ethics, Encyclopedia of Religion, International Encyclopedia of Education, Dictionary of Demography, Encyclopedia of Bioethics, Encyclopedia of World Art, New Catholic Encyclopedia, World Encyclopedia of Peace, International Encyclopedia of Higher Education, Footnotes to World History,* and *World Philosophy: Essay Review of 25 Major Works.*

Similarly, if one looks up "Dance" in the same index, the references will lead to *Encyclopedia of Physical Education, Fitness, and Sports,* to the *New Grove Dictionary of American Music, Encyclopedia of Religion, Dictionary of American History, Dictionary of the Middle Ages, Encyclopedic Dictionary of Semitics, Encyclopaedia Judaica, International Encyclopedia of Education, International Encyclopedia of Higher Education, New Catholic Encyclopedia, Encyclopedia of Practical Photography, American Handbook of Psychiatry, Concise Encyclopedia of Psychology, Funk & Wagnalls Standard Dictionary of Folklore, Mythology and Legend, Handbook of North American Indians, Harlem Renaissance: A Historical Dictionary of the Era, Encyclopedia of the Biological Sciences, Encyclopedia of Sexual Behavior, Cambridge Encyclopedia of Russia and the Soviet Union,* and many other sources as well.

What holds true for indexes and encyclopedias is also true for directories. Students in particular disciplines will learn about the *Directory of American Philosophers* or the *Directory of Historical Societies and Agencies in the United States and Canada* or *Who's Who in Engineering;* but the narrow focus of such specialization often blinds them to the existence of the *Encyclopedia of Associations, Directories in Print, National Faculty Directory,* or *Faculty Directory of Higher Education.* Again, sources relevant to any discipline that do not have the name of a particular discipline in their title tend not to be included on the lists of references given to students within particular subject areas. It then becomes very difficult for such students to see beyond these lists, as they assume that they have been told "everything" they will need to know; furthermore, they are frequently told in explicit terms that scholars should not have to ask for help from librarians.

As I mentioned earlier, the advantage of the Subject/Discipline model is that it provides researchers with an in-depth knowledge of sources specific to their subject area. A particular advantage here is that such lists sometimes include sources that fall between the cracks of the categories devised by librarians. For example, the *Human Relations Area Files,* which is a huge microfiche set of source material that seeks to document comparatively some six hundred aspects of each of over three hundred cultures, is unique to the field of anthropology. It does not fit into any of the "type of literature" categories (see chapter 6) that would enable a naive researcher outside the field to predict its existence. Similarly, the *CIS Congressional Index* in the field of public policy includes a special section on legislative histories whose existence could not be predicted as a type of literature. And so I do not mean to suggest that teaching or learning library research by subject or discipline is a bad thing; I do mean to suggest, however, that it is not an unqualified good thing. While solving some problems of access, it inevitably creates others.

The first of these problems, again, is that it leaves researchers helpless in dealing with subjects in fields outside their own, for it does not enable them to perceive the library as a whole, with predictable systems of access in all subject areas. Second, in concentrating on a particular list of sources within a discipline, it blinds researchers to the existence of cross-disciplinary coverage of the same subject from the perspective of a wide range of sources in other fields. And third, the dependence of this model on lists of particular references leaves researchers at a loss as those lists inevitably become outdated.

Unlike lists of particular sources, *principles* of searching endure; but the Subject/Discipline conceptual model is singularly deficient in principles and rules. It leaves people with no "fall-back" procedures to employ when the specific sources they know about fail them. (The procedures to which they actually do resort in such cases make up the Actual-Practice model, discussed in chapter 7.)

3

The Traditional Library Science Model

Part One:
The Classification Scheme

The conceptual model of research that is based on knowledge of sources within specific disciplinary areas has its parallel in the physical model by which libraries arrange books on their shelves and thereby reveal to researchers something of the extent of what is available to them. Shelf arrangement in libraries is conventionally by subject. The purpose of a library classification scheme such as the Library of Congress Classification (LCC) or the Dewey Decimal Classification (DDC)[1] is thus to arrange printed books in topical or disciplinary categories (i.e., to position volumes treating the same or similar subjects next to one another). The result, ideally, is that a researcher can then browse through *full texts*—not just brief catalog records representing those texts but the texts themselves—in a *systematic* fashion. Such an arrangement provides much greater depth of access to the actual contents of the books than does a card or computer catalog consisting merely of brief surrogate records representing the books. (And at a time when more and more people believe that they can get "everything" from a computer, perhaps a reminder is in order that even catalog or indexing records with abstracts are not nearly as informative as the full texts themselves, most of which cannot be computerized because of very real legal, economic, and preservation impediments [see chapter 10].)

In addition to providing *depth* of access, the physical contiguity of full texts also adds the feature of *serendipity* to searching; that is, it enables one to *recognize* relevant books whose titles, or indeed contents, are phrased so idiosyncratically that they could not be specified in advance by a researcher trying to find them by means of an index file of surrogate catalog records.

The advantages of a subject classification scheme stand out in greater relief if we consider possible alternative methods of shelving books. One is arrangement alphabetically by author. Bookstores frequently use a variant of this approach, first dividing their stock into very broad subject categories (General Fiction, Mysteries, General Nonfiction, History) and then subarranging the categories by authors' names. This is a relatively inexpensive way to bring related books to customers' attention; the problem, however, is that its effectiveness diminishes rapidly with the size of the collection. In a category such as "Social Sciences" in a large secondhand bookstore, for example, Harry Gideonse's *Against the Running Tide* may wind up a whole aisle away from the book to which it is responding, Robert Hutchins's *Higher Learning in America;* and Mortimer Adler's *Philosopher at Large,* which comments on both Hutchins and Gideonse, will be shelved ever farther away simply because of the scattering occasioned by alphabetical filing.

Another alternative method of arranging books is simply by physical size. If all 22 cm books are shelved together in one area and all 25 cm books in another, and so on, then bookshelves can be adjusted very precisely so that there is no wasted space. The books can then be labeled with a simple whole number sequence (1, 2, 3 . . .). As long as a separate catalog of the books exists somewhere, and is itself arranged in some predictable, nonrandom order (e.g., the conventional arrangement by author, title, and subject), then, presumably, the volumes can still be identified and retrieved from the shelf sequence. Furthermore, the considerable expense of reshifting an established sequence because of unanticipated growth in certain subject areas can be entirely avoided: instead of having to interpolate new books into decimally designated interstices in the sequence (1, 1.2, 1.24, 1.26, 1.268, 1.2685, 1.3, 2, 2.1, 2.15, 2.154, 3 . . .), one can simply add any new volumes to the end of the sequence by adding new whole numbers. Moreover, the space costs of having to leave room for such internal growth—over and above the costs of actually doing the shifting—can also be avoided.

Such a random arrangement of books does not theoretically prevent them from being found as long as a nonrandom catalog of the books exists and is keyed to the numbers on the books. This physical configuration, however, does preclude the *systematic* examination of *full texts* because the corresponding catalog can provide systematic access only to the very short catalog records, which can never contain as much browsable information as the books themselves.[2] A few examples may confirm the point.

For a question regarding Abraham Lincoln's pocket knives, I once found useful information in Carl Sandburg's *Lincoln Collector: The Story of Oliver R. Barrett's Great Private Collection* (Harcourt, Brace, 1949); but I could locate the book itself only by browsing the LC classification scheme in the E457 (Abraham Lincoln) area of the stacks. I could not find anything specific on Lincoln's knives in either the card catalog or LC computer catalog, as none of the nonfiction catalog records had both the word "Lincoln" and the word "knife" (or "knives") together. The catalog records simply do not indicate the full content of the books.

For a question on the Civil War ironclad *Barataria,* I found numerous references to the ship in the E591 area of the stacks, which generally corresponds to the catalog heading "United States—History—Civil War, 1861–65—Naval operations." The catalog itself, however, contained no specific references to the *Barataria* which led to precise pages in any of the voluminous E591 material. I simply had to browse the full texts directly because the catalog records were inadequate.

A theology specialist once needed a brief description of an old hundred-volume set called *Corpus Reformatorum,* which is a collection of writings of the Protestant reformers. I eventually found two works each of which contained a one-paragraph description that was right on the button (one was in English, the other in German). I did so by going to the BL class area (Religion) of the reference collection and looking through many different encyclopedias and dictionaries of religion and theology. Since most of these did not mention the *Corpus* at all, there was no way that I could have identified in advance which of the many volumes I consulted had the necessary information, for their surrogate catalog records—even when searched by key word—simply did not contain that depth of information.

For a biographer who needed information on society's attitudes toward traveling saleswomen in the early years of the twentieth century, I had to browse through many volumes in the HF5541 ("Commercial travelers" and "Traveling sales personnel") area of the stacks. I eventually found a few articles that were right on target in a couple of old magazines published for salesmen at the time, *Commercial Travelers Magazine* and *Sample Case.* Again, the library's catalog could not indicate which of the hundreds of volumes in the HF5541 class area had the precise information I needed; it could only get me to the right general area. *Only* systematic browsing of full texts could turn up the desired information.

The point that catalog records—even those exceptional ones with content notes or abstracts—are simply not the same as full texts is worth belaboring, as it is sometimes overlooked even by librarians, and is even more frequently overlooked by some information scientists.

Given, then, that comparatively brief catalog records cannot possibly convey to a researcher the full range and depth of information contained within the books they represent, it is necessary that a method of access be provided that does offer *systematic* (rather than random) access to *full text* features (tables of contents, back-of-the-book indexes, illustrations, chapter subdivisions, individual paragraphs, sentences, and even specific words). Moreover, it is desirable to be able systematically to search full texts in a way that does not necessitate the payment of stiff copyright or royalty fees to publishers or database vendors every time those texts are consulted (see chapter 10).

It is a library's classification scheme for books on the shelves that provides precisely this kind of systematic, royalty-free, in-depth access.

It is immediately obvious, however, that the universe of knowledge records has changed considerably from what it used to be around the turn of the century when the LC and Dewey classification schemes were devised. At that time this universe was understood to consist almost entirely of *books,* and the class schemes were devised with that format of knowledge record in mind. Moreover, the system designers of the time had a different set of assumptions regarding the "departments of knowledge" than we have today. Eric Coates, writing in 1960, makes the point in a comment regarding Charles Ammi Cutter, one of the great library systematizers at the turn of the century.

> To appreciate fully Cutter's viewpoint on this we must bear in mind the half century which now separates him from us. The expression "distinct subject" had more meaning to Cutter and his contemporaries than it can have to us. At the time knowledge still consisted of a number of accepted spheres of thought, each comfortably separate from the others. Subjects were islands of knowledge separated from one another by oceanic voids. This was a great convenience and aid to tidy minds, no longer, alas, available. In our day the various islands have become so thoroughly interconnected that it is often very difficult to see any ocean at all. In fact, the geographical metaphor has to give way to a biological one. Any

subject may impinge upon almost any other and the chances are that such a union will produce a brand-new offspring. (p. 32)

Fritz Machlup notes an analogous concern with "departmentalizing" knowledge in universities during the same period.

> Departmentalization of faculties of liberal arts and sciences was not common until the last decade of the nineteenth century, but was so widespread by the first decade of the twentieth century that a university's reputation came to depend on the excellence of its departments in various disciplines. . . . Departmental structures of faculties of liberal arts and sciences have thus served, at least since the turn of the century, as the principal form in which universities have recognized the autonomy of disciplines as separate branches of learning. (1982:151)

Although the departmentalization of knowledge into separate subjects and disciplines which took place at the beginning of the century persists at the end of it, we are now more aware of the inadequacies, as well as the still valid strengths, of such modeling.

Perhaps the change in perspective is most noticeable in museum displays. When one visits Harvard's Museum of Comparative Zoology, one is immediately aware that its exhibits embody a nineteenth-century perspective on what constitutes the knowledge that ought to be conveyed. One finds, simply, isolated stuffed animals labeled and displayed in separate glass cases. Nowadays, of course, any modern museum with a stuffed hippopotamus would display it in a diorama setting that shows not just the size, shape, and color of the animal itself, but also the whole environment in which it lived, complete with grass, trees, shrubbery, a painted river extending in the background, the birds, insects, and other creatures surrounding it, and some sense of familial or herd relationships within the larger hippopotamus species. (Undoubtedly, too, some museums will offer a button which can be pushed to enable the visitor to hear a tape recording of the *sounds* of the water hole.)

The categorizations and departmentalizations by subject that are represented in a library classification scheme created a century ago reflect shortcomings similar to those of old museum displays—except that major corrections to the inadequacies of a class scheme (that is, those needed to supply the missing linkages and connections) must come mainly from alternative avenues of access to knowledge records (separate catalogs, indexes, databases) that *supplement* the shelving scheme, rather than primarily from enchancements to the classification scheme itself. For the fact is, as long as libraries must continue to deal with knowledge records that appear in physical containers known as books, the placement of such objects next to one another must be accomplished under severe constraints that are inherent in *any* classification scheme, whether it be Library of Congress, Dewey Decimal, Universal Decimal, Bliss, Colon, or any other.

Some of the constraints reflect changes in judgment regarding the relationship or subordination of one subject to another. For example, when the LCC scheme was created at the turn of the century, the state of Czechoslovakia did not exist. Books on that region of Europe (Bohemia) did exist, however, and those on its description and history were given DB196 class numbers, indicating material on a province or region of Austria. After Czechoslovakia became a state in 1918, however, the same class number continued to be used. Catalogers did not wish to separate newer works on that region of Europe from older works, as they all had a common "subject" in spite of the name change.

The political alteration, combination, and fragmentation of central Europe, including Czechoslovakia, throughout the century has inevitably multiplied such problems for library catalogers. Indeed, the problems continue even as this book is being written. Should the physical relationship of books on the shelves continue to reflect political relationships that have undergone massive changes? Should the arrangement of books about states, relative to one another, be patterned on a map of Europe that no longer exists? (Similar problems are reflected in Africa: creating a new class number for a newly independent state can hide from shelf browsers the area's history before independence, shelved in a different class.)

In 1978 the Library of Congress essentially threw up its hands and said, in effect, "Let's start over with Czechoslovakia." Since that year, books on that country's history and description have been classed in DB2011 rather than DB196. The change is that Czechoslovakia now stands on its own, and books about it no longer reflect, *in their physical position on the shelves,* a former relationship of subdivision to Austria.

The concomitant change, of course, is that shelf browsers now have two widely separated areas in which to look for books on this region of Europe. It is a very expensive operation (over seventy-five dollars per volume) to catalog—or recatalog—a book; and, consequently, changes in a classification scheme as a rule do not entail the reclassification of books already on the shelves. Nor can libraries afford to buy multiple copies of the same book and give each a different class number so that shelf browsers may discover it in all of its possible relationships to other books. So each book gets—and keeps—only *one* number within the scheme.[3]

Along with changes in the way a classification scheme treats books on a subject, there is additional—and inevitable—scattering of works on the same subject brought about by the fact that one topic may have many different *aspects* (organizational, philosophical, psychological, historical, numismatic, philatelic, biographical, geographical, social, sociological, economic, political, legal, educational, musical, artistic, literary, fictional, dramatic, poetic, scientific, statistical, technological, military, bibliographical, and so on). And the several different aspects of the same subject may wind up in entirely different areas of the classification scheme.

For example, some books on the subject "Television graphics" are classed, in the LCC system, in the NC area of the stacks, indicating works on "Drawing, design, and illustration" as a subgroup of "Fine arts." About an equal number appear in PN1992, the "Television broadcasts" subdivision of "Drama." Yet another book, *Graphic Design in Educational Television,* appears in LB1044.7, which is the "Television" section of "Visual aids" as an aspect of "Teaching (Principles and practice)." It is likely that a researcher interested in this subject would want to be apprised of the existence of all of these works; and yet any researcher who located one of these classes alone would miss more than he found, and without realizing that he'd missed anything. (There are no cross-reference indications in a library's bookstacks.)

Similarly, a student of English literature who is interested in the Romantic essayist William Hazlitt may mistakenly think that he will find "everything" about the writer in PR4773, the literature class that contains, among other things, Hazlitt's *Complete Works.* Hazlitt, however, wrote on many different topics, and his individual books—apart from their one appearance together in the collected set of his writings—are scattered throughout the classification scheme according to subject. Thus his biography of Napoleon appears not in PR4773 (Hazlitt as subject) but rather in DC203 (Napoleon), and his *Reply to Malthus* appears in HB863 ("Malthus" within "Demography"). What is important to a literature student is that critical works about Hazlitt's writings on these topics appear with the respective subjects in the class scheme, and not in PR4773. Thus, Robert Robinson's *William Hazlitt's Life of Napoleon: Its Sources and Characteristics* has a DC203 class number, and W. P. Albrecht's *William Hazlitt and the Malthusian Controversy* is in HB863. A further complexity for the student arises from the fact that all bibliographies about Hazlitt appear in class Z8394.4; and since these are indispensable in listing the various and widespread critiques of the author, the student who browses PR4773 alone will, again, miss more than he finds without realizing he's missed anything.

Although the examples I provide are exclusively from the Library of Congress classification scheme, the same problems are inherent in any library classification system for placing books on the shelves in subject groupings. A single book may have various aspects that would make it useful to researchers browsing in several different areas of the stacks, in quite different subject categories. Yet each book can be given only one call number; and no library can afford to buy multiple copies of a single book and give each copy a different class designation.

Barbara Christian's *Black Women Novelists* (Greenwood, 1980) illustrates the problem faced by any classification scheme: if the book is cataloged in the "American fiction" section of the stacks (PS), then shelf browsers in the primary "Afro-Americans" (E185) or "Women" (HQ1101–2030) areas will miss it. But if it goes into either of those areas, then browsers in "American fiction" will miss it. The same book cannot be put in three places even though it may be of interest to three different groups of searchers. Classifiers simply have to make a choice. Unfortunately, most researchers who use the class scheme for browsing purposes are unaware of how very many such choices have been made.

The problems of pursuing research in a Subject/Discipline model embodied physically in a classification scheme that groups books together by subject are thus analogous to the problems this model entails simply as a mental construct: (1) the model makes it very difficult to see outside or beyond the subject the researcher begins with; (2) the model conceals rather than reveals the multidisciplinary range of the subject's various aspects; and (3) the groupings of a class scheme, like the list of references "covering the subject" given as a guide to students, are themselves apt to become outdated in the relationships they display and in the separation of recent materials from older works if the scheme is changed.

These problems obtain in any system devised for organizing a large collection of books on shelves. Further problems are added when the scheme is called upon to house or contain knowledge records that are not monographic. The subject content of most journal articles, for example, cannot be adequately revealed by a classification scheme for one obvious reason: a long run of bound volumes of the journal may contain articles on thousands of subjects (often dozens within a single issue). The individual articles cannot be separated and individually interfiled among the books; and the entire aggregate of articles formed by the full journal set can receive only one class number within the system.

Indexes to journal articles (e.g., *Readers' Guide to Periodical Literature, Biological Abstracts, Social Sciences Citation Index*) present an even greater problem: each index may cover hundreds or even thousands of journals, and so has a logical subject relationship with each one, and even with each different subject *within* each journal. Browsers who are examining the journal sets themselves could thus profit from having the index placed adjacent to each set that it indexes. But this is a physical and economic impossibility. One result is that most researchers routinely neglect the journal indexes, as their existence is concealed rather than revealed to people who are using the subject groups defined by the shelf scheme.

Neither can the classification system reveal the contents of knowledge records in formats that cannot be interfiled with books (microforms, sound recordings, newspapers, motion pictures, photographs, posters, CD-ROMs, dial-up databases, and so on). The operation of the class scheme as a subject-access tool is predicated on the assumption that anything within it can be easily *browsed* in relation to its neighbors; and so those physical formats that do not allow browsing must be accommodated elsewhere.

An inevitable problem follows, then: when their own mental sets expect nothing more than a Subject/Discipline arrangement of records, researchers tend too readily to accept the classification scheme's array as the entire universe of what is available. Those knowledge records that are concealed within the scheme (unperceived because of widespread scattering of the subject's many aspects) or those that are entirely omitted from it (either not interfiled with the books, or not even present within the library) tend as a consequence to be disproportionately overlooked.

The problem, then, is not merely that a subject classification scheme can no longer be considered the primary model or universe within which library research is done; that is too simple an assessment. The complicating factor is that most researchers are themselves still thinking only in terms of *subject-content* arrangements of sources for research. When they come into libraries, then, the Principle of Least Effort (see chapter 8) induces them to follow the only path they see (the subject approach as created by the class scheme), which appears to embody the one avenue of access they *expect* to see.

Other models do exist besides the Subject/Discipline "universe"— indeed, it is the purpose of this book to spell out what they are—but they aren't as obvious, and for that reason alone the classification scheme's arrangement of books in subject groups continues to exert a powerful pull on researchers. Moreover, the scheme does indeed continue to be useful—often indispensable—because it provides an avenue for the systematic examination of full texts, most of which cannot be duplicated in any database. Computers can provide such access to only a very limited extent, in comparison with the volume of printed sources that continue to be produced, for the mounting and searching of full texts in electronic form entails the payment of copyright royalty fees to the text producers each time they are used. Economic and legal realities—which are just as important in the total system of access as are engineering capabilities— effectively prevent databases from replacing classification schemes for printed volumes.

As much as a subject-class scheme is still necessary, however, it cannot be considered the whole of the universe in which researchers must work. It must be seen, rather, as *one element* in a still larger model or universe. Some, though not all, of the additional necessary elements of this larger model may also be found in what I call the Traditional Library Science model. At this point, however, I continue the discussion of this model exclusively in terms of the Library of Congress version of it (rather than the Dewey Decimal, Bliss, Colon, or other forms) because the LC model has been found to be the most capacious class scheme for accommodating the growth of large collections (i.e., those in research libraries rather than, say, small public libraries). Moreover, the LC model is much larger than the classification scheme alone—a point that is sometimes misunderstood even within the library and information science community. It actually has three components, each of equal importance to the proper functioning of the whole system. And the other two elements—a vocabulary-controlled catalog and a specially emphasized collection of published bibliographies and indexes—go a long way toward correcting the defects of the class scheme component.

4

The Traditional Library Science Model

Part Two:
The Vocabulary-Controlled Catalog

A library's catalog of its holdings (whether computerized or in card format) is the second element of the Traditional Library Science model, and it can be viewed in two ways. On the one hand, it can be seen by itself as a more or less complete "universe" or model by which the totality of a library's book records are organized in a predictable manner. (Nonbook records will be discussed later.) This function is evident in those libraries, such as remote storage facilities, that do not have any subject ordering of books in the stacks, but where shelf arrangement is determined by size of volumes or by recency of acquisition. Here, systematic subject access is provided not by the shelving of volumes in a classification scheme but rather by subject cataloging of the books. More precisely, the catalog provides systematic and predictable paths of access *to catalog records representing the books,* not to the full texts themselves. These catalog records are then linked to shelf-location marks *on* the books which allow the texts to be found within the storage scheme, even when the latter is not itself arranged by subject.

On the other hand, when the library also has a classification scheme arranging the books by subject on the shelves—and this is the usual pattern in research libraries—then the catalog can be seen as having the additional function of serving as the *index* to the subject categories in the shelf arrangement. And in this capacity it corrects many of the defects and shortcomings that are inherent in the classification scheme alone.

A major virtue of a library set up according to the LC system, then, is that its catalog functions both independently of the class scheme to reveal relationships or groupings that the shelf arrangement cannot show and also in concert with it as its index, thereby enabling the various class groupings within the scheme to be identified in the first place (and then browsed) much more efficiently.

The *system* of the catalog is created by vocabulary control of entries within it, and this "control" extends to authors and titles as well as to subjects. Basically this system may be understood as a formal mechanism for grouping together under one term the many synonyms, variant spellings, or variant phrasings referring to a single concept that would otherwise be widely scattered in an alphabetical or key word arrangement. The essence of the system lies in its creation of predictable categorizations. The predictability of which categorizing terms have been selected is a function of the cross-reference structures leading to them. (See chapter 10 for a fuller discussion).

One function of the catalog is thus to establish a standardized form for every author within it so that each author's works will be grouped together in one place. The idea is to prevent the scattering that would result if, for example, some books appeared under "Mark Twain" while others were filed under "Samuel Clemens" (or "Clemens, Samuel").

The existence of pseudonyms is not the only problem, however. Sometimes the literature simply contains variant spellings of the same name. An extreme example is provided by "Muammar Qaddafi." The Library of Congress, which collects material from all over the world, has received works by and about him with all of the following spellings:

> Qaddafi, Muammar
>
> Gadhafi, Mo ammar
>
> Kaddafi, Muammar
>
> Qadhafi, Muammar
>
> El Kadhafi, Moammar
>
> Kadhafi, Moammar
>
> Moammar Kadhafi
>
> Gadafi, Muammar
>
> Mu ammar al-Qadafi
>
> Moamer El Kazzafi
>
> Moamar al-Gaddafi
>
> Mu ammar Al Qathafi
>
> Muammar Al Qathafi

Mo ammar el-Gadhafi
Muammar Kaddafi
Moamar El Kadhafi
Muammar al-Qadhafi
Mu ammar al-Qadhdhafi
Qadafi, Mu ammar
El Kazzafi, Moamer
Gaddafi, Moamar
Al Qathafi, Mu ammar
Al Qathafi, Muammar
Qadhdhafi, Mu ammar
Khaddafi, Muammar
Muammar al-Khaddafi
Mu amar al-Kad'afi
Kad'afi, Mu amar al-
Ghaddafy, Muammar
Ghadafi, Muammar
Ghaddafi, Muammar
Kaddafi, Muamar
Quathafi, Muammar
Gheddafi, Muammar
Muammar Ghaddafy
Muammar Ghadafi
Muammar Ghaddafi
Muammar Al-Kaddafi
Muammar Quathafi
Muammar Gheddafi
Khadafy, Moammar
Qudhafi, Moammar
Qathafi, Mu'Ammar el
El Qathafi, Mu'Ammar

Kadaffi, Momar

El Gaddafi, Moamar

Moamar el Gaddafi

The Library's catalog chooses *one* of these forms (Qaddafi, Muammar) and then groups together all of the variations under this one spelling—and also provides cross-references leading to it—so that researchers themselves do not have to expend the effort of thinking up all the different forms to achieve complete retrieval. Note that the catalog, in creating standardized author groups, thereby reveals a relationship among knowledge records that is not displayed by the classification scheme, which scatters an author's works according to *subject*.

Similarly, the catalog serves to "control" titles, which often show more variation than most researchers realize. Editions of *Hamlet,* for example, have been published with all of the following alphabetically scattered forms on their title pages:

Amleto, Principe di Danimarca

Der Erste Deutsche Buhnen-Hamlet

The First Edition of the Tragedy of Hamlet

Hamlet, A Tragedy in Five Acts

Hamlet, Prince of Denmark

Hamletas, Danijos Princas

Hamleto, Regido de Danujo

The Modern Reader's Hamlet

Montale Traduce Amleto

Shakespeare's Hamlet

Shakspeare's Hamlet

The Text of Shakespeare's Hamlet

The Tragedy of Hamlet

The Tragicall Historie of Hamlet

La Tragique Histoire d'Hamlet

Still other editions appear in such nonroman scripts as Greek, Hebraic, and Cyrillic.

In such cases catalogers must create a *uniform title* in order to group all variant forms in one place so that a scholar may conveniently notice together the entire range of editions that would otherwise be scattered throughout the catalog. The creation of standardized *names* and *titles* is usually referred to as "authority control"; I use this term interchangeably with "vocabulary control," which is the expression usually used in speaking of the creation of standardized *subject* terms.

Most library searches are done by subject rather than by author or title (many title searches being themselves misguided attempts to do subject-category inquiries), and so I wish to concentrate on subject searching in discussing the Library of Congress model.

Subject control in the LC system is brought about by the *Library of Congress Subject Headings* (*LCSH*) list, currently in four volumes and often referred to simply as "the red books." It is a roster of terms that are acceptable to computer and card catalogs as valid subject headings; its purpose is to provide a standardized vocabulary for categories of knowledge, even at very specific levels. The terms thus serve to bring together in convenient groups the literature of the world—no matter the language of the works being cataloged—so that materials on the same subject can be noted and retrieved together.

The problem the list attempts to solve is apparent both within any individual language and across the range of languages: different terms, synonyms, and phrasings are used to describe the same subject. For example, the terms "capital punishment," "death penalty," "execution," "legal execution," "penalty of death," *pena capitale,*" *"peine de mort,"* *"smertnaia kazn',"* and *"Todesstrafe"* can all be understood to refer to the same thing. Authors who write on this subject may also use still other terms (e.g., *A Life for a Life, To Kill and Be Killed, The Ultimate Coercive Sanction*) in the titles of their works. The range and sequential order of key words involved, then—even within English, let alone across other languages—would cause works under all of these terms to be scattered from one end of the alphabet to the other; and the result would be that researchers who think of only one or two terms would miss most of the material available on the subject without realizing they've missed anything. (To anticipate a point made in a later chapter, this is precisely the problem with *key word* searching.)

A major principle in the construction of the *LCSH* list is that of *uniform heading,* and it addresses just this problem. Librarians who create a catalog using this system choose *one* term from the many possible key words, and then group all relevant titles together under that

one category term (in this case "Capital punishment") rather than re-
peating the same list of works under each of several terms scattered
throughout the alphabet. Finding the approved term, then, is crucial to
efficient searching. For example, as of early 1990 the Library of Congress had 103 books with the words "death penalty" in their title; but it
had *846* books listed under the subject heading "Capital punishment."
Since most of the books on this topic do not use the words "death
penalty" in their title, a reader using that search term rather than the
proper subject heading would miss most of what is available.

As the full list of relevant books appears under only one of the many
possible terms, the catalogers will place cross-references at several of
these other possible subject terms to steer researchers to the one main
grouping. The first type of cross-reference in the system is thus between
terms that are not used to terms that are used.

Additional cross-references are then created between and among the
terms that are used. The headings "Dreams" and "Children's dreams,"
for example, are obviously related to each other; and yet in an alphabetical display they would be widely separated. The *LCSH* list, therefore,
establishes cross-references from one to the other to bring to researchers' attention the existence of additional category terms that might
otherwise be overlooked. Linkages to broader terms (BT), narrower
terms (NT), and related terms (RT) are established in both directions
(see Figure 1). An additional designation, UF, or "used for," indicates
possible terms that are *not acceptable* in the *LCSH* system.

The first task the vocabulary-controlled catalog undertakes, then, is
that of solving the problem of scattering created by variant forms of
author, title, and subject terms. In each case the attempt is made to
create a uniform *category term* under which all variants are grouped
together. Furthermore, cross-references *leading to* the term are added,
as well as cross-references *among* the established headings, so that the
groups themselves can be meaningfully related. Note, however, that all
of this categorizing takes place entirely within the catalog itself, *independently of any shelf-arrangement or class scheme* for the actual books
or documents to which the catalog refers. A library can have a systematic catalog, in other words, at the same time that it has nonsystematic
shelf arrangement of its holdings.

When the shelf arrangement is also systematic, however—as in the
LC classification-by-subject scheme—then the catalog functions to
solve still other problems *within the classification scheme.*

Dreaming
  USE Dreams
Dreams
    ₍*BF1074-BF1099 (Parapsychology)*₎
    ₍*QP426 (Physiology)*₎
    ₍*RC499.D7 (Hypnosis)*₎
  UF Dreaming
  BT Sleep disorders
       Subconsciousness
       Visions
  RT Sleep
  NT Children in dreams
       Children's dreams
       Fantasy
       Fortune-telling by dreams
       Lucid dreams
       Men's dreams
       Monsters in dreams
       Nightmares
       Sex in dreams
       Water in dreams
       Women's dreams
— **Religious aspects**
— — **Buddhism,** ₍**Christianity, etc.**₎

Figure 1

The first such problem is that shelf arrangement by subject does not and cannot group together in *one* place within the bookstacks *all* of the works on one subject. As I noted in the previous chapter, a single subject may have many different aspects, and each aspect can appear in an entirely different class number. For example, books on the economic aspect of clocks appear in HD9999.C6; those on the artistic aspect of clocks appear in NK7480–7499; and those on their technological aspect appear in TS540–549. Since there are *no cross-references in the book-stacks,* browsers who discover only one of these areas are likely to be entirely unaware that the others exist.

Works that are scattered in the bookstacks, however, are grouped together in the vocabulary-controlled catalog. In this example, books on all of the various aspects of clocks are grouped together under the one heading "Clocks and watches." In other examples the widespread scattering on the shelves of works on "Leeks," "Metal-working machinery," and "Shipwrecks" is corrected in the catalog by the grouping of the works together, in each case, under one *LCSH* term (see Figure 2).

A more far-ranging example of books being widely distributed in the classification scheme and yet grouped together by means of surrogate

Clocks and watches *(May Subd Geog)*

→ { *[HD9999.C6 (Economics)]*
    [NK7480-NK7499 (Art)]
    [TS540-TS549 (Technology)]

UF Timepieces
    Watches
BT Chronology
    Horology
    House furnishings
RT Clock and watch making
    Time measurements
NT Astronomical clocks
    Atomic clocks

Leeks

→ { *[QK495.L72 (Botany)]*
    [SB351.L5 (Vegetables)]

UF Allium porrum
    Allium tuberosum (Allium odorum)
BT Onions
RT Cookery (Leeks)
NT Frozen leeks

Metal-work *(May Subd Geog)*

→ { *[NK6400-NK8450 (Fine arts)]*
    [TS200-TS770 (Manufactures)]
    [TT205-TT273 (Handicraft)]

UF Metal industries
    Metalwork
BT Arts and crafts movement
    Decoration and ornament
    Manufacturing processes
RT Metals—Coloring

Shipwrecks *(May Subd Geog)*

→ { *[G525-G530 (Narratives)]*
    [JX4436 (International law)]
    [VK1250-VK1299 (Reports)]

UF Marine disasters
    Wrecks
BT Adventure and adventurers
    Marine accidents
    Voyages and travels
RT Collisions at sea
SA *names of wrecked vessels*
NT Refloating of ships
    Wreck
— **Law and legislation** *(May Subd Geog)*
— **Religious aspects**

Figure 2

records in the catalog is provided by the subject "Afro-Americans." As of late 1989 the Library of Congress had 6,057 works cataloged (since 1968) under this one subject heading (with various subdivisions), which were thus brought together in the catalog. The books themselves, however, appeared in the bookstacks throughout the entire classification scheme from A to Z. Moreover, the titles of the books were also widely scattered within the catalog itself because of the wide variety of key words employed by their authors. The *LCSH* category term "Afro-Americans" thus served to solve the problem of key word title scattering within the catalog and also the problem of scattering of the subject's various aspects within the class scheme:

• The A classes in the Library of Congress classification system (General Works) included 15 works on "Afro-Americans," mainly studies done by the Rand Corporation grouped together in AS36 (Academies and Learned Societies), with titles such as *Race Differences in Earnings* and *Employment and Income in the Black Community.*
• The B classes (Philosophy/Psychology/Religion) had 166 works, such as Richard Tristano's *Black Religion in the Evangelical South,* with the LC subject heading "Afro-Americans—Southern States—Religion."
• The C classes (Auxiliary Sciences of History) held 47 works, mainly family histories under the subject heading "Afro-Americans—Genealogy."
• The D classes (History: General and Old World) included 74 works, many of them on the topic of Americans settling in Liberia, under the subject heading "Afro-Americans—Colonization—Liberia."
• The E classes (including "United States [General] History") held the largest single aggregate of works, 2,841, under a variety of headings such as "Afro-Americans—History—To 1863," "Afro-Americans—Social Conditions," and "Afro-Americans—Biography."
• The F classes (including "United States Local History") had 565 works with titles such as *The Blacks of Pickaway County, Ohio, in the Nineteenth Century* and *Minority Military Service, Rhode Island, 1775–1783,* under headings such as "Afro-Americans—Rhode Island—Genealogy."
• The G classes (including "Folklore," "Recreation," and "Sports") contained 210 books with titles such as *Black Dance: From 1619 to Today, Jesse Owens, Olympic Hero,* and *Afro-American Folktales:*

Stories from Black Traditions in the New World. Subdivided heading forms in the catalog pointing to these classes included "Afro-Americans—Dancing—History," "Afro-Americans—Biography," and "Afro-Americans—Folklore."

• The H classes (Social Sciences) had 324 titles such as *Social Security and Race, Homicide Among Black Americans,* and *Trends, Prospects, and Strategies for Black Economic Progress.* Subject headings such as "Afro-Americans—Mortality," "Afro-Americans—Social work with," "Afro-Americans—United States—Crimes against," and "Afro-Americans—Employment" tended to fall in H class numbers.

• The J classes (Political Science) included 86 works such as *Blacks and the 1988 Democratic National Convention* and *Jesse Jackson's Campaign* under subject headings "Afro-Americans—Politics and government" and "Afro-Americans—Suffrage."

• The K classes (Law) held 158 titles, among them *The Criminal Law of Slavery and Freedom, 1800–1868, Race Relations and the Law in American History,* and *Black Labor and the American Legal System.* Common subject headings that pointed to these classes were "Afro-Americans—Civil Rights—History," "Afro-Americans—Legal status, laws, etc.—Southern States," and "Afro-Americans—Employment—Law and legislation."

• The L classes (Education) held 311 works such as *Inside Black Colleges and Universities* and *The Education of Blacks in the South, 1860–1935,* with category headings "Afro-Americans—Education" and "Afro-Americans—Education (Higher)."

• The M classes (Music) contained 220 items such as *The Cash Box Contemporary Album Charts, 1975–1987, Ella Fitzgerald,* and *Black Musical Theatre: From Coontown to Dreamgirl.* The headings "Afro-Americans—Music" and "Afro-Americans—Biography" were common, the latter including dozens of life stories of figures such as Whitney Houston, Duke Ellington, and Janet Jackson.

• The N classes (Fine Arts) held 14 books, among them *Black Collectibles Sold in America, Winslow Homer's Images of Blacks,* and *Protest Drawings: A Graphic Response to the Civil Rights Drama,* with subject headings "Afro-Americans—Collectibles," "Afro-Americans—History—1863–1877—Pictorial works," and "Afro-Americans—Civil Rights—Pictorial works."

• The P classes (including "Languages" and "Literature") had 597 works such as *Invisible Poets: Afro-Americans of the Nineteenth Century, Black and White Speech in the Southern United States, Langston Hughes and The Blues, Ralph Ellison,* and *Sounder,* with subject headings "Afro-Americans—Intellectual life," "Afro-Americans—Southern States—Language," "Afro-Americans—Folklore," "Afro-Americans—Biography," and "Afro-Americans—Fiction."

• The Q classes (Science) included 16 books such as *Blacks, Science, and American Education* and *Seven Black American Scientists,* with category headings "Afro-Americans—Education—United States—Science" and "Afro-Americans—Biography."

• The R classes (Medicine) contained 70 books, among them *Health Policies and Black Americans, Cancer Among Blacks and Other Minorities,* and *Hypertension in Blacks.* Subject headings that tended to point to R classes were "Afro-Americans—Health and hygiene" and "Afro-Americans—Diseases."

• The S classes (Agriculture) had 23 books, most of them biographies of George Washington Carver (Afro-Americans—Biography), with an occasional exception such as *History, Growth, and Transition of 4-H Among Negroes in South Carolina* (Afro-Americans—South Carolina).

• The T classes ("Technology," including "Cookery") contained 13 books such as *Gordon Parks: Black Photographer and Film Maker* (Afro-Americans—Biography) and *Soul Food* (Afro-Americans—Nutrition).

• The U classes (Military Science) also included 13 books, such as *The History of Black Servicemen* and *The Air Force Integrates, 1945–1964.*

• The V classes (Naval Science) had only 5 books, including *The Integration of the Negro into the U.S. Navy.* As with the U classes, corresponding subject headings usually had "Afro-Americans" as a subdivision of another heading (as in "United States—Armed Forces—Afro-Americans") rather than as a heading itself. (A computer catalog, however, can search for such subdivisions at the same time that it retrieves the term as a heading.)

• The Z classes (Bibliographies) held 301 works with an amazing variety of titles and subject headings. The reason is that, in the LC system, bibliographies on a particular subject are not shelved with the regular books on the same subject; instead, they are all grouped together in Class Z (see chapter 5). Thus, the Zs offered works such as:

Afro-American Sources in Virginia: A Guide to Manuscripts (Afro-Americans—Virginia—History—Sources—Bibliography)

*Generations Past: A Selected List of Sources for Afro-American Genealogical   Research   *(Afro-Americans—Genealogy—Bibliography)

Black Studies: A Catalog of Selected Doctoral Dissertation Research (Afro-Americans—Bibliography—Catalogs)

Black American Health: An Annotated Bibliography (Afro-Americans—Health and hygiene—Bibliography)

Black Holiness (Afro-Americans—Religion—Bibliography)

Black Labor in America 1865–1983: A Selected Annotated Bibliography (Afro-Americans—Employment—Bibliography)

A Bibliography of the Dr. Martin Luther King, Jr., Collection in the Mississippi Valley Collection (Afro-Americans—Civil Rights—Southern States—Bibliography—Catalogs)

As inclusive as it is, the groupings of works together (both key word variant titles and class variant call numbers) under the one heading "Afro-Americans," with appropriate subdivisions, is not the only collocation function performed by the catalogers for works on this subject. The term "Afro-Americans" is itself part of a larger display of alphabetically grouped terms in the *LCSH* list, and, therefore, in the catalog as well. This is but a sample of the full list:

Afro-American actors
             architecture
             beauty operators
             diplomats
             families
             historians
             leadership
             painting
             parents
             preaching
             quilts
             radio stations
             students

veterans
wit and humor
women composers

Afro-Americans—Biography
—Civil rights
—Folklore
—History
—Legal status
—Religion

Afro-Americans and mass media
as consumers
in business
in the newspaper industry
in veterinary medicine

"Afro-Americans" as one category (including all of its subdivisions) is, in fact, nested within a display of 170 other subject headings starting with "Afro-American(s)"; and again, while these terms themselves appear next to one another as a single "meta-group" in both the *LCSH* list and the catalog, the books they refer to are scattered from A to Z in the classification scheme on the shelves, and also from A to Z when listed by title (rather than by subject heading) within the catalog itself.

The *Library of Congress Subject Headings* list thus creates category terms that, by themselves, solve certain problems of scattering. And the alphabetical collocation of these terms within the list (as well as within the catalog itself), and the extensive provision of cross-references to other terms elsewhere in the list, solves additional problems of scattering.

But the operation of the *LCSH* system in providing vocabulary groupings and linkages of groups does not end here. The system provides still other linkages between knowledge records through what are called *tracings*.

Within the research library's catalog itself (I am speaking now of the *LCSH* terms not as they appear in the "red books" set but as they appear within the actual catalog), each record contains a field listing all of the *LCSH* terms assigned to the book represented by that record. Thus, for example, the unit record for Robert Saudek's *Anonymous Letters: A Study in Crime and Handwriting* (see Figure 3) has four subject trac-

```
75-38671                          ITEM 1 OF 1 IN SET 1          (LCCC)

Saudek, Robert, 1880-1935.
  Anonymous letters : a study in crime and handwriting / by Robert Saudek ;
and with a new pref. by William F. Butterworth.  New York : AMS Press, [c1976]
142 p., 7 leaves of plates : ill. ; 19 cm.

LC CALL NUMBER: HV8074 .S3 1976

SUBJECTS:
  Writing--Identification.
  Forgery.
  Evidence, Expert.
  Graphology.

SERIES TITLES (Indexed under SERI option):
  Foundations of criminal justice

DEWEY DEC:  364.12/2
```

Figure 3

ings: "Writing—Identification," "Forgery," "Evidence, expert," and "Graphology." For librarians this means that, for record-keeping purposes, copies of this unit record (or catalog card) will be duplicated at each of these four points in the catalog. For researchers using the catalog who find the Saudek record when doing an author or title search, the tracings on it mean that *other, similar* books will be found under these category terms.

There are two points here that are useful to researchers. To reiterate the first: the tracings enable them to progress from the discovery of one particular author or title (here, Saudek's *Anonymous Letters*) to the larger discovery of the proper *category terms* that will group together many similar titles, albeit with different key words.

The second point is that the appearance of several subject tracings on one record effectively provides cross-reference linkages between these terms, *linkages that often do not appear in the* LCSH *list itself*. Thus, here, the *LCSH* term "Writing—Identification" is linked to "Forgery"; but there is no cross-reference between the two within the red books set. Should the researcher then look up "Forgery" in the catalog, he could find Doris Williamson's *Cross-Check System for Forgery and Questioned Document Examination* (see Figure 4), which provides additional connections through *its* tracings. Specifically, it links "Writing—Identification" to the additional *LCSH* term "Signatures (Writing)"; and, again, this is a relationship that is not explicitly indicated within the red books list itself.

The vocabulary control of subject headings is thus not accomplished entirely by the *LCSH* red books set. The tracings that appear on the records for books that are actually cataloged within the system make virtually every entry in the catalog a source of cross-references to other, related entries.

Similarly, the actual records within the catalog serve as an index to the classification scheme in ways that the *LCSH* list by itself cannot. The "Forgery" heading, for example (see Figure 5), indicates only three areas of the class scheme which correspond to that subject:

> HG1696–HG1698 (Economics. Finance. Banking. Drafts. Checks. Forgeries.)
>
> HV6675–HV6685 (Sociology. Social pathology. Social and public welfare. Criminology. Embezzlement. Forgery, etc.)
>
> Z41 (Bibliography. Books [General]. Writing. Autographs. Signatures, including forgery, collecting of autographs, etc.)

A search under "Forgery" *in the catalog,* however, will indicate that books appearing under this subject heading can also be shelved in several other areas of the stacks, such as:

> HV8074 (Sociology. Social pathology. Social and public welfare. Criminology. Penology. Police duty. Investigation of crimes. Identification of documents.)
>
> KF8947 (Law of the U.S.—General. Courts. Procedure. Civil procedure. Trial. Evidence. Documentary.)
>
> KF9367 (Law of the U.S.—General. Criminal law. Particular offenses. Offenses against property. Fraud. Fraud by forgery. Bad checks.)

In other words, books listed in the catalog under the heading "Forgery" can have HV8074, KF8947, or KF9367 call numbers assigned to them,

```
Williamson, Doris M.
    Cross-check system for forgery and questioned document examination / Doris
M. Williamson, Antoinette E. Meenach.  Chicago : Nelson-Hall, c1981.  xix, 115
p. : ill. ; 23 cm.

LC CALL NUMBER: HV8074 .W5 1981

SUBJECTS:
  Forgery.
  Legal documents--Identification.
  Writing--Identification.
  Signatures (Writing)

ADDED ENTRIES:
  Meenach, Antoinette E.

DEWEY DEC:  363.2/565 dc19
```

Figure 4

Forgery   *(May Subd Geog)*
     ⌈*HG1696-HG1698 (Checks)*⌉
━━━▶ { ⌈*HV6675-HV6685*⌉
     ⌊*Z41 (Autographs)*⌋
   BT Criminal law
        Fraud
        Offenses against property
        Swindlers and swindling
   SA *subdivision* Forgeries *under names of*
           individual persons and under types
           of art, objects, documents, etc., e.g.
           Postage-stamps—Forgeries
   NT Arts—Forgeries
        Blanks in legal documents
        Cancellations (Philately)—Forgeries

Figure 5

even though these options are not spelled out explicitly in the red books' note under "Forgery."

A single subject heading can thus comprise several different aspects reflected in various places within the classification scheme. When creating a particular catalog record, the LC librarians usually indicate which aspect they consider to be most important for the book in hand by linking the *first* subject tracing to the classification number. Thus, in Figure 4, the first tracing, "Forgery," on the record for the Williamson book is linked to the class number HV8074. This number does not appear under "Forgery" within the *LCSH* list (see Figure 5); but it does appear under "Writing—Identification" (see Figure 6). The *aspect* of forgery that the cataloger wished to emphasize for this particular book, then, was its investigation by police rather than its perpetration by criminals or its prosecution by lawyers.

Not all aspects of the linkages between the vocabulary-controlled subject headings and the classification scheme are thus indicated by the *LCSH* red books. The catalog records themselves must be consulted within the particular library that uses the overall LC model for a more complete indication of which *LCSH* terms point to which subject areas of the bookstacks.

How, then, does all of this relate to the Traditional Library Science model and its adequacy or inadequacy as an overall "universe" of arrangement—both as a mental set held by researchers and as a physical model actually used by libraries—for providing access to knowledge records? There are a number of major points to be made here.

Writing

[Z40-Z104.5]

Here are entered works on the process or result of recording language in the form of conventionalized visible marks or graphic signs on a surface. Works on the writing of a particular language are entered under the name of the language with subdivisions Alphabet and Writing, e.g. Greek language—Alphabet; Egyptian language—Writing. Works on systems of writing used by several peoples are entered under Writing, followed by the name of the system, e.g. Writing, Arabic.

General and comparative works on the Semitic alphabet and its ancient and modern derivatives, or with similar series of characters employed to represent the sounds of a language, are entered under Alphabet.

Works on variations in the style of writing in the past, and especially with ancient and medieval handwriting, are entered under Paleography.

Works on written languages as a form of communication or discourse are entered under Written communication.

- UF   Chirography
        Copy-books
        Handwriting
- BT   Language and languages
- RT   Ciphers
        Extinct languages
        Penmanship
- NT   Abbreviations
        Agraphia
        Autographs
        Calligraphy
        Children—Writing
        Cryptography
        Cuneiform writing
        English language—Writing
        Graphemics
        Graphology
        Hieroglyphics
        Japanese language—Writing, Cursive
        Japanese language—Writing, Seal style
        Language and languages—Orthography
            and spelling
        Library handwriting
        Mirror-writing
        Numerals, Writing of
        Paleography
        Pasigraphy
        Picture-writing
        Shorthand
        Signatures (Writing)
        Stoichedon inscriptions
        Transcription
        Typewriting
- — Copying processes
        USE   Copying processes
- **— History**
        [P211]
        BT   Hieroglyphics
- **— Identification**
        [HV8074-HV8076]
        UF   Identification of handwriting
        BT   Criminal investigation
                Evidence, Criminal
                Evidence, Expert
                Evidence (Law)
                Legal documents—Identification

Figure 6

41

The first is that only one component of the Traditional Library Science model is *perceived* by most researchers. People notice the classified arrangement of books on the shelves and routinely use it for browsing, *but they usually do not notice the vocabulary-control system in the catalog*. The experience of reference librarians is that it is truly unusual to find any readers who can locate on their own the proper subject heading(s) for their topic (see chapter 7). It is not at all uncommon for graduate students—who are usually taught "methods of research" by professors within their own discipline, using the Subject/Discipline model, rather than by librarians—to go through their entire degree program without even being informed of the existence of the *Library of Congress Subject Headings* list. Nor are librarians blameless here; the classes that we teach are often organized by the Type-of-Literature model (see chapter 6), and so students are never taught the *LCSH* system (both within the red books and on tracings on actual catalog records) as the *index to the classification scheme*. Students do not then clearly perceive the difference between a *title* search and a *subject heading* search in the catalog; and so, more often than not, they find only an individual title or two that looks good, which leads them to only one area of the classification scheme, whereas the discovery of the proper *LCSH* term, such as "Clocks and watches" or "Afro-Americans," would lead them to many titles and also to several areas of the bookstacks.

Most people who use the classification, in other words, unwittingly find themselves in the position of the fly crawling across the face of the Mona Lisa: they don't see the whole picture. Nevertheless, since they come in with the mental set of the Subject/Discipline model in their heads, the one portion of the library scheme that they do see *matches their low expectations* of what they ought to see—that is, the classification scheme *apparently does* group books together by subject or discipline—and so they are satisfied by finding *any* apparently relevant subject grouping. (What is not apparent is that the scheme does not group *all* relevant books together in one place, but that there is a great deal of scattering of the various aspects of the same subject into many different class groups. Again, there are no cross-references in the stacks.) The Principle of Least Effort (see chapter 8) then leads them to conclude that they've found "everything" available.

There are further implications to this situation. The first is that the Traditional Library Science model is capable of functioning *much more efficiently* than it usually does. The reason for many of its apparent failures is that usually only one component of it is *taught:* "When you find one relevant book on the shelves, look around for others in the same area." What this advice fails to teach is how to find the first "relevant book" with which the process begins, that is, it fails to indicate the crucial distinction between title and subject heading searches in the catalog. Moreover, with or without such (bad) teaching, only one component of the whole model is readily *perceived:* researchers can simply *recognize* the utility of subject groupings of books on the shelves without any formal instruction at all, but they cannot easily recognize the vocabulary-control system in the catalog. The distinction between title records and subject headings is simply not obvious to most people.

The second implication is that calls to abandon the classification system because "it no longer works" or "it cannot provide the access needed today" are based on seriously mistaken notions of the function of the classification scheme. The classified arrangement of books was never designed to be the *whole universe* of the Traditional Library Science model. It is and always has been only *one component* of that universe. Of course it does not—and cannot—work in displaying cross-disciplinary connections between various subjects, for by its very nature it can display only some relationships among books as physical objects at the expense of displaying other possible relationships. Of course the knowledge categories created at one period of history will not always reflect the thinking of later decades; and of course books arranged in the earlier configurations cannot economically be recataloged and relabeled to reflect later understandings.

Critics who expect such wonders from a class scheme simply do not understand the whole system. It is the vocabulary-controlled catalog—not the classification system for shelving the books themselves—that must be consulted to reveal cross-disciplinary connections. It is the catalog's subject heading system which enables works that appear in only one subject group on the shelves to be listed within *several* subject categories in the catalog. It is the catalog and the cross-references that appear within it that allow changes in knowledge categories to be economically updated. Condemnation of the *classification system* for lacking features appropriate to the *catalog* betrays an ignorance of how the two components work together; specifically, it betrays an unawareness of the subject heading system's function (and frequently a parallel ignorance of the function of name authorities and uniform titles). Furthermore, other criticisms of the classification scheme display an ignorance of the continuing need for *deep* access to full-text features (tables of contents; back-of-the-book indexes; illustrations; chapter subdivisions; individual paragraphs, sentences, and words within the text) *in a systematic way*—which is entirely lost if the classified arrangement of full texts is forgone in return for only systematic access to the very superficial surrogate records in the catalog.

Now, I do not by any means intend to suggest that a library's catalog solves all of the problems of access to knowledge records that the class scheme does not handle. Far from it. Within the Traditional Library Science model, neither the shelf-classification component for arranging monographic full texts nor the vocabulary-controlled catalog provides even a nearly adequate solution to the problem of access to journal articles. Nor do these components provide anything like efficient access to the contents of newspapers, microforms, CD-ROMs, or dial-up databases. Nor do they provide acceptable access to government documents, which libraries usually shelve by a Superintendent of Documents classification that is not compatible with LC (or Dewey) class designations. Nor do they provide access to special collections, which often include—or may be entirely composed of—nonbook formats such as photographs, prints, maps, sound recordings, motion pictures, and so on. Nor, of course, do they provide access to the holdings of other libraries, which may be just as vital to the success of a research project as are local holdings.

The fact remains that the class scheme and the catalog system were designed to provide access to books, and not to knowledge records in the many other formats that have proliferated, especially since the turn of the century (when the Library Science model was designed), and only to books within one facility, not to those held elsewhere. Obviously, if these two components by themselves constituted the entire Library Science model, then it could justifiably be criticized for any number of glaring deficiencies.

Such criticism is nevertheless premature, and also subject itself to criticism by those who have a better understanding of the model in dispute. Even though, as we shall see, a number of these objections to the Library Science model are indeed valid, the fact remains that the model is still much more capacious and efficient than its critics usually perceive. For there is a third component of the model that does solve many of the problems just enumerated; and, in spite of its usually being overlooked, it is equal in importance to the other two components.

5

The Traditional Library Science Model

Part Three:
Published Bibliographies and Indexes

The third component of the Library Science model for providing access to knowledge records is the structured aggregate of published bibliographies (including journal indexes) that the library contains within its holdings. While the classification scheme by itself enables researchers to perceive some, though not all, of the library's resources on subjects of interest, and while the vocabulary-controlled catalog enables them to perceive many other relevant sources that are "blind spots" to the shelf browsing approach, published bibliographies allow readers to identify still more sources that neither of the other two avenues of access is capable of revealing. Specifically, bibliographies and indexes are the traditional means of gaining detailed access to journal articles, government documents, microforms, special collections, nonbook formats, and the holdings of other libraries. The Library Science model therefore assigns particular importance to published bibliographies and indexes, and gives them a special emphasis in placement and arrangement.

The business of librarianship, in other words, has at least two major functions. The first is *to create the basic access systems* of the classification scheme and the vocabulary-controlled catalog; the second is to *present to researchers in a systematic way* those additional sources created by others (scholars, commercial companies)—sources that provide access to knowledge records in ways that the librarian-created systems of class scheme and catalog cannot.

How do librarians attempt to provide such systematic access to these other sources? The answer lies primarily in the creation of two groups of sources that are "outside" the regular subject classification scheme. Specifically, in the Library of Congress scheme there are two classes, A and Z, that are unlike the others (B through V). The latter constitute groupings of material by particular subject or discipline (e.g., B–BJ for "Philosophy and Psychology," E–F for "American history," PR for "English literature"). Class A, by contrast, is for "General works." Its function within the whole system is to serve as a kind of "table of contents" to what follows in all of the other classes. It contains sources that provide introductions, general overviews, and starting points for research on any subject, but not the in-depth literature itself that is found in the B through V classes. The A groupings thus hold all of the general encyclopedias such as the *Britannica, Americana, Great Soviet, Brockhaus,* and *Espasa.* Such sets provide overview articles on all subjects, with very brief bibliographies of selected and especially recommended works for further reading, rather than comprehensive or in-depth reading lists. They enable researchers to perceive initially the "lay of the land." The A classes also contain general factbooks such as the *World Almanac, Encyclopedia of Associations,* and *Research Centers Directory.* The general and non–discipline-specific indexes such as *Readers' Guide to Periodical Literature* and the *Essay and General Literature Index* (an index to essays appearing within anthologies), as well as all indexes to newspapers, are also in the A classes. *Readers' Guide* is the most general of indexes; it is used most appropriately by those who are not doing in-depth research, or who don't need a lot of information on their subject. (In a sense, one could say the same about newspaper indexes, at least insofar as they can be contrasted with discipline-specific indexes.) Those who are doing more scholarly research will almost always be better served by the scores of specialized and discipline-oriented indexes that can be found elsewhere.

The Z classes are even more important; and they have a different function within the whole scheme. Their purpose is to serve as a detailed, in-depth index to material shelved in the other classes, much as the index volume at the end of an encyclopedia provides better and deeper access to the set than the simple alphabetical arrangement of the articles themselves. The crucial point here is that, in the LC system, subject bibliographies on a particular topic, and discipline-specific indexes, are not shelved with the "regular" books on that topic; rather, all subject bibliographies are removed to the very end of the classification scheme and grouped together in the Z classes.[1] The Dewey Decimal Classification has a somewhat analogous pattern of segregating subject bibliographies; in it the base number 016 is reserved for bibliographies.

A further extension of that number then corresponds to the subject of the particular bibliography. The point here is that this system, too, separates bibliographies into a special class rather than placing them with monographs on the subject: thus a bibliography on civil engineering would not go in class 624 with books on that topic; rather, it would go in 016.624.

The latter part of the Z classes in the LCC system serves this indexing function. The lower Z numbers (Z4 through Z1199) indicate specific subject and disciplinary groupings ("History of books," "Libraries and library science," "Book collecting") just like the B through V classes. These ranges, however, are followed by higher numbers at the very end of the scheme:

Z1201–4980   National bibliography

Z5000–7999   Subject bibliography

Z8001–8999   Personal bibliography

The "National" range includes subject bibliographies by or about whole countries or smaller regions, and on topics particularly associated with those geographic areas (e.g., bibliographies on English or American literature are in this range; and, more specifically, those on Afro-American, Catholic, Jewish-American, or women authors in the United States are also to be found here). Bibliographies on the history and inhabitants of the area(s), including their smaller geographic regions, are also in Z1201–4980. Arrangement is generally by continent (in the order of North America, South America, Europe, Asia, Africa, Australia), with regional or country subdivisions within each continent.

The next range, Z5000–7999, is an array of detailed bibliographies on specific subjects or classes of subjects that do not have the geographic associations found in the preceding sequence. What is particularly noteworthy (and often confusing, even to some librarians) about this sequence is that while it is indeed arranged by subject, the subject categories are not arranged in relation to one another in a disciplinary or logical manner as is usually the case elsewhere in the classification scheme. Rather, they are simply arranged in *alphabetical* order, which often makes for strange bedfellows, as in this sequence:

Z6041–6045   Geophysics

Z6046   Glass

Z6055   Gold- and silversmiths' work

Z6081	Graphology
Z6121	Gymnastics
Z6151–6155	Handicrafts (including Blacksmithing, Textile crafts, and Woodwork)
Z6201–6209	History
Z6240	Horses and horsemanship
Z6250	Hotels
Z6260	Human engineering
Z6270	Ice cream
Z6293	Indexes
Z6297	India rubber; Rubber
Z6331–6335	Iron and steel
Z6366–6375	Jews
Z6461–6479	Law, international; and international relations

The logical groupings of subjects within the B through V classes, in other words, is not mirrored by a parallel sequential grouping of bibliographies about those subjects in the Z classes above Z5000.

The reason for this apparently lies in a bit of library history that has been obscured over the last century. When the LC classification system was devised in the early 1900s, most large research libraries had closed stacks (as LC still has today), so readers were dependent on catalogs and bibliographies in an open reference area to identify which sources they needed to request (by call slips) from the closed bookstacks.

The Z class ranges were thus devised for public use in an open area. The bibliographies were segregated from the monographs in the first place because readers did not have direct access to the shelves where the monographs were kept. Moreover, even the reference librarians who did have access to the stacks could not continually be running back into miles of bookshelves to find the bibliographies they needed to identify specific sources that were blind spots to the subject heading system in the card catalog. The librarians, too, needed them out in an open and easily accessible area.

The question then became something like this: Given that these bibliographies are unusually important to the functioning of the whole access system, and that they must therefore be given special emphasis by being placed in an open area, how should they be *arranged* in that open area so that they can most easily be found by users of the library?

The first option, of course, would be to arrange the index-Zs (let me use this term for those sources with class numbers of Z1201 or above) in a classified sequence parallel to the arrangement of the monographs in the closed bookstacks. The problem, however, is that the convolutions of the regular classification scheme from B through V are simply not perceptible or graspable by anyone except experienced library specialists. This is not to say that the scheme cannot be used by lay people; obviously it can. But their use of it consists entirely of browsing limited areas for particular subjects. What nonspecialists always fail to perceive is the arrangement and structure of the whole scheme from beginning to end; furthermore, they routinely overlook the scattering of different aspects of a subject among many classes. To use the regular monograph classification sequence (as opposed to that of the index-Zs), nonspecialists always require an external source such as the library's catalog to let them know at which starting point within the sequence they should begin their browsing.[2] Even reference librarians, I must add, have difficulty perceiving the details and internal structure of the whole scheme.

But it must be remembered that the real purpose of the B through V classification system is precisely to provide in-depth access to full texts within predictably limited subject areas, not to provide browsers with an overview of how specific subjects are related to all other subjects. Again, there are no cross-references in the bookstacks, and the same subject may have many different aspects that cause books on the subject to be far separated from one another in the classification scheme.

The index-Zs have a different purpose: they serve to round up *bibliographical listings* of works on all aspects of particular subjects when the works themselves that are listed in the bibliographies may be *widely scattered* throughout B through V, or may not be in the class sequence (e.g., nonbook formats), or even in the library. They therefore do not require an arrangement that is designed for a different purpose; and, indeed, if the complexity of the B through V arrangement is such that it cannot be readily grasped as a whole, then it is simply not appropriate for arranging critical index material in an open area for high-volume use by people who have limited interest in, and less memory for, library technicalities. A system of arrangement that is *more immediately perceptible and graspable* is required for the indexes that provide access to the more complicated areas of the library. What is necessary for the unusually important index-Zs, then, is a categorization that can be *recognized* without having to be remembered.

The resulting system thus makes heavy use of two categorizations that library users already know: the continents and the alphabet. Presumably, then, users could simply recognize these patterns if they looked for them. Again, the index-Zs break down as follows:

Z1201–4980   *National bibliography* (arranged by continent in the order of North America, South America, Europe, Asia, Africa, Australia; subarrangement usually by country, often—though not always—in alphabetical order)

Z5000–7999   *Subject bibliography* (arranged alphabetically by subject group)

Z8001–8999   *Personal bibliography* (arranged alphabetically by the surname of the subject)

This is probably as good a system as could be devised, given both the complexity of the material to be contained within it and the need to use as simple and as predictable an arrangement as possible.

Certainly the Z8000s (Personal bibliographies) can be considered highly successful, at least for people who know enough to look for them (a point to which I shall return). For example, I once helped a reader who had a very specific question about Benjamin Franklin. He told me that a friend of his had read an article that said Franklin had once made an anti-Semitic speech to the Constitutional Convention in Philadelphia, and he wanted "a copy of that speech." A quick search of the Library's computer catalog, combining "Franklin" with "Jew," "Anti-Semitism," and other such terms produced no hits. Similarly, a computer search of the major dial-up database covering the field of American history, *America: History and Life,* produced nothing but irrelevant articles (e.g., material on Benjamin Franklin Peixotto, an American consul to Romania who tried to alleviate the situation of Jews there; an article on Benjamin Franklin Davega, a Sephardic Jew who lived in California in the nineteenth century; an irrelevant article on the right Franklin abstracted by someone named *Jews*bury; and so on). Since the computers were failing, I simply walked over to the Z8000s, looked for the F section, and found a huge bibliography of nearly everything published about Franklin from 1721 through 1983: Melvin H. Buxbaum's

Benjamin Franklin: A Reference Guide (G. K. Hall, 1983–88; 1130 pages in two volumes). The index to this set, under the entry "Franklin, Benjamin—alleged anti-Semitism" led immediately to seventeen annotated entries that were right on the button, and which indicated decisively, without the reader's even having to call up articles referred to, that the alleged speech was known to be a twentieth-century forgery.

For some inquiries, the Traditional Library Science model, *when used according to its design,* can thus spectacularly outperform even the best computer databases. And reference librarians must deal with many more such inquiries than most nonlibrarians realize. Indeed, for the numerous questions librarians receive from students seeking literary criticism of particular works, a good collection of index-Z personal bibliographies will routinely outperform even the *MLA International Bibliography* online.

The personal bibliographies sequence within the index-Zs is thus very easy to use. Its alphabetical arrangement is very effective in providing immediate access; and the alphabet will remain effective no matter how many volumes are added to the sequence. (The Library of Congress itself has 840 linear feet of Z8000s—nearly the length of three football fields).

Other subjects, however, do not lend themselves as easily to alphabetization as do personal surnames. The first part of the index-Zs, then— the "National bibliography" sequence in Z1201–4980 arranged by continent—is thus an attempt to take as many topics as possible out of the "what's left" hodgepodge sequence of "Subject bibliography" in Z5000–7999. In the Z1201–4980 sequence there are *fewer categories* to have to think up, and there is much less need for thought about *which term is being used in an alphabetical sequence* ("Jews" or "Hebrews"? "Cards" or "Gambling"?) when the arrangement is *geographical* rather than *alphabetical.* The world conveniently divides itself up into only a few continents; and a great deal of subject matter can be categorized *more predictably* by these few locations than by alphabetical tag. Thus, as I have mentioned, bibliographies on literature, history, ethnic studies, travel, cultural or military affairs, and the like tend to be grouped together in the index-Zs according to the geographic area of their subject, whereas in the classification scheme itself, the monographs on these subjects are widely scattered in the D and E (History), P (Language and literature), and U and V (Military subjects) classes, and so on.

Whenever the alphabet must be used as a device for arranging subjects, the problem of synonyms and variant phrasings inevitably asserts itself. A system of vocabulary control, such as that in the library *catalog,* solves such problems; but vocabulary control, dependent as it is on cross-references, cannot be used to arrange books *on the shelves.* Vocabulary control on the shelves would require "dummies" to be inserted between the books, with the necessary cross-reference information; and no library has the money or the shelf space to create all of the dummies necessary to make the requisite links between terms not used and terms that are used, and further references among the used terms to display relationships to one another. It is simply not cost-effective to duplicate an avenue of access on the shelves that is already available elsewhere, in the catalog. Again, the classification scheme and the vocabulary-controlled catalog are *two different systems of access,* and, when dealing with access to print sources such as books, system users only get into trouble by demanding that one take on an access function that properly belongs to the design of the other.

The middle sequence of the index-Zs (Z5000–7999) does not function as predictably, then, as the geographic or personal name sequences because its alphabetical arrangement of subject categories lacks the vocabulary-control mechanisms that enable a searcher to predetermine which alphabetical label is being used as the key to a particular subject's placement in the sequence. Thus, for example, bibliographies of published diaries appear not in the *D* section but in the *B* (Biography) category. Bibliographies on medieval studies appear not in the *M* but in the *C* (Civilization) group. And bibliographies and indexes on architecture appear not in the *A* but in the *F* (Fine arts) class. In spite of such problems, however, it cannot be said that all of the categorizations are this confusing; there is indeed a discernible alphabetical sequence that can be perceived by those who know enough to look for it (see Appendix 1).

Now, I wish I could report that training in the recognition and use of the index-Zs is a customary part of library instruction classes. But it simply isn't. The approaches that are used are those of the Subject/ Discipline (see chapter 2) or the Type-of-Literature (see chapter 6) model. Indeed, it is truly exceptional even for reference librarians— who, unlike the general public, are taught according to the Library Science model in addition to the other two—to learn the internal structure of this index-Z component of the model. And yet a knowledge of it makes it easy to find information in areas that are blind spots to the catalog and the class scheme for monographs (criticisms of literary works being the most obvious example). Reference librarians *are* educated in the use of free-floating subdivisions in the *Library of Congress Subject Headings* system, which forms much of the internal structure of its vocabulary control; and they learn what to expect there from alphabetical lists of these components (e.g., *Free-Floating Subdivisions: An Alphabetical Index* [LC, 1991]). Parallel formal training in the recognition and use of the alphabetical and geographical sequences of the index-Zs would be similarly useful.

A major point of this book is that the Library Science model continues to work at a much greater level of efficiency than it is usually given credit for—and that it works in many ways that still cannot be matched by the Computer Workstation model (see chapters 9 and 10)—*if* each of its three components is recognized in the first place as of equal importance, and if each is used *according to its design*. While this model simply can no longer be considered the entirety of the universe within which researchers must work, its components nevertheless retain their value as necessary elements of the still larger model that is required today (see chapter 11).

Originally, then, the index-Zs were designed to provide an easily understood avenue of subject access to library collections which would identify topical materials that were in blind spots to both the subject heading system of the card catalog and the subject groupings of full texts created by the classification scheme. When specific works were identified by subject by means of bibliographies and journal indexes (also in the index-Zs), they could then be searched for by author or by title in the library catalog for the call numbers that would allow them to be retrieved from the stacks.

Fortunately, the arrangement of the index-Zs by continent or by alphabetical sequence is not the only avenue of access to these crucial bibliographies. While this arrangement is quite useful to those who know enough to look for it, it is still inadequate and often very inefficient, even for knowledgeable searchers. The Library Science model, however, provides an additional systematic avenue of access to bibliographies—one that works much better than their arrangement itself because the additional avenue solves the problems of vocabulary control. This additional avenue of access is found in the second component of the overall model, the controlled-vocabulary subject heading system of the library catalog. Bibliographies are given *special treatment* there, too, by the routine employment of standard, free-floating subdivisions that can attach themselves whenever appropriate to any valid heading in the whole system; these subdivisions are:

[LC Subject heading]—Bibliography

—[Geographic subdivision]—Bibliography

—Periodicals—Indexes

Researchers who find the right subject category terms in the first place, then, will automatically be informed through these subdivisions that special bibliographies or journal indexes exist for that subject. The bibliographies and indexes, in other words, are made to *stand out prominently* in the vocabulary-control system so that they will be emphasized and therefore noticed even by people who are not specifically looking for them. This is the preferred way to gain access to the index-Zs. Even reference librarians use this approach much more frequently than the avenue provided by the physical arrangement of the Zs.

Over the years a number of additional avenues of access to published bibliographies have also been developed; in general, however, these are sources that librarians are trained to remember directly, without having to go through any system to find. They include:

• *Bibliographic Index* (H. W. Wilson, 1937–). This publication appears three times a year with annual hardbound cumulations. According to its own "Prefatory Note," it is "a subject list of bibliographies published separately or appearing as parts of books, pamphlets, and [about three thousand] periodicals. Selection is made from bibliographies that have fifty or more citations. The Index concentrates on titles in English, other Germanic languages, and the Romance languages."

• *Bibliographische Berichte* (Klostermann, 1959–). Somewhat comparable to *Bibliographic Index,* this annual provides better coverage of German and east European bibliographies.

• *A Guide to Published Library Catalogs* by Bonnie Nelson (Scarecrow Press, 1982). This is an extensively annotated listing of the published catalogs of research libraries that specialize in collecting within certain subject areas. Each such catalog is in effect a huge bibliography on its subject.

A number of other such sources exist[3]; to discuss them further here would be inappropriate, however, as the point of this chapter is to explain the *aggregate* of published bibliographies collectively forming one segregated and thus emphasized component of the access system provided by the Library Science model. I do not wish to lose the primary focus on the forest by looking at individual trees.

To recapitulate the important point, the aggregation of the index-Zs provides an effective means of solving many of the problems laid at the doorstep of the Library Science model by those who mistakenly perceive it as composed solely of a classification scheme, or even of a class scheme plus a catalog. (The usual mistake is to perceive its "universe" as simply coextensive with the classification scheme alone; this misperception comes very close to reducing the Library Science model, in effect, to the Subject/Discipline model.) Published bibliographies and indexes reveal to researchers the existence and contents of journal and periodical articles, government documents, microforms, special collections, and nonbook formats (including *computer databases* as well as maps, prints, photographs, and so on) that are not shelved in the regular bookstacks; and bibliographies also reveal the contents of *other libraries* and repositories throughout the world. Note that in doing so they provide much of the "access" to other collections that many contemporary theorists mistakenly assume to be available only through direct computer linkages. The Library Science model thus has a self-correcting component that compensates for the weaknesses of the classification scheme and the card or computer catalog of (primarily) book holdings. Nevertheless, other blind spots remain in this model; despite its self-correcting features, it still cannot be viewed any longer as the totality of the universe within which researchers must operate.

Specifically, the aggregation of index-Zs—even if its existence and tripartite internal structure is taught to researchers—still hides as much as it reveals. It does not distinguish between *more important* and *less important* indexes, for example—a distinction that becomes crucial in large library collections. Nor does it distinguish among vocabulary-controlled subject heading indexes, key word indexes, and citation indexes, or bibliographies arranged in classified order; nor does it actively bring to anyone's attention the possibility of related-record searching on certain CD-ROMs.[4] Moreover, while it can provide references and citations to computer databases, it cannot provide a way of physically displaying or arranging the actual computer terminals themselves in a way that relates them to other sources that provide access to knowledge records which lie in blind spots to the computers.

I spoke earlier of two major functions of librarianship, namely, to create two of the major avenues of access to knowledge records and to present to researchers, in a systematic way, the additional avenues and sources that are created by others.[5] It is especially in its ability to present the proliferation of these other sources that the Library Science model, in its traditional form, is showing its age.

As we shall also see, however, what are weaknesses or blind spots in this model are areas of light in other models (and, conversely, what are blind spots in other models are areas of light in the Library Science model). What will be required, ultimately, is a larger model that systematically incorporates the advantages of all the other schemes.

6

The Type-of-Literature Model

Bibliographic instruction in graduate schools tends to be offered along the pattern of the Subject/Discipline model; that is, resources within one subject area are studied, with an emphasis on a particular list of sources. The obvious reason for such an approach is that graduate schools by their very nature seek to promote specialization and in-depth familiarity with *one* slice of the pie of knowledge. The consequent blindness that students schooled in this model exhibit to resources in other subject areas has been discussed in chapter 2.

Undergraduate instruction in library research is not always so discipline-specific. If it is simply based on another list of particular sources, however—even though the sources may cover a wide variety of subject areas—the disadvantages that accrue to any such list will still assert themselves. Students who cannot answer their research questions by means of the titles given there will be powerless to find other titles efficiently; and the list itself will tend to go out of date relatively quickly. The problem, in a nutshell, is that simple rosters of sources arranged by subject do not convey *principles* of searching that can be used in any situation. They do not give a student the *power to predict* the likely existence of other sources that would answer his or her question when the sources on the given list are insufficient.

One alternative to the Subject/Discipline model, however, does provide such principles and (at least to some extent) systematic predictability of reference sources even in subject areas with which the researcher has no prior familiarity. This is the Type-of-Literature model. It tends to be taught to undergraduates more than to graduate students because it is not discipline-specific; and it is usually taught in library schools to students learning how to do general reference work. This model is based on the fact that there are certain types of literature (almanacs, dictionaries, encyclopedias, directories, indexes, chronologies, bibliographies, and so on) that can reasonably and predictably be expected to exist in all subject areas. If, then, researchers have a foreknowledge of the range of such types of literature, and an understanding of the kinds of questions that each type is best at answering, they will be able to move with some confidence through the reference literature of any subject or discipline.

For example, questions such as "Where can I get a list of schools for nannies?" or "How can I find what celebrations are planned worldwide to usher in the year 2000?" tend to lie beyond the personal expertise of anyone trained in a discipline-specific manner. And yet both questions have something in common that permits them to be answered efficiently—something that has nothing to do with the *subject* of the question. And this common element is that both questions are *amenable to being answered by a particular type of literature*—in this case, directories. In the first instance, reference to the *Encyclopedia of Associations* (Gale, annual) immediately turns up a descriptive entry, with address and phone number, of the American Council of Nanny Schools; and, in the second, the *Encyclopedia of Associations: International Organizations* (also Gale, annual) leads one easily to similar information on the World Association for Celebrating Year 2000.

Another example is provided by a writer I once helped who needed confirmation of the point that turn-of-the-century "normal schools" for training teachers were not considered academically on a par with colleges and universities. In a very important way, this question was quite similar to another that I mentioned in chapter 2, from the woman who wanted information on the "fourteenth-century sociologist" Ibn Khaldun. Obviously, the *subjects* of the two questions do not have any common ground. Nor could I have hoped to provide an answer to either question by drawing on any subject expertise of my own. Nevertheless, it was a very simple matter to provide on-target answers to both questions within a matter of minutes because my training as a librarian enabled me to perceive that both could be answered by a particular type of literature—encyclopedias—whose existence I could reasonably predict even though I did not have exact titles in mind beforehand. In one case the *International Encyclopedia of Education* did the trick, in the other the *Encyclopaedia of Islam*.

The Type-of-Literature model, then, represents a genuine advance beyond the Subject/Discipline model as a conceptual structure with which to pursue library research, for it enables its adherents to find with relative ease and efficiency the reference literature of *any* subject, even—or, rather, especially—a subject entirely beyond the realm of their personal knowledge.

There are many different types of literature whose existence can reasonably be predicted within most subject areas, among them:

Almanacs. These are general fact books and compendia of miscellaneous information. They are particularly good for answering questions having to do with statistics, weights and measures, awards, brief news items, dates or anniversaries, geography, weather and climate, and sports.

Atlases. These are compendia of maps or tables that graphically display information not just on geopolitical matters but also on subjects such as crop production, spread of diseases, military power balances, climate variation, ecological conditions, status of women, literacy levels, technological levels, population trends, soil conditions, occupational distributions, area histories, trade patterns, and the like.

Bibliographies. These are compendia of citations (sometimes with annotations) to books, journal articles, and dissertations on particular subjects. They are especially useful in historical or literary research, as they frequently include references to older works that tend to be overlooked by computer databases.

Catalogs. Catalogs provide listings of merchandise, art objects, publications, equipment, and so on which are located at particular places or are available in a particular market; they often provide descriptive details, specifications, and prices.

Chronologies. These present facts arranged by the time sequence of their development. Usually chronologies offer parallel listings that display the temporal contexts of different areas of study (e.g., politics, arts, technology, religion) simultaneously, so that a reader may correlate the events of one area with contemporaneous, earlier, or later developments in the other subject areas.

Computer databases. Such electronic sources of information can be either in-house (mainframe or CD-ROM) or dial-up (connecting to external suppliers) in format; and they can provide, variously, bibliographic citation information (often with abstracts), full-text material or tabular data, or library locations of print (and other) sources in virtually all subject areas, though not all subjects are covered to the same extent. They are often more limited than print sources in their range of coverage, however; they tend to favor recent sources; and the full-text types usually favor sources of less than book length, which do not entail difficult problems of copyright restriction.

Concordances. These are word lists associated with particular texts (usually literary classics) that enable researchers to determine exactly where any particular word(s) appear within a text.

Dictionaries. These reference sources provide an alphabetically arranged list of words with their definitions, pronunciations, etymology, scope of usage, and so on. Often they contain biographical and geographical information. The term "dictionary" is often synonymous with "encyclopedia," referring simply to an alphabetical (rather than a systematic) arrangement of entries, regardless of length.

Directories. Directories provide information for identifying or locating knowledgeable people, organizations, or institutions in various subject areas. They list names, addresses, and telephone or fax numbers.

Encyclopedias. Encyclopedias seek to provide an overall summary of the important facts established in a given subject area. They are intended to offer initial overview access to the knowledge of a field, and are usually written with a nonspecialist audience in mind (unlike review articles or treatises). They are good at answering questions about history, biography, geography, philosophy, theory, and physical nature; they are useful, too, in providing highly selective bibliographies of recommended sources for in-depth study. Their entries are arranged alphabetically rather than systematically (as in treatises); and they can usually be counted on to have a detailed index that will reveal much more of their contents than the simple alphabetical sequence of entries can.

Guides to the literature. The literature of any subject may be thought of in terms of different levels. *Primary literature* deals directly with a particular problem or concern, presenting original insights about it or creative expression of it. *Secondary literature* generally comprises scholarly studies of the primary literature rather than (or at least with less emphasis on) direct studies of the matter that gave rise to the primary literature; popularization is often a function of this level. *Tertiary literature* consists of reference works (dictionaries, encyclopedias, handbooks, indexes) that identify, point out, summarize, abstract, or repackage the information provided by the other two levels. Guides to the literature ideally seek to provide an intellectual structure that orients a researcher to the most important sources at all three levels of literature for a given subject. In practice, however, many such "guides" fall short of this mark, and present instead an overview only of the tertiary reference literature for their field.

Handbooks and manuals. These are a type of reference source intended to be easily transportable for actual use "in the field" rather than just in libraries. They are related to encyclopedias and treatises in that they try to provide the principles and important facts of a subject area, and in that they can be arranged alphabetically or systematically. Their major distinction from these forms is in their emphasis on practice, procedures, and "how to" directions for producing actual results rather than just intellectual understanding. Also, they tend to be much more concisely written, again, so as to be more easily carried about in field situations.

Indexes and abstracts. Journal articles and reports in any subject field are not efficiently revealed to researchers by library catalogs or classification schemes, which were designed to provide access to monographs. Indexes fill in this gap by providing subject and author access to such literature. Abstracts go a step further in also providing brief summaries of the articles or reports; they thus provide similar avenues of access but penetrate to a deeper level of content revelation.

Newsletters. These are current sources, providing up-to-date information in fields that tend to develop or change with some rapidity. They can appear daily, weekly, or monthly.

Review articles. These are articles that appear in journals, annuals, or essay anthologies that seek to provide a "state of the art" or "state of the situation" overview or assessment of a particular subject. Unlike encyclopedia articles, they are usually written for specialists, and so may assume familiarity with technical or occupational jargon. Furthermore, in seeking to provide an exhaustive analysis and evaluation of the literature of the topic, they include a bibliography that seeks to be comprehensive rather than merely selective. Review articles, too, tend to place a greater emphasis on the current state of a subject, whereas encyclopedia articles tend to emphasize its historical aspects.

Treatises. Like encylopedias, treatises attempt to present a comprehensive summation of the established knowledge of a particular subject; unlike encyclopedias, however, they tend to be arranged systematically rather than alphabetically, and they tend also to seek their audience among specialists rather than lay people.

Union lists. These are location devices; they enable researchers who have already identified specific sources to determine which libraries actually own a copy of the desired works.

Yearbooks. This type of literature seeks to provide a historical record of, and usually an evaluative commentary on, the year's developments in a particular field. Such annuals provide a more permanent, and often better indexed, cumulation of the updating information contained in newsletters.

A foreknowledge that the reference literature of any subject will have the internal structure defined collectively by these (and other) types of literature, each having a particular strength in answering certain types of questions, can thus alert the researcher to distribute his efforts among a variety of avenues of access to knowledge records. It will enable him to avoid wasting time on avenues whose strengths do not correspond to his needs, and to focus his energies more efficiently on those that will most readily answer the kind of question he has in mind. The Type-of-Literature model actually allows a researcher to *ask more focused questions in the first place*—especially in unfamiliar subject areas—because it provides him with a better *a priori* understanding of the literature that is *likely to exist*. It enables the searcher to see more than just a blur lying beyond the list of specific sources provided by the Subject/Discipline model; it provides him with a road map that clearly distinguishes likely paths leading to payoffs in the literature of *any* subject area. It also permits him to anticipate the existence of, and therefore to search more efficiently for, kinds of sources that may not be displayed in the groupings that are created on the bookshelves by the library's classification scheme (i.e., the first component of the Library Science model, which is all that most people see of it). With this model, in other words, a searcher is not simply dependent on recognizing whatever the class scheme may offer. The Type-of-Literature model gives him a tool that enables him to perceive categories of sources that may not be physically adjacent to one another on the shelves.

With all of its advantages, however, there are also problems with the Type-of-Literature model. Foremost among these is the fact that it just doesn't "take" as well with many researchers as does the Subject/ Discipline model. Students schooled in the Type-of-Literature approach, once they have left the classroom and actually come into the library, very often demonstrate that they grasp only the concrete, particular sources (e.g., *Readers' Guide, InfoTrac, Encyclopaedia Britannica*) which they have been given as examples of the types of literature, without perceiving the predictive intellectual structure itself of which these examples are only limited instances. The teaching of this model, too, has a tendency to reduce itself to being another exercise in presenting a specific list of sources, much as in the Subject/Discipline model— the only differences being that many subjects may be covered on the list rather than just one, and that the "type" list will be more explicitly arranged by categories of literature.

Now, some lists are better than others. Professional reference librarians themselves are often dependent on the *Guide to Reference Books* (American Library Association, revised irregularly), a listing of some 1,500 pages which specifies the various type-of-literature sources that are available within all subject areas. For example, in its "History" section it lists atlases, bibliographies, chronologies, dictionaries— including encyclopedias—directories, dissertation guides, fellowship and grant guides, guides to the literature, manuscript sources, periodical directories, periodical indexes and abstracts, and so on.

Each specific discipline also has one or more published guides which attempt to do within that one subject area what the ALA *Guide* tries to do as an overall source for all of them. The individual guides, of course, go into greater detail. Ching-chih Chen's 824-page *Scientific and Technical Information Sources* (2nd ed.; MIT, 1987) is a good example; it lists the following chapter headings:

1. Selection Tools
2. Guides to the Literature
3. Bibliographies
4. Encyclopedias
5. Dictionaries
6. Handbooks

7. Tables, Almanacs, Databooks, and Statistical Sources
8. Manuals, Source Books, Laboratory Manuals and Workbooks, and How-To-Do-It Manuals
9. Guides and Field Guides
10. Atlases and Maps
11. Directories, Yearbooks, and Biographical Sources
12. History
13. Important Series and Other Reviews of Progress
14. Treatises
15. Abstracts and Indexes, and Current-Awareness
16. Periodicals
17. Technical Reports and Government Documents
18. Conference Proceedings, Translations, Dissertations and Research in Progress, Preprints, and Reprints
19. Patents and Standards
20. Trade Literature
21. Nonprint Materials
22. Professional Societies and Their Publications
23. Databases

A good listing of such type-of-literature rosters within all subject areas is Martin Sable's *Research Guides to the Humanities, Social Sciences, Sciences, and Technology: An Annotated Bibliography of Guides to Library Resources and Usage* (Pierian Press, 1987).

The main problem with any such list—whether it be a mimeograph prepared by an instructor or the ALA *Guide* or the Chen science list or Sable's overall bibliography itself—is that it will inevitably become dated. There will always be a succession of new directories, new encyclopedias, new databases, and so on that come out after the publication of any such guide, no matter how comprehensive it aspires to be. An additional problem is that the list may not be comprehensive enough in the first place to indicate to researchers the full range of reference sources that are already available.

The question, then, is this: even if you do understand the predictive intellectual structure of the Type-of-Literature model, how do you find concrete instances of the type you're looking for, within the subject area of your interest, if the published list or bibliography you're working with isn't adequate to reveal the source that you think is likely to exist?

The answer lies in the vocabulary control of the *Library of Congress*

Subject Headings (*LCSH*) system employed by most libraries' catalogs—and which is also employed by larger dial-up catalogs available through the Dialog system or OCLC's EPIC service. New type-of-literature sources, as well as old, can themselves be found in a predictable manner through a series of standard or "free-floating" form subdivisions that catalogers can attach, as appropriate, to any *LCSH* category term. Both old and new examples of types of literature can thus be found easily within any subject area, according to standard patterns of subdivision.

     [LC Subject Heading]—Abstracts
                 —Archival resources
                 —Atlases
                 —Bibliography
                 —Case studies
                 —Catalogs
                 —Charts, diagrams, etc.
                 —Chronology
                 —Concordances
                 —Data bases
                 —Dictionaries
                 —Directories
                 —Discography
                 —Encyclopedias
                 —Film catalogs
                 —Guidebooks
                 —Handbooks, manuals, etc.
                 —Illustrations
                 —Indexes
                 —Inventories
                 —Manuscripts—Catalogs
                 —Microform catalogs
                 —Patents
                 —Periodicals—Bibliography

　　　　—Periodicals—Bibliography—Union lists
　　　　—Periodicals—Indexes
　　　　—Phonotape catalogs
　　　　—Photograph collections
　　　　—Pictorial works
　　　　—Portraits
　　　　—Posters
　　　　—Quotations
　　　　—Registers
　　　　—Reviews
　　　　—Sermons
　　　　—Slides
　　　　—Statistics
　　　　—Tables
　　　　—Textbooks
　　　　—Translations
　　　　—Union lists
　　　　—Video catalogs
　　　　—Yearbooks

Obviously not all of these subdivisions exist under every heading; but the standardization of the vocabulary terms gives one a predictable way of looking for the types that do exist in any field.

This points up another problem with the Type-of-Literature model: over and above the difficulty of the rapid dating, even obsolescence, of bibliographies arranged by type categories, the alternative means of identifying the types (through continuously updated *LCSH*-controlled catalogs) involves so *many* possible form subdivisions that they are difficult to remember, and when one cannot remember the range and articulation of the model's components in the first place, then one obviously has less predictive power in using the model. There are, in fact, scores of form subdivisions distinguished within the *LCSH* system (see Appendix 2); and while not all of them are as important as the ones I have listed, nevertheless, the sheer size and complexity of the model makes it difficult to teach and to learn. Additionally, students who are merely exposed to the list of types rather than actually drilled in its use, through *many* concrete experiences of its utility in answering questions, tend to forget it quickly. What happens is that they tend instead to remember only the individual titles offered to them as representative of the various types of literature, rather than the intellectual framework or structure of the model itself, which is what gives it its predictive power.

It is their special expertise in the Type-of-Literature model—including a greater foreknowledge of the range of possible form subdivisions of *LCSH* headings—that usually enables reference librarians to find material in unfamiliar subject areas even more efficiently than full professors within those areas. The librarians have an *intellectual structure* to work with that predisposes them to expect the existence of resources in areas that are blind spots to the Subject/Discipline model—a structure that also gives them a systematic and predictable method of *finding* the sources that they suspect will exist, through both static bibliographies arranged by types of literature and form subdivisions in continuously updated library catalogs using the *LCSH* system of subject headings.

I think that the usual failure of the Type-of-Literature model to "take" with most students, in spite of its tremendous potential for getting them beyond the limitations of the Subject/Discipline model, is attributable in part to its complexity to begin with, in part to instructors' failure to teach the *LCSH* form-subdivision component of the model, and in part to the fact the one really must get a certain amount of actual experience in using it successfully in order for it to register as a "mental set." Part of the problem with this model is that it goes against the grain of a natural tendency to think only in terms of subjects, rather than in terms of abstract categories of sources that *transcend* particular subjects or disciplines. Whatever the reasons, however, the model as it is taught frequently degenerates from a universal intellectual structure to a mere list of particular sources, often incomplete to begin with and soon to be outdated in any event.

In passing, it should be noted that the widespread availability of commercial computer databases in various subject areas has now considerably extended the range and flexibility of the Type-of-Literature model, for these databases now permit journal and report-literature sources to be searched by types of literature within them. Previously these types were blind spots even to this model because the traditional Type model developed as a way of categorizing only sources that would appear within library catalogs in the first place; this limitation excluded journal articles and, usually, technical reports and those of any nature published in microformats. These sources were better covered by commercial indexes, and library catalogs developed in a cost-conscious way that tried not to duplicate avenues of access available elsewhere.

Thus, for example, it has always been impossible to find either journal article reviews of specific books or state-of-the-art review articles—both of which are extremely important types of literature—through the *LCSH* form subdivisions in the catalog because the catalog itself was never intended to reveal the contents of individual journal articles within the library's collections. (The "—Reviews" form subdivision in an *LCSH* catalog works only for collections of reviews published in book form.) The new systems of access to journal articles provided by computer databases, however, solve these problems, as they enable one to do "document-type" searches of this literature. For example, the *Psychinfo* database in the field of psychology allows researchers to look specifically for the following document types:

- Audio Tape
- Bibliography
- Book
- Book Chapter
- Dissertation
- Journal Article
- Review
- Technical Report

Similarly, the *Social Scisearch* database, covering approximately 1,400 journals in all fields of the social sciences, enables a searcher to look specifically for these document types:

- Abstract
- Article
- Book Review
- Chronology
- Correction/Addition
- Database Review
- Discussion
- Editorial
- Fiction/Creative Prose
- Film Review

- Hardware Review
- Item about an individual
- Letter
- Meeting Abstract
- Note
- Poetry
- Review/Bibliography
- Software Review

The ERIC database in the field of education has a similar feature, enabling one to look for almost three dozen document types, including teaching guides, review literature, audiovisual material, geographic material, tests and questionnaires, and bilingual materials.

Again, however, the document-type-of-literature search feature of these databases—like the standard form subdivisions of *LCSH* in the library catalog—is seldom taught to anyone but reference librarians. For most students who are learning about databases, it is often considered sufficient if they can be taught to understand clearly the differences between controlled-vocabulary and key word searching, and between Boolean "and" and "or" operators. Classroom presentations, especially if confined to one hour, often do not allow time for the extra consideration of document-type search features.

In any event, the overall Type-of-Literature model does not take very well among students, especially when they are not taught the predictability of its *LCSH* component. It also is not absorbed very well by desultory researchers who don't have occasion to use the model frequently, and thereby to develop a "feel" for the kinds of problems it solves or for the efficiency with which it solves them. Part of the problem here is that most researchers tend to follow a Principle of Least Effort (see chapter 8); and a major implication of this is that they tend to pursue those sources or avenues which they can easily recognize above those they have to remember. Also, the books in a library are not physically arranged according to type of literature; rather, they are arranged according to subject or discipline by the classification scheme. The class scheme, then—the first component of the traditional Library Science model—is all that most people can easily recognize. The Type-of-Literature model depends for its success not only on prior training but also on a knowledge of the working of the *LCSH* vocabulary-control system—and even, to some extent, on knowledge of index-Z bibliographies such as the ALA *Guide* and the Chen and Sable volumes. It depends, in other words, on a knowledge of the two other components of the Library Science model besides the classification scheme; and this is a knowledge that most researchers do not have.

I do not mean to suggest that the Type-of-Literature model is reducible to the lesser-known components of the Library Science structure. It isn't. It is dependent on them but not identical to them. One major difference between the two models is that the Type model usually functions well in identifying only tertiary, rather than primary or secondary, literature—that is, it's good for turning up *reference* sources. It's better for addressing *factual* questions that have a definite answer ("How tall is the Eiffel Tower?" "What was the population of Chicago in 1940?") than for answering open-ended *research* questions ("What does the library have on Peruvian ceramics?"), although it is useful in the latter cases, too. The problem, though, is that the Type model does not "see" or distinguish among monographs, whereas the Library Science model does. Thus, the *LCSH* system includes hundreds—indeed, thousands—of monograph subdivisions that have nothing to do with types of literature such as:

> [LC Subject Heading]—Antiquities
> —Armed Forces
> —Biography
> —Civilization
> —Criticism and interpretation
> —Discovery and exploration
> —Economic conditions
> —Foreign economic relations
> —Foreign relations
> —History
> —Manufactures
> —Officials and employees
> —Religion
> —Social life and customs
> —Study and teaching

A knowledge of the Library Science model will thus enable one to see a way beyond the Type-of-Literature model; yet a knowledge of *only* the former may very well cause one to miss the types of literature revealed by the *form* subdivisions in *LCSH,* as they may get buried among all of the *topical, geographic,* and *chronological* subdivisions with which they are usually mixed. Often, though not always, one has to know that the form subdivisions are there in order to search for them effectively; this is especially the case with subject headings (e.g., "Afro-Americans") that have scores or even hundreds of subdivisions of all four types.

There is an additional reason for the Type model's greater success in dealing with specific-answer reference questions than with open-ended research questions: it fails to distinguish *methods of searching* within its "Indexes" and "Databases" categories. For example, I once helped a woman who wanted information on "managing sociotechnical change." She had already been referred to one of the best indexes to journals in the management field, *Business Index;* but she'd had no success with it. The reason for its failure is that it uses *LCSH* category terms, and there simply is no category term for what she wanted. (Its "Management" subject heading was much too broad.) What was required, then, was an index to management journals that allowed searches by key words rather than by *LCSH* terms. The *Social Sciences Citation Index* nicely filled this bill: it enabled her to find the exact word "sociotechnical" paired with the word "management" or "planning" in a dozen articles.

The colleague who had referred her to *Business Index* was simply following the prescription of the Type-of-Literature model that an "index" to journals in the management field should be consulted. The Type model, however, has a shortcoming in that it simply lumps together all indexes or databases that cover a field; it does not distinguish further whether the sources permit searches by subject heading categories, by key words, or by footnote citations. The last is a method of searching that is, unfortunately, relatively unknown to many researchers. It enables one to find which journal articles have footnoted any given source. The major reason for its neglect is that the citation indexes, when mentioned in *subject* bibliography lists, are simply mixed in indiscriminately with the other indexes which cover that subject. Neither the Subject/ Discipline nor the Type-of-Literature categorization reveals the distinctive properties of citation indexes. What is required to give them proper emphasis is a Methods-of-Searching model (see chapter 11).

Another problem with the Type model is of relatively recent origin; it consists in the blurring of an important distinction. Whenever a particular index exists in both paper-copy and computer database formats, it is often asserted simply that the two are "the same," and usually there is a concealed proposition that the hardcopy version may be dispensed with. Frequently, however, the paper version covers earlier years that are not included in the database, offering information that becomes automatically "unimportant" because it is not computerized.

A more subtle difference, however, concerns the years of coverage that do overlap in the two formats. For example, I mentioned in my earlier book, *A Guide to Library Research Methods* (Oxford, 1987), an instance in which I had helped a woman who was looking for articles on "blended families" or "stepfamilies." At the time I searched three databases with these two key word terms and found fifteen items initially; but then I noticed the additional term "reconstituted families" being used in some abstracts on the printout. Searching under this term, I found an additional nineteen articles.

Two years later I was asked the same question by a different researcher; but this time I was working in a library that did not have public access to the dial-up commercial databases, and so I had to use the print version, *Social Sciences Citation Index,* of what I had searched before in database form. The print version is arranged in such a way that if you look up one key word of interest ("families"), you can then see in a column below it all other key words that have appeared with it in the title of any article within five-year periods. I could thus quickly point out to the researcher the "blended," "reconstituted," and "step-" parings that I'd used before in the database version. The print version that I was using this time, however, enabled me to spot two other terms that I had overlooked before: "reintegrated families" and "remarried families."

The distinction, then, is this: not only are print and computer versions not "the same" for search purposes, but the advantages of searching one format rather than the other are not *all* on the computer side. They usually are, of course; such marvelous search capabilities as word truncation, Boolean combinations of multiple terms simultaneously, and document-type retrieval capability are possible—or at least maximally efficient—only with the electronic formats. But the databases also have some limitations, and these do show up in some research problems: in addition to lacking earlier years of coverage, a database often makes it harder to *browse* because computers tend to display only what is explicitly specified in the first place. A print version of "the same" information, however, enables one more easily to *recognize* important search terms that cannot always be specified fully in advance.

I have seen this problem not only with the *Social Sciences Citation Index* but with the print and CD-ROM versions of *Dissertation Abstracts* as well. One researcher who was interested in the history of iron companies in the United States achieved only indifferent results with the CD-ROM. In scanning the print index, however, she noticed a good entry on an iron *foundry,* a word she hadn't been able to spot using the computer. Another researcher interested in Canadian *beef* exports noticed only when she searched the print version that the word *cattle* was also important.

The moral of these examples is that the mere *presence* of information within a source does not ensure *access* to it. Access is determined by the *format* of its presentation, not by its mere existence. And the Type-of-Literature model, as it is taught to prospective librarians these days, is tending to blur the distinction of format between print indexes and databases, to the detriment of the efficiency of some inquiries. While it is true that the computer sources are usually best regarded as the first choice among formats, it is also true that they do not *always* work; and librarians (if not their patrons) must know what else can be tried in such situations. There are times when the print-version distinction is important (see Dolan [1979], Elcheson [1978], Johnston [1978], Johnston and Gray [1977], Rowland [1982], and Standera [1985]). Again, what is required here is a perspective from the Methods-of-Searching model to highlight a difference that tends to be blurred in the Type-of-Literature model.

How does the Type model stack up, not just as an intellectual structure but as a device for the actual physical arrangement of library resources? The answer is implied in the fact that it is primarily a method for structuring the categorization of reference sources rather than monographs. It could thus not be used to arrange the library's entire general collection of books; a Subject model, as reflected in the classification component of the Library Science model, is preferable. It has been used on occasion to organize reference collections; but such instances have been confined to relatively small special libraries in the medical field (see Truelson [1962], Jenell [1976]). Here, an arrangement by type-of-literature is effectively a subarrangement of a library devoted to a single discipline. If the library were to provide general coverage of thousands of subjects, the Type model alone would be insufficient to arrange its reference sources, although it still might be very useful as one component of a larger arrangement.

The Type-of-Literature model as a whole, then, is primarily useful as an intellectual construct enabling researchers to see predictable similarities among reference sources across the entire range of subjects. Since libraries are not *arranged* by this model, it tends to be neglected more than it should be. A failure to teach the model's *LCSH* form-subdivision component also undercuts its effectiveness. Nevertheless, for those who do learn it, it is extraordinarily effective. It lets researchers see beyond the confines of specific lists of recommended sources, and of specific groupings of books arranged by library classifications, to *abstract* groupings that cannot go out of date or suffer from localized collection gaps, and that can always be exemplified by concrete sources in *predictable* ways.

7

The Actual-Practice Model

A number of studies of the actual information-seeking behavior of scholars indicate that, after leaving the compulsory environment of the classroom, they tend not to use even the Subject/Discipline model for doing library research in their own fields. Specifically, they neglect the available journal indexes and abstracts to a surprising degree, and place extraordinary emphasis instead on simple footnote chasing from known sources, especially those in their personal libraries, or on talking to colleagues.[1]

The same scholars also neglect the Traditional Library Science model. Specifically, they use only one of its three components, the classification scheme, for browsing; and they use it with only minimal efficiency because very few of them perceive the extent of scattering of a subject's various aspects throughout the classification system. Additionally, very few researchers understand the second component of the model, the vocabulary control provided by authority work for names and titles, and by *Library of Congress Subject Headings* for subjects; and they fail to perceive that efficient browsing is itself a function of first finding the proper *LCSH* terms in the catalog, which terms round up in the catalog the different subject aspects that are scattered in the stacks, and which thereby point out the variety and range of class areas that need to be browsed for more in-depth information.

There is widespread confusion among scholars about how to find the proper subject headings for their topics, and most researchers who do try to use the catalog wind up with only a few titles that happen to start with the key words they've searched for. Furthermore, even those who do find a proper *LCSH* category term tend often to rest content with whatever they find under a very general term, thereby missing the majority of books that are most relevant because, unknown to the searchers, the library usually catalogs books only under the most specific headings available in *LCSH*.

Published bibliographies and indexes—the third component of the Library Science model—also tend to be overlooked because they are not shelved with the monographs on their subjects but rather are separated off in the Z classes; they are thus routinely missed by scholars browsing the other parts of the classification scheme.

The Type-of-Literature model also tends to be ignored by most researchers; for the reasons given in chapter 6, this abstract intellectual structure tends in practice to be perceived only in terms of a specific list of individual sources that can never be complete and that, in any event, tends to go out of date rapidly.

The somewhat depressing fact, then, is that most researchers follow no formal procedures at all that would *systematically* reveal to them a research library's contents. Instead, they follow a Principle of Least Effort (see chapter 8) and rely heavily on only those search techniques that are obvious (footnote chasing, superficial use of the library catalog, general browsing, talking to colleagues) and that they would have pursued anyway even if they had never been exposed to any formal bibliographic instruction programs. This is the Actual-Practice model. It is worth emphasizing, with examples, just how much material researchers miss, without being aware that they've missed anything, when they follow this model.

In chapter 4 I discussed the concept of *uniform heading* as a principle in the construction of the *Library of Congress Subject Headings* system. A second principle of *LCSH* is that of *specific entry*. This concept may perhaps be best introduced by several examples of mistakes that even experienced researchers routinely make.

• A student interested in nightmares made the usual mistake of looking under "Sleep" and "Dreams." The proper heading is "Nightmares." Works on nightmares, as a rule, are filed *only* under the latter term; they are not duplicated under "Sleep" or "Dreams."

• A researcher interested in the effects of divorce on children made the usual mistake of looking under "Divorce." The proper heading is "Children of divorced parents."

• A biologist looking for books on blue crabs made the usual mistake of looking under general terms such as "Crustaceans" and "Chesapeake Bay." The proper heading is "Blue crabs."

• A reporter looking for material on televising court proceedings made the usual mistake of looking under "Media" and "Television." The proper heading is "Television in the courts," which files alphabetically much farther back in the catalog (or on a computer "browse" screen) than "Television" alone.

• An ethnologist looking for works on the Chibcha Indians of Colombia made the usual mistake of looking under the general heading "Indians of South America." The proper term is "Chibcha Indians."

• A student looking for books on costume in Great Britain made the usual mistake of looking under a general heading, "Great Britain—Social life and customs." The proper heading is "Costume—Great Britain."

In each case, material cataloged under the proper, specific heading was *not duplicated under the general terms* under which the researcher was looking. Thus, most of the material on "Children of divorced parents" is found *only* under that term and *not* under the broader term "Divorce." This is what *specific entry* means: librarians, as a rule, will catalog a book only under the most specific category terms in the *LCSH* list, not under the relevant general terms. The general terms are used only when the books themselves are very general in nature. The more specific a book is, the more specific its subject headings in the catalog will be. And the same book, as a rule, will not usually appear under both specific and general headings. The catalogers always make a choice (that is the principle of *uniform heading*); and their choice, predictably, will be for the narrower term(s). The predictability of this choice gives an intellectual structure and "direction" or "grain" to the use of *LCSH,* and thus makes it a *system* of access rather than a matter of guesswork.

It is therefore very important for researchers always to find the most specific subject headings available in the *LCSH* list; and yet very few people do this. As a result, they miss most of the best books on their subject.

The question, then, is, "How do you find the most specific term?" One answer lies in following the cross-reference structure given in the *LCSH* list itself. Figure 1 in chapter 4 gives a variety of cross-references, each group preceded by a code designation.

UF = Used for (Thus "Dreams" is *used for* "Dreaming." In other words, terms preceded by UF are not acceptable; readers instead, should refer to the boldface heading above them.)

BT = Broader Term(s)

RT = Related Term(s)

NT = Narrower Term(s)

The BT, RT, and NT headings are all acceptable in the *LCSH* system. The important point, however, is that they are not subdivisions or subsets of the term under which they appear. Rather, they are entirely separate headings, and if you want them, you must look for them directly in the catalog. Thus, material under "Children's dreams" appears only under that specific term in the C section of the alphabet, and not in the D section under "Dreams." The most important cross-references are thus usually the NT, or Narrower Term, headings, and it is crucial to begin a catalog search with them. Scholars following the Actual-Practice model, however, routinely fail to do this.

It is the widespread experience of reference librarians that most researchers do not even know that the *LCSH* list exists. Scholars, in doing catalog searches, usually wind up with a few individual titles of books rather than categories of relevant titles. Thus, for example, one reader at the Library of Congress searching for books on "Hovercraft" in the Library's computer catalog found ten books whose titles started with that word. In calling up the full catalog record for one of those books, however (see Figure 7), the reference librarian showed him that the proper *LCSH* category terms for similar books were listed in the tracings at the bottom of the record; these were "Ground-effect machines" and "Hydrofoil boats." In searching these catalog terms, the reader found *an additional 61* relevant works, most of which—forty-eight of sixty-one—used key words other than "Hovercraft" in their titles (e.g., *Surface Effect Ships for Ocean Commerce; Water, Air, and Interface Vehicles; Air Cushion Vehicles;* and so on).

People who do not know about the *LCSH* system routinely miss much more than they find. But since they usually can find a few relevant titles, they have no idea that they've missed anything, let alone most of what is available.

This example also shows that there is a second way to find the proper *LCSH* terms for whatever subject needs to be searched: in addition to the

```
Hovercraft and hydrofoils / edited by Roy McLeavy.  London : Jane's Publishing
Company, 1980.  255 p. : ill. ; 13 x 19 cm.

LC CALL NUMBER: VM363 .H68

SUBJECTS:
  Ground-effect machines.
  Hydrofoil boats.

ADDED ENTRIES:
  McLeavy, Roy.

SERIES TITLES (Indexed under SERI option):
  Jane's pocket book ; 21

DEWEY DEC:  629.3/24 dc19
```

Figure 7

cross-references (especially the NTs) in the *LCSH* list, there are the tracings that appear at the bottom of virtually every catalog record. If you can identify one good source through an author or a title search, in other words, you can then look at the tracings to find the proper subject headings to search under for similar books.

Unfortunately, it is also the widespread experience of reference librarians that most library users are as ignorant of the existence of tracings as they are of the *LCSH* list itself. Even senior scholars can go along for decades without ever catching on to the *system* of how to find the right subject headings. As eminent a pair of historians as Jaques Barzun and Henry Graff, in their classic *The Modern Researcher* (4th ed.; Harcourt, 1985), do not get their readers beyond the inefficient Actual-Practice model in finding subject headings.

> [S]ubjects frequently go by different names. For example, coin collecting is called Numismatics. More complicated is the way in which one who wants information about the theory of the divine right of kings arrives at the term "Monarchy." One might conceivably have reached the same result by looking up "Right, divine," or even possibly "Divine Right," if the library owns a book by that title or is fully cross-indexed. What is certain is that there is little chance of success if one looks up "King" and no hope at all if one looks up "Theory." In other words, one must from the very beginning *play* with the subject, take it apart and view it from various sides in order to seize on its outward connections. (p. 22)
>
> To find a subject other than a person, you must bring to bear on the problem a little more knowledge and imagination. As was shown in Chapter 2 with regard to the divine right of kings, you must guess under what word or words your subject has been catalogued. (p. 68)

Well, no, you do not have to "guess." And in this case "Monarchy," a general heading, is not the best term. If you look in the

Library of Congress Subject Headings list (which is not even mentioned in *The Modern Researcher*) under either "Kings and rulers" or "Monarchy" (see Figure 8), you will find in either instance a Narrower Term cross-reference to the specific heading "Divine right of kings." Moreover, in looking next under this term itself, you will find two other useful bits of information. One is that books under the subject heading "Divine right of kings" will tend to be assigned to the JC389 classification area; and from the corresponding list of class areas under "Kings and rulers" you can tell immediately that works in this class range will be connected with "Political *theory.*" Furthermore, there is an additional NT cross-reference under "Divine right of kings" itself, to the heading "Kings and rulers—Religious aspects," which is likely also to repay a search in the catalog. The *LCSH* list all by itself, then—even apart from any subsequent examination of tracings—enables you to find two precisely relevant subject headings to look under, and also defines what will be the best area of the stacks to browse. Familiarity

Kings and rulers *(Not Subd Geog)*	**Monarchy** *(May Subd Geog)*
⌜*D107 (Biography: comprehensive)*⌝	⌜*JC374-JC408*⌝
⌜*D352.1 (19th century)*⌝	UF Sovereigns
⌜*D399.7 (1871-1900)*⌝	BT Executive power
⌜*D412.7 (20th century)*⌝	RT Democracy
⌜*JC374-JC408 (Political theory)*⌝	Despotism
⌜*JF253 (Constitutional history)*⌝	Royalists
UF Kings and rulers, Modern	NT Divine right of kings ◀━━━━━━━
Monarchs	Emperors
Royalty	Kings and rulers—Succession
Rulers	Ministerial responsibility
Sovereigns	Prerogative, Royal
Sultans	Queens
BT Heads of state	Sovereignty
History	— **Denmark**
Political science	UF Danish monarchy
RT Despotism	Monarchy, Danish
Queens	BT Denmark—Kings and rulers
Regency	
SA *subdivisions* Kings and rulers *and*	
Queens *under names of countries,*	
cities, etc., and ethnic groups	
NT Caliphate	
Caliphs	
Civil list	
Courts and courtiers	
Dei gratia in royal titles	
Dictators	
Divine right of kings ◀━━━━━━	

Figure 8

with the Traditional Library Science model thus eliminates the guess-work.[2]

Unfortunately, the majority of library users, who follow the rather haphazard procedures of the Actual-Practice model, do not perceive the various *systems* of library retrieval. If we stay with *LCSH* a bit longer, it is evident that there will be several undesirable results if you fail to find the proper subject headings.

You will miss most of what the library's catalog has to offer on your subject, and you will miss all *of the* best *material.* Again, most of the books under "Children of divorced parents" will not be duplicated under "Divorce," and most of the books under "Divine right of kings" will not be duplicated under "Monarchy." The books under the more general terms may have *chapters* on the topics that you seek, and this may be enough to mislead you into thinking you've found the best sources; but the proper, narrower terms will turn up *whole books* on these subjects, which is preferable.

You will miss most of the range of call number areas to browse in the bookstacks. There is much more scattering of subjects in the library's classification scheme than most people are aware of; for example, books on "Drug abuse" (a proper *LCSH* term) can be classified, in a large library, in many different areas of the stacks: several different sequences within the HV5800s (Social pathologies), AS36 (Societies), BV4470 (Pastoral theology), several H classes (Social sciences) other than HV, several KF classes (U.S. law), LB1044 (Teaching), a number of P (Fiction) and R (Medical) areas, QP37 (Human physiology), TX943 (Food service), and two different Z classes (Subject bibliographies). Several other examples may be found in chapter 4 (see "Clocks and watches" and "Afro-Americans").

As I mentioned in that same chapter, a single subject can have many different aspects, *and each aspect can appear in an entirely different class number.* Moreover, those who follow the Actual-Practice model of plunging directly into the bookstacks after locating only a few relevant titles in the catalog will be utterly blinded to this scattering because there are no cross-references in the classified shelves.

The different aspects that are scattered in the stacks, however, are grouped together in the catalog by the *LCSH* headings. Thus, all of the works on "Drug abuse" that are separated on the shelves are listed together under the one subject heading.

It is especially important to note that libraries which use call numbers supplied by the Library of Congress without modifying the numbers for local use (which is always permissible) will separate bibliographies from other books on the same subject, just as LC itself does.[3] In conventional Library of Congress cataloging, subject bibliographies are never classed with the regular monographs on the same topic; rather, bibliographies are all grouped together in the Z classes. As I noted in chapter 5, the original idea behind this arrangement was that the Z-class works would thus serve as a detailed index to the whole library, much like the index volume of an encyclopedia. Researchers who follow the Actual-Practice model, however, simply do not perceive this predictable aspect of the *system* of classification, any more than they perceive the *system* of *LCSH*. The result is that most researchers who browse the regular stack areas for books on their subject miss all of the relevant published bibliographies.

This can be disastrous. To pursue another example, a search on the Library of Congress computer catalog under the heading "School discipline—United States" turns up 74 books (as of mid-1990). If a researcher then has access to the stacks (most do not at LC), and goes simply to the primary KF and LB class areas while neglecting the Z group, he would miss E. L. Karnes's *Discipline in Our Schools* (Greenwood, 1983), which is a *700-page annotated bibliography* that lists *hundreds* of relevant sources beyond the 74 that appear on the computer printout.

In fact, a researcher following the Actual-Practice model would probably not find even those 74 to begin with. If he had begun his search in the catalog by looking for the likely sounding phrase "Discipline in the schools," he would instantly have found two books with that exact title, and two more listed immediately below it on the browse screen, *Discipline in the Secondary Classroom* and *Discipline in the Secondary School*. Since he would not have access to the stacks at LC, he would wind up with only four sources rather than 74. Even if he did have access to the stacks, however, in pursuing only these four titles he would wind up only in the LB3012–3013 stack grouping. This, of course, would lead to other titles in the area; but he would still be missing all of the additional sources in both the Z and KF classes. In other words, he would be making haphazard rather than systematic use of both the catalog and the class scheme.

If you fail to find the proper subject heading you will miss the array of standardized topical, geographic, chronological, and form subdivisions that can greatly focus your research efforts and prevent you from wasting time. I have already discussed form subdivisions in chapter 6. It is useful, however, to exemplify how they can be mixed in with the other types of subdivision.

[LC subject heading]—Bibliography
    —Criticism and interpretation
    —Description and travel
    —Dictionaries and encyclopedias
    —Directories
    —Economic conditions
    —Foreign economic relations
    —Foreign relations
    —Great Britain
    —History [with period subdivisions]
    —History—Sources
    —Japan
    —Management
    —Maps
    —Pictorial works
    —Social life and customs
    —Soviet Union
    —Statistics
    —Study and teaching
    —United States
    —United States—Bibliography
    —United States—History

Such subdivisions are the primary means by which the library distinguishes the many possible aspects of the same subject and yet also groups together under one heading records for works that are themselves widely scattered in the bookstacks. (A more extensive example, "Afro-Americans—," may be found in chapter 4.)

Many of these subdivisions are "free-floating" and can be attached to a wide range of *LCSH* terms. They may not always be explicitly listed under the headings in the *LCSH* list itself; nevertheless, they will often appear in the catalog. If, for example, you are looking for books on the economy of Greece, it is important to realize that such works will appear under "Greece—Economic conditions"; and books under this heading will tend to fall in the HC (Economic history and conditions, by region or country) and HJ (Public finance) areas of the stacks. Note, however, that the books about Greece *in general* (i.e., those without the "— Economic conditions" subdivision in the catalog) will tend to be shelved in the DF (Greece) area of the stacks. A researcher following the Actual-Practice model by simply looking up a few titles that start with the word "Greece" may therefore wind up, unknowingly, in a class area that is far removed from the best grouping for the subject *aspect* he really wants.

Note that *subdivisions* of an *LCSH* heading are considered to be subsets of it. In this respect they are quite different from BT, RT, and NT cross-references, which are not subsets and must be looked up separately.

It is particularly important to look for the form subdivision "— Bibliography." This is the way to identify and locate the important Z-class material that you would otherwise miss in browsing the non-Z areas of the bookshelves. But in order to find this subdivision, you must *first* find the proper *LCSH* category term of which it is a subdivision. Researchers who follow the Actual-Practice model usually fail to do this. They thus overlook the bibliographies *twice,* first by browsing the wrong areas of the stacks for them, and then by looking under the wrong category terms in the catalog. Finding published bibliographies efficiently is a function of first finding the right subject heading(s).

If you fail to find the proper LCSH *category term, you will miss all of the cross-references to other, related terms.* In library catalogs, subject cross-references to the crucial narrower terms (NTs) are inserted only with the subject entries, not with title entries, which many researchers mistake for subjects. And in many of the new computerized library catalogs no cross-references are included at all; with such systems you must consult the *LCSH* set itself for the listings of broader, related, and narrower terms.

Cross-references are crucial for thorough research; they are the webbing that holds together the intellectual structure of the library's retrieval systems. For example, a reader who is interested in "Children's dreams" will find that most of the books on this subject have class numbers in the BF1099 (Dreams) area of the stacks. But if she fails to find this exact heading in the *LCSH* list or in the catalog itself, she will miss an important cross-reference to the related heading "Children—Sleep"; and most of the books under *this* heading have class numbers in the RJ (Pediatrics) area of the stacks. Note that simple browsing of the BF1099s would fail to alert her to the RJ area; and looking under the wrong heading to begin with ("Dreams" rather than "Children's dreams") would also cause her to miss the important cross-reference.

If you fail to find the relevant English-language LCSH *term, you will miss most of the relevant foreign-language material.* Many readers who are specifically looking for foreign-language works make the same mistake that English-speakers make: they erroneously find—and then settle for—only a few *titles* when they ought to find the corresponding subject heading *category* term(s) instead. For example, one scholar who was looking for Italian-language books on the subject of "Venice" mistakenly searched under the Italian form "Venezia." This, predictably, led him to find only those few titles that happened to begin with this word. The proper subject heading is the English form; and the grouping of books that it creates includes all books on that subject in the library's collection, no matter what their language.

The English-language *LCSH* terms perform an especially useful function in grouping together in one place those foreign-language works that are scattered because of inflected case endings (e.g., *anthropos, anthropou, anthropoi, anthropon, anthrope, anthropois, anthropous*). The presence of such variant forms of the same word may severely undercut the alternative search technique of computerized key word retrieval, especially if the software of the library catalog does not permit word truncation.

If you fail to find the proper LCSH *category term in a computerized catalog, you will not be able to limit your inquiry to only the most recent material, or to only works in a certain language.* Computerized catalogs often allow a retrieved set of records to be limited by a further specification, and not just by date or language. Limitations by presence or absence of a bibliography, illustrations, maps, index, and so on may also be possible, as well as limitation to a certain geographic subject area by continent, region, or country. Such limitation cannot be achieved nearly as efficiently by the technique of browsing through the books on the shelves, for in the bookstacks the recent and the older works will all be mixed in together, often in identical maroon buckram library bindings, as will the English and foreign-language works. And, often, titles indicating language are not recorded on the spines of the slimmer volumes. In a large library, the very size of the class areas to be browsed— let alone the extent of scattering according to subject aspects—can greatly diminish the efficiency of identifying all of the best sources on a topic.

From all of these indications of what Actual-Practice researchers miss by failing to find the right subject headings, it should be apparent that there is much more of a *system*—an *intellectual structure* with a certain "direction" or "grain"—to subject searching than most people realize, and it is a system with definable rules that need to be followed for optimal results. There are integral relationships and connections that are established in a predictable manner among subject headings and cross-references to them; and there is a discernible internal structure by which the books arranged on the shelves are tied to the (subdivided) headings in the catalog that refer to them and by which the classification groupings are collocated or scattered.

There is even a system to proper *browsing* procedures. This technique is unusually important in the Actual-Practice model; and yet most researchers who rely so heavily on it regard its operation as primarily fortuitous or haphazard. Efficient browsing, however, is truly systematic: it is a function of first finding the right LC subject headings in the catalog. Failure to do so will effectively blind Actual-Practice stacks browsers to the possibly widespread scattering of the various aspects of their subject.

It is important to note, further, that the working of *LCSH* as a *system* extends considerably beyond just the library's catalog and the classification scheme it indexes. LC subject headings also play a key role in providing access to journal articles, government documents, and catalogs of special collections—that is, to sources not efficiently retrievable through either the library's catalog or the class scheme—because so many commercially produced indexes rely on *LCSH* as the basis for their own subject vocabularies. The Actual-Practice model, however, usually tends to neglect such indexes entirely, relying instead on simple footnote chasing from already known sources to provide whatever level of access it can. And even when footnotes fail to offer good access to journal articles, documents, and so on, these sources still tend to be overlooked as an alternative.

LCSH terms, however, provide at least a basic level of access to thousands of these sources. If you find a good heading that works in the catalog, you can usually use the same term in a wide variety of different disciplinary indexes. This enables you to find not only relevant material within a given discipline but also perspectives on the same subject from many other disciplines, all of which tend to use the same basic subject heading system. Thus, to reiterate a crucial point from chapter 2, if you have a good subject heading—whether "Tea," "Shipwrecks," "Shakespeare," "Women," "Computers," or "Religion"—you can plug it into all of the following indexes with a reasonable expectation of successful retrieval:

Magazine Index

Business Index

Legal Resource Index

National Newspaper Index

Readers' Guide to Periodical Literature

Social Sciences Index

Humanities Index

Business Periodicals Index

General Science Index

Applied Science and Technology Index

Biological and Agricultural Index

Index to Legal Periodicals

Education Index

Art Index

Bibliographic Index

Subject Collections

Subject Guide to Books in Print

American Book Publishing Record

Cumulative Book Index

Fiction Catalog

Index to U.S. Government Periodicals

Public Affairs Information Service (P.A.I.S.)

P.A.I.S. International

Monthly Catalog of U.S. Government Publications[4]

Now, not every index covers every subject in each annual volume; for example, you will not find "Shakespeare" in every volume of *Biological and Agricultural Index* or *Business Periodicals Index*. But you *will* find that heading if you are persistent in searching several of the annuals. The important point is that no index is simply limited to subjects "within" its discipline. All of them can—and do—cover *other subjects from the perspective of their discipline*. And the fact that they all tend to use *LCSH* terms binds them together in an extension of the regular cataloging system for books.

Those scholars following the Actual-Practice model who do not perceive the *LCSH* system in the first place will obviously not perceive its widespread extension into journal indexes either. This is unfortunate, as a greater awareness of this system of retrieval would encourage the more routine use of generally overlooked sources, and would also allow cross-disciplinary research to be done in a very efficient and systematic manner.

Even though most adherents of the Actual-Practice model are not aware of how much material they miss, they nevertheless do suspect that all is not well when they can find almost nothing on their topic. Such situations, of course, would not come up nearly as often as they do if researchers knew how to find the right subject headings to begin with. But, failing that, what do these searchers perceive as the alternative avenues of searching?

Browsing in the stacks is one preferred method; but this approach has serious weaknesses, already discussed, when it is not done according to the internal structure of the library's *system*.

Talking to colleagues is another preferred method; this can produce either spectacularly successful results or miserable failure (and all points in between). If the colleagues who are consulted are themselves governed by the limitations of the Actual-Practice model, then *systematic* retrieval of library sources is still precluded.

Footnote chasing is an obvious method that requires the researcher simply to have common sense rather than any particular knowledge of library systems. The problem, however, is that this technique can lead only to *previous* sources—those earlier writings cited by the work in hand. The Actual-Practice model at this point routinely overlooks two other library systems of access: citation searching and related-record searching.

Citation searches enable you to find *subsequent* articles—those written *after* the date of the work in hand, and which cite *it* in a footnote. If you already have a good source, in other words, you can use citation searching to generate a list of more recent journal articles that refer to the one you started with.[5]

Related-record searches, available only in the CD-ROM versions of the citation indexes, take a different approach. They enable you to find articles published *in the same year* as the one you started with which are related to it in that they have footnotes in common. You can thus tell, within a given year, who is playing in the same intellectual ballpark— the ballpark being defined by clusters of footnotes held in common rather than by title key words shared in common. (Indeed, the surprising feature of related-record searching is that it turns up so many relevant records that have entirely different title key words.) A few multiyear cumulative databases are available for this method of searching; but mostly it can be done only within pools of articles that have been published within a single year. Where footnote chasing enables you to search backward in time to previous sources, and regular citation searching enables you to search forward in time to subsequent articles, related-record searching enables you to search "sideways" in time to find related articles published simultaneously.

These methods of searching, while they can produce spectacular results, are nevertheless usually overlooked because they are not as obvious as browsing, talking to colleagues, or footnote chasing.

Another major omission in the Actual-Practice model is the use of published bibliographies, especially those that are separately published as opposed to the ones that appear at the end of monographs or journal articles. The separate bibliographies wind up in the index-Z classes, and the explanation for their being overlooked has already been given.

Yet another problem with this model is that, in failing to recognize the systematic aspects of a vocabulary-control apparatus such as that of *LCSH,* it also fails to perceive clearly the *nonsystematic* aspects of the opposite type of vocabulary searching: that done with key words. Key word searching, which is used more frequently nowadays because of the widespread availability of computer databases, is an *avenue* of access to knowledge records; but it is not a *system* of access because it lacks the crucial element of predictability. There is no intellectual *structure* or *direction* that enables you to proceed from the little that you know to the retrieval of whole *categories* of sources that contain works whose key words you could not specify in advance. Key word searching gives you precisely what you do specify in advance, and nothing more; if your specification is even slightly off, you may miss whole ranges of relevant material. (You may also wind up with large numbers of irrelevant sources that happen to have the right key words in the wrong contexts.) And it is easy to miss such relevant material because you have to guess the right words to search under, for there are no cross-references in key word searches to lead you to the right terms. There is no synonym control or "uniform heading," and no predictability of the choice between general or specific headings. The examples given in chapter 6 are relevant: a search that looked only for the key words "stepfamilies," "blended families," and "reconstituted families" unwittingly missed articles that used different words—"remarried families" and "reintegrated families." A search for "iron companies" missed those records with the words "iron foundry," one specifying "beef" missed "cattle," and so on.

A lot of the key word searching that is being done in the new computer indexes is thus not nearly as efficient as the Actual-Practice searchers think it is. They often believe that the databases give them "everything," regardless of which words they type in. Its failure to reveal the radical difference between two distinct *methods of searching,* using controlled-vocabulary subject headings on the one hand and natural language key words on the other, is one of the greatest deficiencies of the Actual-Practice model.

Nonetheless, in spite of its weaknesses, this model—just like all of the others discussed so far—does have its advantages. And the successful aspects of footnote chasing, browsing, and talking to colleagues must be integrated into any larger model that seeks to improve on such Actual Practice.

8

The Principle of Least Effort

The various models that we have looked at so far, especially when they are considered as structures for the actual physical arrangement of library resources, were all developed prior to the library profession's understanding of what may be called the Principle of Least Effort. This principle states that most researchers (even "serious" scholars) will tend to choose easily available information sources, even when they are objectively of low quality, and, further, will tend to be satisfied with whatever can be found easily in preference to pursuing higher-quality sources whose use would require a greater expenditure of effort. I do not mean to say that this principle cannot be discerned in prior models; but the lack of explicit emphasis on it has influenced the ways in which the models have been taught—or not taught—and their often suboptimal performance.

The Principle of Least Effort is not itself an overall model for the conceptual or physical arrangement or categorization of the materials available to researchers; but, now that librarians know as much about it as we do, it must be a design factor incorporated into any new model that would seek to go beyond the existing ones. This may seem obvious, but my experience is that it is not. What happens in the real world is that librarians are quite willing to pay lip service to the principle, but when its implications are raised (i.e., that existing arrangements and practices must actually be changed), then the principle tends to be dismissed as insignificant or insubstantial. For this reason the present chapter, and this book's bibliography, both seek to establish the reality of the Principle of Least Effort in information-seeking behavior in a way that cannot be casually ignored. Part of the reason for its neglect in practice up to now is that the various studies and review articles documenting it have not been assembled with any cumulative force. Mere references to them are not nearly as persuasive as quoting from them (the latter entailing much more work, which explains its not having been done thus far). There are so many of these studies that the library profession truly does not need any more of them. What it does need, however, is a crystallized understanding of the information that we already have.

The point is this: if one is to create a model that makes use of what we now know about people's information-seeking behaviour, it must be a system that makes the best sources for researchers' inquiries, *or at least the most promising avenues of research,* easily available. In other words, if a system makes only *some* sources easily available—especially if those sources are very superficial or of poor quality—then it can do real damage to the quality of research, for it will encourage users simply to make do with whatever sources are *readily retrievable* within it, regardless of their quality or completeness.

All library stystems are based on assumptions about what kinds of behavior can reasonably be expected from the system users. If these basic assumptions are wrong—if we assume that users will act in a certain way when they really will do no such thing—then any systems based on such mistaken premises will simply not succeed in connecting researchers with the information they need. What such systems will actually do instead will be to give their designers an excuse for blaming system failure on "user laziness." But *shifting the blame* for the problem is not at all the same thing as *providing a solution.* And if we are to do the latter, we cannot avoid our responsibility to learn the body of facts repeatedly established in the professional literature.

Before we get into the details of this literature, however, let me try to summarize it by means of a common-sense analogy. Let us compare doing library research to playing a pinball game. In a pinball game there are two factors, not one, that determine where the balls will wind up. The first is the skill of the players—their ability to manipulate the flippers and to shake the machine without tilting it in order to make the balls go where they want. The second factor, which is easier to overlook, is *the overall slope of the gameboard itself.* If the game designer were to change the slope of this surface by making it significantly steeper and also tilting it to the left side, then it would be inevitable and fully predictable that more of the balls would wind up in the lower left corner *regardless of the players' skill or experience.*

What the professional literature on information-seeking behavior consistently tells us is that, of the two factors, the "slope" of the system is much more important in determining results than is the skill or experience of the information seeker. There are, of course, exceptions, but as a general rule of thumb, people tend to choose perceived ease of access over quality of content in selecting an information source or channel; that is, they usually follow the slope of the system *regardless of whether it is leading them to the best sources.* Moreover, they tend to "satisfice" (Simon, 1956), that is, to set moderate goals to begin with, and to stop searching as soon as these goals are approximated, regardless of the fact that they may be overlooking better material. This may sound irrational, but it is nonetheless true; it has been observed and verified repeatedly. Information seekers tend to follow a "principle of least effort," a "principle of least action," or a "principle of information-processing parsimony." The aggregate of literature on these points is substantial.

Victor Rosenberg (1966) concludes his investigation of information-seeking behavior by stating: "The results of the study [imply] that the ease of use of an information gathering method is more important than the information expected for information gathering methods in industrial and government environments, regardless of the research orientation [i.e., proficiency] of the users" (p. 1). And: "From the results of the experiment, it is reasonable to conclude that: (a) research and non-research professional personnel in industry and government do not differ to any appreciable extent in their evaluation of information gathering methods; and (b) the preference for a given method reflects the estimated ease of use of the method rather than the amount of information expected. These conclusions in conjunction with the results of observation studies imply further that the basic parameter of the design of any industrial information system should be the system's ease of use, rather than the amount of information provided, and that if an organization desires to have a high quality of information used, it must make ease of access [to it] of primary importance" (p. 19).

Peter Gerstberger and Thomas Allen (1968) reach similar conclusions: "A direct relationship is found between perceived accessibility of information channels and several objective measures of utilization, whereas no definite support is found for the hypothesis that the channels perceived highest in technical quality are those used most frequently" (p. 272). And: "Any assumption that engineers act in accord with a simple instrumental learning model in which they turn most frequently to those information channels which reward them most often should now clearly be laid to rest. Engineers, in selecting among information channels, act in a manner which is intended not to maximize gain, but rather to minimize loss. The loss to be minimized is the cost in terms of effort, either physical or psychological, which must be expended in order to gain access to an information channel. Their behavior thus appears to follow a 'law of least effort' (see, e.g., Zipf, 1949). According to this law, individuals when choosing [among] several paths to a goal, will base their decision upon the single criterion of *least average rate of probable work.* . . . The implications of this finding are very important. . . . More investment in library holdings, for example, will be wasted unless at the same time this material is made more accessible to the user'' (p. 277; see also Allen, 1977).

John Salasin and Toby Cedar (1985) conclude from their survey of 1,666 researchers, practitioners, and policymakers in the field of rural mental health services: ''These findings are consistent with research showing that information sources tend to be chosen on the basis of perceived ease of use, rather than on the basis of the amount of information expected from the source'' (p. 113).

An important review article by Saul and Mary Herner (1967) notes (citing Columbia University, 1966): ''In all, descriptions of 1,036 'episodes' were collected. These were analyzed, tabulated, and types of information were correlated against the means by which obtained. The preliminary results, described in the interim report, tend to confirm the oft-observed conclusion that scientists and engineers follow those paths in seeking and obtaining information that place the smallest amount of strain and effort on them'' (p. 8). Also (citing Kenney, 1966): ''The sample of interviewees consisted of 75 users of International Labour Office documentation services. The interviews dealt with the mode and degree of available services, their shortcomings, and user preferences and habits in regard to card catalogs and indexes. . . . The obvious conclusion, confirming Rosenberg's findings [1966], is that people do not like to work too hard or travel to any extent for their information, even at the risk of losing some'' (p. 29).

Esther Bierbaum (1990) reports: ''In an extensive examination and content analyis of journal articles about the information behavior of scientists, Herbert Poole [1985] found that 43 of 51 studies (84%) directly exemplified least effort and pain avoidance'' (p. 18).

William Miller and Bonnie Gratch (1989) note: "One longitudinal study over eleven years compared MEDLINE transaction logs of several groups—faculty, graduate students, and a mixture of staff from a school of pharmacy and a department of pathology. Its findings reveal that the convenience of terminal location affected use, that convenience of doing online searches was more important to end users than the quality of search results. . . . Peischl and Montgomery (1986) analyze some of this research and conclude that, for most types of users, the responsibility for quality searches rests with the library, because infrequent or disinterested users do not perform effective searches" (p. 398).

Harry Back (1972) extends these findings to researchers in most disciplines, not just engineers and scientists: "It is reasonable to conclude from these studies that in most disciplines researchers and educators rely primarily on informal sources and on citations in relevant documents to find references. Formal methods are an important source of references in a few fields only and even there the formal methods are usually secondary to semi-formal and informal ones" (p. 160). The reason is that "[a]lthough they do not supply all relevant references, informal methods are used because they generally deliver a few relevant references with the least amount of effort" (p. 162). "In a similar study," Back writes, "Rosenberg reported that research and nonresearch personnel do not differ to any appreciable extent in the factors affecting their preference for information gathering methods. . . . Thus, the findings obtained by Gerstberger and Allen apply to researchers and educators as well as engineers" (p. 161).

Further confirmation that the findings of Rosenberg and Allen and Gerstberger are not limited to engineering or the hard sciences comes from Herbert Menzel (1966), who summarizes an American Psychological Association survey of its members on how they found books: "Most of the cited books had been discovered through a colleague's recommendation, prior knowledge, browsing, or other informal means" (p. 54)—in other words, those means that require the least amount of effort. L. Uytterschaut's (1966) survey of social scientists reveals a similar concern to get research done "as quickly as possible" and with surprisingly little use of formal library avenues of access. The reliance on footnote chasing and the neglect of indexes by social science faculty is also reported by Patricia Stenstrom and Ruth McBride (1979) and by Mary Folster (1989). Eldred Smith (1990) offers a lengthy bibliographic essay with extensive additional footnotes on "the importance that scholars attach to convenience'' (p. 41) in doing research in all fields (sciences, social sciences, and humanities). Dierdre Stam (1984) reports similar results in a study of the information-seeking practices of art historians. Maureen Pastine (1987) notes the same practices among other humanities scholars.

Mary Ellen Soper's article "Characteristics and Use of Personal Collections (1976) observes, regarding scholars' behavior: "Both evidence and informed opinion support the assumption that ease of accessibility to information affects its use, quite apart from the value of the information. . . . [A] seeker of information, for whatever purpose, will go first to a source he perceives to be the most accessible to him. In spite of the possibility that the information he needs may exist in a more authoritative form elsewhere . . . he will tend to be satisfied with what he finds nearest and not search further. The cost to the user of going beyond his immediate environment may outweigh the cost of using sources that are judged inferior by other knowledgeable people" (p. 401).

The National Enquiry into Scholarly Communication's landmark 1979 study *Scholarly Communication* (described as the "[r]eport of a comprehensive three-year research effort conducted under the auspices of the American Council of Learned Societies") points out an extremely important fact (confirming Soper): most scholars try to avoid using libraries in the first place, preferring by a large majority to use thier personal collections instead (pp. 133, 135). This finding is endorsed by many librarians, among them one quoted by William Paisley (1968): "The levels of frustration in using libraries are awfully high for most people. . . . [Y]ou are conditioned to feeling that the library is a place you almost have to drag something out of" (p. 18). Paisley also notes the "obvious solution": *"make high-quality channels more accessible and easy to use"* (p. 9; emphasis added).

Charles O'Reilly (1982) confirms the point that even professionals are not exempt from the Principle of Least Effort. In a review of the literature prior to presenting the results of his own study, he notes that "decision makers may choose information sources based on criteria other than quality of information. Corroboration of this fact is available from a number of studies. For example, in a now classic study Menzel and Katz (1955) demonstrated that physicians often learned of innovations in drugs, not from the most qualified sources such as reputable medical journalists, but from accessible sources such as drug salesmen. In a study of research and development scientists, Gerstberger and Allen

(1968) also found channel accessibility to be an important determinant of use. Similar findings have been reported in studies of education, rural sociology, and the diffusion of technical innovations (Rogers & Shoemaker, 1971). Studies of this type have revealed that often the information source is chosen for reasons other than factors associated with quality. . . . It is important to note, however, that it is the accessibility, not the quality, of the source that often is the critical determinant of its use" (p. 758). And later, in discussing the results of his own study, he states: "It is important to note that accessibility predicts frequency of use independent of a set of other variables that might affect information usage, such as uncertainty in the task, education, and tenure in the job. These factors are significant determinants of use in some instances, but it is accessibility of the source that consistently determines usage" (p. 767).

Richard Miller (1986) writes: "Moreover, there is a limit to the lengths faculty will go to obtain information, even when the information is known to be highly important to research. The principle of least effort has been shown to have a major influence on faculty research techniques and attitudes toward using libraries. Briefly stated, the principle of least effort says that in any problem situation that admits of more than one possible solution, people will tend to choose the solution that produces a minimally acceptable result with the least expenditure of effort" (p. 463).

Edwin Parker and William Paisley (1966) point out: "Accumulating data have not been kind to normative assumptions of ways in which scientists *ought* to use information. We have been forced to broaden our investigations to include . . . 'inefficient' and 'irrational' information-seeking, and so on" (p. 1061).

Further discussion and extensive documentation of the validity of the Principle of Least Effort may be found in the bibliography at the end of this book.

What are we to make of the mass of this literature? In brief, there are two conclusions that we cannot responsibly avoid. First, given a choice between a system of access to information that is perceived as easy to use and one that is perceived as difficult, most researchers will choose the easy path alone, regardless of the fact that it may offer lower-quality content. And second, *even experienced researchers and senior scholars* tend to follow the slope of a system that makes some channels easy and others difficult to use—or difficult even to perceive in the first place.

It is necessary to belabor the reality of the Principle of Least Effort for a specific reason, namely, that system designers who ignore it— apparently in favor of what they regard as their own unchallengeable "common sense"—often assert that it is not their fault when their systems fail to deliver the best information. Rather, they say, the system is good; the problem is that its users are lazy, and this is a factor for which they cannot be held responsible. It is acceptable, in other words, for the problem to remain unsolved as long as the blame can be shifted.

If, however, it can be demonstrated that we already *know* that most researchers will not expend much effort in seeking information, then this is something that information professionals and library designers must take into account in creating any overall system. It is irresponsible to view the creation of information systems as merely a technological problem, for to do so is to ignore a great deal of information that we have about the *people who must use* the systems. Ironically, disregarding the Principle of Least Effort is itself a result of the same principle at work: it is easier for many library managers and information scientists to concentrate on "hard" problems of technology than to do the difficult library research on "soft" human behavior. As Robert Fairthorne (1969) has noted: "The unwillingness, o[r] inability of information retrieval specialists to retrieve information about information retrieval is notorious. It is also extremely expensive" (p. 338).

Still, although the requisite awareness may be lacking in individual cases, the library literature indicates a widespread recognition of the need for change.

James Dwyer (1979), referring to an unpublished paper by Marcia Bates, "User Studies: What Are They Good For?" notes: "Bates proposes that we reconsider assumptions about our clients and reformulate our service patterns accordingly: '[The traditional] model is the industrious searcher who does for him or herself, and if not willing to is considered 'lazy' and not deserving of our attention. I'm not suggesting that we turn library service inside out and do everyone's searching for them. But I do suggest that it is our responsibility as information professionals to know and understand people's search behavior and to design services to optimize the likelihood for people getting the information they need *given* their patterns of behavior" (p. 137).

James Bettman and Pradeep Kakaar (1977) make the point emphatically: "The major result of these two studies is that the strategies used to acquire information are *strongly* affected by the structure of the information presented. . . . The results above have important substantive implications for decisions on how to present information to consumers. For example, the public policy maker must make decisions with respect to the provision of information to consumers. In the past, such decisions have concentrated on simply making information available. However, this focus is not sufficient. Even if information is available, if it is not easily processible it cannot be used by consumers. . . . The point is that processability is as important as availability. Thus there is a need to determine which forms of processing and rules are most 'effective' and 'easiest' for consumers, and then *information displays need to be designed which will encourage such rules or forms of processing*" (pp. 239–40; emphasis added). To anticipate a future point here, let me simply note that other studies indicate that some information requests are more processable by way of manual or print sources than through computer searches; see Dolan (1979), Elcheson (1978), Johnston (1978), Johnston and Gray (1977), Rowland (1982), and Standera (1985). Print sources, therefore, will have to have an important place in any overall library system design.

Richard Dougherty (1973), citing R. S. Taylor (1968), draws the inevitable conclusion: "[A] system which provides easier access, specifically physical convenience, will be more effective than a system which is concerned only with the quality of the scheme of subject organization. . . . If ease and convenience are such potent influences on a user's behavior, then why not develop mechanisms to improve the ease [with] which a library's rich resources can be accessed?" (p. 29).

The Committee on Scientific and Technical Communication of the National Academy of Sciences–National Academy of Engineering (1969) says that "the lack of awareness of the existence of information sources rather than their (imputed or experienced) ineffectiveness continues to contribute in a major way to the heavy dependence on informal channels. Finally, there is little effort to apply or implement what is learned from user studies; for example, what steps should be taken to deter users from returning to familiar and easily accessible sources, even when the expected yield is low, and to tap instead sources that promise a higher yield, albeit at greater effort" (p. 107).

Don Swanson (1966) spells out the implications of the "principle of least effort": "The design of any future information system should be predicated on the assumption that its customers will exert minimal effort in order to receive its benefits. Furthermore they won't bother at all if the necessary minimum is higher than some fairly low threshold'' (p. 9).

Herner and Herner (1967) provide a succinct statement of the professional responsibility involved: ''While the user can furnish *insights* as to how he get his information and how he prefers to get it, it falls ultimately to the information specialist to devise the best and most efficient means of supplying it'' (p. 3).

James Leisener (1984) concludes: ''It is high time that this profession confront these issues and redesign library media instruction and services in the light of our primitive but growing understanding of information seeking behavior. . . . It is also clear that we need to reconsider the concept of self sufficiency in information seeking activities . . .'' (pp. 85–86).

With the development of the library profession's understanding of the realities of actual information-seeking behavior, it will no longer do to assert that researchers' failure to find necessary information is simply the result of their own laziness. If we truly hope to solve the problem of overlooked information, we must take into account library *system design* in addition to *researchers' skills*. We must consciously manipulate the ''slope of the gameboard'' to make the best channels easier for researchers to perceive.

One distinction is important here, however: while we cannot know in advance the information content of particular books, journal articles, or other sources, we can know in advance that some *methods of searching* are clearly superior to others for given inquiries. Thus, subject heading category searching is usually more effective than natural language key word searching, provided that appropriate subject headings exist. If they do not exist, then key word search sources are preferable as the *first* avenue of attack. In some instances citation searching will be a preferable first point of attack rather than either *LCSH* or key word approaches. At other times, the use of published bibliographies rather than computer-generated lists will be the best first step; and so on. *How* the readers can search in the first place is a function of the configurations of the ''gameboard'' that the librarians have waiting for them. It is necessary that the full range of search options be embodied in distinct groups of sources that will allow the different search methods to be readily perceptible (and distinguishable), with any one of them then being easily available as the *first* option for a given inquiry. Such a configuration is the system-design responsibility of the librarians, not of the researchers themselves. These are points that need to be kept in mind, especially in any attempt to integrate computerized-access resources into a model of library research in the future.

9

The Computer Workstation Model

Part One:
The Prospect

A new model of the overall universe of information available to researchers has recently developed as an outgrowth of the rapid advances in computer technology for storing and retrieving knowledge records. Given the realities of human nature and the Principle of Least Effort in information-seeking behavior, the Computer Workstation model has become enormously attractive; indeed, its adherents hold out the prospect that "everything"—a "virtual library," or "the entire Library of Congress"—will be available immediately and completely to anyone with access to such a workstation. Gone would be the need to travel to a library; instead, the "electronic library" would be available anywhere, to anyone with access to the inexpensive equipment needed to tap into it.

The roots of this idea of the obsolescence of libraries as physical places goes back to the Documentation movement that flourished in the 1940s and 1950s (Rayward, 1983), and that reflected a justified impatience with the concept of libraries as storage facilities for printed texts, especially books, to the comparative neglect of other formats of knowledge records (e.g., reports, journal articles, photographs, typescripts, memoranda, manuscripts, and maps). These other records often tended to be held in repositories other than libraries, such as archives, corporate offices, or government agencies, but were validly perceived by the Documentalists as being, in their own way, just as important as books in the totality of the universe of knowledge records. Moreover, even when such formats were collected by libraries, they tended not to be granted the same priority, and also not to be indexed or classified as systematically as the books.

In terms of the present analysis, one could say that the Documentalists were justifiably dissatisfied with the Traditional Library Science model—or at least with the classified book-collection component of it, which they tended to perceive as the entirety of that model's universe, having only dim perceptions of the second component, the vocabulary-control system of the catalog. Their virtual neglect of the third component, bibliographies and indexes which do indeed provide access to material in other locations and to the nonbook formats within the library itself, was unfortunate and yet perhaps unavoidable, since librarians themselves have often failed to see this component as being on a par with the other two.

A further impetus toward the idea that libraries-as-places are obsolete came with the Documentalists' fascination with microfilm as a way of freeing the intellectual content of written or graphic works from the physical confines of books. The new microformats held out the hope of two profound improvements in providing access to knowledge records: (1) they could physically reduce the size of library collections to the point that whole collections could be stored conveniently not only in library buildings themselves, but also in individual researchers' own offices or homes; and (2) they could greatly reduce the cost of obtaining such collections in the first place, as microforms could be duplicated (as well as stored) much less expensively than printed-paper formats.

One thus finds a host of optimistic predictions along these lines in the literature of the 1960s and 1970s:

"UMF [ultramicrofiche] has the potential of providing anyone with his own portable reader. In the future a person may be able to acquire a sizeable library of selected titles in a package no larger than a standard dictation machine, complete with reader and microfiche, weighing less than five pounds" ("Real Future Is Seen for Ultramicrofiche," 1968, p. 288).

"For the average person, [microprinting] could mean the possession of an almost unlimited supply of low-cost 'volumes' in a library no larger than a file cabinet. And if he wanted a set of encyclopedias in every room, he could easily afford it" ("Microbooks—A Future Revolution in Printing," 1964, p. 216).

"Tomorrow's businessman will have the information necessary to do his job, right at his fingertips, due to the growing acceptance of micro-imagery as the solution to the information explosion" (Steel, 1974, p. 213).

"College libraries of the future will lend microfiche cards instead of books and students will use their own portable readers to study the cards without leaving their rooms in the opinion of Rutherford Rogers, the librarian of Yale University'' (''Microfilm to Replace Books,'' 1973, p. 28).

"How would you like to have the Library of Congress, occupying 270 miles of bookshelves, in your house?

"Sounds impossible? Well through a new microphotography process, PCMI (photochromic microimages) you may, one day, be able to have the entire contents of the great library in your den on film—all contained in about six standard filing cabinets. A viewer is already available to project the filmed images'' (''Putting a Library in a Shoebox,'' 1965, p. 77).

It is noteworthy that the microfilm ''solution'' to the problems of libraries wound up creating still more problems for the Traditional Library Science model. Microforms, not being comfortably readable without bulky machines, could not be browsed like books, and so could not reasonably be included in a library's classification scheme for shelving books; instead, they had to be shelved in separate areas close to the viewer machines. And the maintenance and user-service requirements of the machines meant that they had to be arrayed together in such areas, near their attendants, rather than distributed throughout the bookstacks. The inability of the classification scheme—which, again, was and still is often misperceived as the whole of the Library Science model—to deal with microforms thus led those of the Documentalist mind-set to see microforms as achieving their full potential *outside* traditional library buildings (as the quotations indicate), thus lending further impetus to the notion of the obsolescence of libraries-as-places where (obsolete) books are stored.

Microforms, of course, failed to ''replace'' either printed books or libraries-as-places, although they proved to be wonderful supplements to print formats; but what is most interesting at present is the remarkable similarity with which the current rhetoric about computer workstations mirrors the earlier rhetoric about microform workstations.

A *New York Times* article of May 13, 1990, asserts that ''mass data storage and information networks erase the physical requirements of storing documents. Whether corporate or public, tomorrow's library will not necessarily be a place to go . . . but rather a focal point for a variety of services. Such 'libraries without walls' are beginning to appear in schools and businesses, and the silent, musty stacks are giving way to high-technology centers, available to personal computers everywhere . . ." (p. 8F).

An official of the Library of Congress is quoted in the *Wall Street Journal* of February 23, 1990, as saying: "Libraries of the future will be a service, not a place. . . . What you once had to go to the Library of Congress to see can be viewed at home. That's the capability" (p. B4). This prediction is echoed by the chairman of the Senate Subcommittee on Science, Technology, and Space, who writes in the *Washington Post* of July 15, 1990: "If we had the information superhighways we need, a school child could plug into the Library of Congress every afternoon and explore a universe of knowledge, jumping from one subject to another, according to the curiosity of the moment" (p. B3).

A brochure, "Academic Libraries: Your Campus Information Centers," published by the Association of College and Research Libraries and the American Library Association, tells students: "It's likely that library's [sic] services will become more decentralized than they are now, and users would not always have to come to a physical building to use the library's resources. Instead, when institutions of higher education are networked and faculty members and students have individual computer workstations, the resources of the library will be accessible with just a few keystrokes." (Note the characteristic assertion that "the" resources, not merely "some" resources, will be available in this manner.)

A corporate futurist with a large commercial computer company has predicted "that the pocket office will arrive in the 1990s, to be quickly followed by the 'information centre' worn as an ornament—the equivalent of the Library of Congress tappable from your wrist" (Large, 1984: 17).

Evidently there is an intellectual niche that cries out to be filled by the thought of having "everything" one needs available through one-stop shopping. Certainly the Principle of Least Effort in information-seeking behavior impels researchers to drift in this direction; but the Computer Workstation model provides additional inducements toward belief in "one-source" research by holding out the prospect of several advantages over the Traditional Library Science model.

First, the Library Science model, which originated in an era of manual and print technology, depended for decades on card catalogs as a major avenue of access to libraries' holdings; and a printed-card technology enforces a certain economy in the intellectual structure of subject access that it can provide. If, for example, the librarian-catalogers wished to provide access to a certain book through its author's name, its title, and three subject category terms, they had to create a separate card for each such point of access and then file the five cards separately at the appropriate places in the catalog's alphabetical sequence. Under the constraints of such a model it would be out of the question to index a book under fifteen or twenty subject headings, or to create and file a separate card under each word in the book's title, or in its table of contents. The labor-intensive cost of creating and filing so many different cards for only one book would be prohibitive; moreover, any such catalog would soon become physically very bulky, resulting in both increased costs for storage space and increased frustration for users trying to find their way through so large a file.

A computerized catalog, by contrast, obviates such constraints. In an electronic catalog, each work can be represented by only one record; but that one record can have as many points of access as there are different words, numbers, or codes on it. In such a situation, presumably, catalogers can add many subject headings beyond the traditional two or three, as well as tables of contents or descriptive notes; and they can make each of these extra elements a directly searchable point of access while at the same time circumventing the prohibitive cost of creating, filing, and storing separate records for each one.

Second, the Library Science model traditionally depended on a vocabulary-controlled system of approved subject category terms, such as *Library of Congress Subject Headings.* A frequent problem with any such system is that sometimes there just isn't any approved heading that corresponds to what a researcher wants to find. For example, someone who needs information on "the interoperability of military parts in the NATO system" or on "nonbank banks" will not find any appropriate *LCSH* term. With a computer catalog, however—assuming that it has the proper software—one can search directly for the key words "interoperability" and "nonbank" anywhere on any record, as the third word of the title, or the twenty-fifth word of the note field, and so on. The computer model thus enables one to "see" information in areas that are blind spots to the old library model.

Third, in the old model, direct access to full texts (as opposed to surrogate catalog records) is provided by the classification scheme; that is, the contiguous shelving of books on the same subject enables readers to search not just brief catalog records or subject headings but the full texts themselves in a systematic manner. The elements of the knowledge records that could not be included in the catalog (tables of contents, back-of-the-book indexes, illustrations, individual paragraphs and even words) could still be searched for systematically, and in predictably limited areas, because of the subject groupings of full texts brought about by the class scheme.

As I pointed out in chapters 3 and 4, however, there are inevitable and unavoidable problems that are entailed in the classifier's choice of *which* subject area any one book will be assigned to, for many books could usefully be categorized in a variety of different subject areas (e.g., *Black Women Novelists* or *Graphic Design in Educational Television*). The classification of each book in only one area of the stacks thus cannot reveal the full range of its possible subject ties to all other related books. Again, the economics of a printed-book–based system preclude purchasing multiple copies of the same work and cataloging each in a different area of the stacks.

The computer model, by contrast, holds out the prospect of a solution to this problem. If all of the full texts of a library collection can be digitized, then all of them can be searched simultaneously for any inquiry. In this model, one's range of vision into the texts is not constrained by the proximity—or lack of proximity—of printed books necessarily confined to certain physical locations. To return to an example from chapter 3, stacks browsers who look for books on "Television graphics" in the NC area of the shelves (Drawing, design, illustration) will probably miss those on the same subject that are shelved in the PN1992 (Television broadcasts) and LB1044.7 ("Television" within "Teaching") class areas. The computer searcher, however, would retrieve all of the related texts together at the single location of his workstation.

The ability to search digitized full texts by computer has other implications as well. The speed of retrieval is much greater, as is the completeness of the in-depth access. For example, a linguistics scholar looking for appearances of the word "ripped" as a body-building term would, in using a classified array of printed texts, go to the area of the stacks dealing with this subject and then individually skim likely looking volumes. While this technique will turn up some instances of the word, it can also lead the searcher to overlook others, for a human searcher cannot take the time to actually read every word on every page of every possible relevant text.

The computer, however, can search for every instance of the word in every text in its digitized database, and do it at very high speed. The completeness and rapidity of access that it can provide to full texts is thus potentially much greater than that allowed for by a classification scheme of subject-grouped printed books. Whether the potential becomes actual, however, obviously depends on the extent of the full-text collection that is digitized in the first place, a point to which I shall return.

Fourth, the old library model necessarily treated books and journal articles differently. A library's card catalog traditionally provided author, title, and subject access only to books, not journal articles. To provide such access to every article in every journal in the library's collection would have meant creating a card catalog hundreds of times larger and bulkier than a books-only file, and this would have been precluded by economic reasons alone. As an alternative, however, libraries could and did provide access to the journal articles through special indexes and bibliographies (the third component of the Library Science model), and so there was no need for the card catalog to duplicate an avenue of access that was readily available elsewhere. For searchers, however, this meant that more than one source had to be consulted if they were to find both books and journal articles.

The computer model, however, holds out the prospect of searching all knowledge records in the same way, at the same time, and at the one location. At a computer workstation it is technically just as easy and convenient to search digitized journal indexes as it is to search book catalogs—and some software configurations already allow the search of both simultaneously. Moreover, it is technically just as easy to digitize the full text of journal articles as it is to scan books into the database; and so, again, researchers have the potential to see "everything" in one location, instead of having to look at a catalog in one place and indexes in several others.

Fifth, the equality of treatment that the computer model allows for books and journal articles extends to other formats as well, including reports, government documents, manuscripts, typescripts, prints, photographs, maps, posters, animated illustrations, video and movie images, and music and sound recordings. *All* can be digitized and reproduced at a computer workstation. (Perhaps even three-dimensional holographic images will be similarly accessible in the future.) Furthermore, the equality of storage capability holds out the potential for vastly

superior linkages among the various formats through hypermedia connections. Theoretically one could read a play, call up criticisms of it in
journals, examine a copy of the author's manuscript to study revisions
during the creative process, watch a movie based on it, listen to a
symphony inspired by it, and view a roundtable discussion of critics
arguing with one another over all of the above, all at the same workstation. Hypermedia linkages would allow a researcher to go back and forth
among all formats of knowledge records, all at one workstation.

Sixth, the linkages that can be created among various media of knowledge records at one library can also, theoretically, be created among
other computerized knowledge records that are stored in computers in
other locations—whether in other campuses, other cities, other countries, or other continents. Electronically digitized information can be
transmitted across the world just as readily as across a campus; the
prospect of a networked "library without walls" is thus another appealing aspect of the ideal Computer Workstation, and it is one that cannot
be duplicated by the place-bound Traditional Library Science model.

Seventh, again, the classification scheme is usually perceived as the
main (or even sole) component of the Library Science model; and the
classification scheme obviously cannot incorporate computer workstations. Where would a device capable of displaying, variously, any kind
of knowledge record on any subject be physically located in a scheme
devised to reveal subject relationships among printed books? The classification scheme, then, can obviously no longer be considered the "universe" of which knowledge records are available. The ideal workstation, however, is seemingly capable of containing everything that could
be placed within the class scheme, plus a wide variety of formats that
never could find a home in it—and that have always been a problem for
the Library Science model. And so proponents of the ideal Workstation
model view the computer as forming in and of itself the entire new
"universe" of records, making the Library Science class scheme obsolete at the same time.

The combination of these factors thus holds out a very powerful and
attractive inducement for researchers to believe that the Computer
Workstation model represents the entirety of the "new" universe of
knowledge, that "everything" one would want to know can be included
in it, and that all of this knowledge can be searched at once through a
single source. Moreover, it is emphasized that this single source is
definitely not a traditional library. In fact, it is usually spoken of in terms

that explicitly contrast it to books and libraries. Thus, for example, a 1990 mass-mailing advertisement from C&P Telephone for the Bell Atlantic Gateway Service reads, in part:

> Now you can access a world of information vital to your everyday life— easily and affordably—just by dialing one local number to go on-line with. . . .
>
> You need the right tools to help you maximize the utilization of your time . . . keys to rapid problem solving . . . and a sharper edge to help you cut through the clutter and get right to the heart of an important issue.
>
> Now, C&P Telephone brings you an exclusive, innovative way to accomplish *all* of that and more . . . productively, efficiently and economically! . . .
>
> So easy and convenient, Bell Atlantic GATEWAY opens up an immediate reference for educational and practical information on *everything* from travel arrangements . . . through financial planning and on-line shipping systems, health care, self-help and social interaction services . . . to reviews on [*sic*] the best restaurants in your area and top box-office movies! So it's a vital *one-stop source* for every member of the family—regardless of age.
>
> Think about it! A round-the-clock, *total* information service available 365 days a year—right in your own home or office! So *no matter what type of data* you require—you'll always have access to it for work, school, home, and community living.
>
> No more endless hours of research . . . no more expensive, outdated reference books. *All you need* is this *one-stop* information service. (emphasis added)

Who, at least in the copywriter's mind, could pass up such a millennial system?

Who indeed?

10

The Computer Workstation Model

Part Two:
Qualifications

There are a number of problems with the Computer Workstation model if it is represented as encompassing the total universe of knowledge records, either now or in the future. These problems tend to lie in concealed propositions that are assumed by proponents of the model, and that are seldom fully articulated.

Concealed Propositions

Specifically, two of these propositions arise from the frequent practice of setting the Workstation model in opposition to the traditional Library Science model. They are: (1) that the new avenues of access to catalog records provided by computerized key word, word-truncation, word-proximity, and Boolean-combination search capabilities are making vocabulary control and authority work (standardization of variant forms and linkage of categories) unnecessary; and (2) that the technical possibility of mounting full texts online or in CD-ROMs makes irrelevant the continuation of a classification scheme for printed books. In other words, the retrieval capability of the computer is assumed to be so powerful that any records within it—whether catalog surrogates for full texts or the texts themselves—no longer require the standardization, categorization, and integrative relational linkages provided by the work of professional library catalogers.

An explicit statement of the first proposition appears in a 1984 article by the director of the University of Guelph Library, who expresses the opinion that research is proving that it will soon be possible to ignore structured, thesauri-driven approaches to information retrieval such as LCSH. They can be replaced with natural language systems that might contain abstracts, tables of contents, and indexes—if not full texts—derived from electronic publishing. The searcher will use natural language to develop and carry out a search. The key to this type of retrieval system is the artificial intelligence supplied by programming, which leads to dynamic search results. (Beckman, 1984: 252)

The writer does not cite any of the research to which she alludes; nor does she give any examples of an artificial intelligence system capable of dealing not merely with a relatively small collection of literature focused on a single subject or discipline, and entirely in one language, but rather with a research-library–sized collection of multilingual holdings in all subject areas. In any event, her statement is not entirely typical of those who see no continuing need for a "thesauri-driven" approach; most such thinkers believe that the mere possibility of enhanced key word searching, even without artificial intelligence programming, is enough to "replace" vocabulary control.

The first question that arises, then, is this: Can key word or natural language searching on computers replace rather than merely supplement *Library of Congress Subject Headings?* The answer entailed by the usual portrayal of the Computer Workstation model is that it can.

An example of the second concealed proposition is stated in a 1982 book on the Library of Congress:

[I]t is easy to see that traditional answers to the traditional questions fall apart with videodisc technology—or at least traditional cataloging techniques do. If every disk has some 3,000 books on it, we can no longer shelve "books" by call number and keep inserting the latest volume in among its subject peers. Subject classification by class number on open shelves can be forgotten. The present guess is that disks will be loaded in the manner of a bookstore: all fiction on one "wall," political science on another, cookbooks, history by country, psychology, children's books, biology, et cetera. Within each broad category, it is assumed that books will be stored by acquisition number. . . . (Goodrum, 1982: 302–3)

The second question, then, is this: Since it is technically possible to digitize full texts of books and store them on optical disks or other electronic media, is it necessary for libraries to maintain classification schemes whose purpose is to collocate printed books as physical objects in browsable subject groupings? The answer entailed by the usual portrayal of the Computer Workstation model is that the class scheme is indeed obsolete.

These answers, however, are not really as sensible as they may appear on the surface.

Knowledge Records That Cannot Be Retrieved Without Vocabulary Control and Classification

As a reference librarian who is called on to use both key word searching and *LCSH* every day, and also the classification scheme for printed books as well as full-text databases, I must point out some of the very real difficulties that result from a naive acceptance of these two propositions. Let me first give some concrete examples of what I have in mind, to establish a baseline understanding of the function of the LC subject heading and classification systems.

My first example concerns a fiction writer who once told me she needed background books on ''what life is like for people who live along highways out in the country, not near cities.'' A question like this is impossible to research with natural language key words, for that search technique will produce a superabundance of utterly irrelevant hits (e.g., crossing ''life'' and ''highways'' turns up *Effect of Prestress on the Fatigue Life of Concrete,* a study conducted for the Texas State Department of Highways and Public Transportation). It will also miss the large majority of works that *are* relevant. In this instance I asked the writer if she had in mind something like people who lived along the old Route 66, and she said yes. In searching the Library of Congress computer system for ''Route 66,'' then, we found four titles. From the subject category *LCSH* tracings on these titles, and on other records to which they led, I finally made a set composed of the *LCSH* elements ''(Automobiles or Roads) and (Road guides or Guide-books),'' then limited it with the geographic area code for the United States. (The code, like the *LSCH* terms, is an artificial indexing element added to the record by the subject catalogers, as opposed to being a natural language feature that could simply be transcribed from the book titles or contents pages.) We came up with a set of over 150 titles including:

> *Roadside History of Colorado*
> *Where the Old Roads Go*

Roadside History of New Mexico

RVing America's Backroads

The Roadside History of Vermont

A Field Guide to Interstate 95

Arkansas Roadsides

Backroads, USA

Back Roads of the Central Coast

Travelers Guide to Interstate 80, Coast to Coast

Idaho for the Curious

Back Roads of New England

Tour the Country Roads

The writer was delighted. Suddenly she had dozens of titles that seemed right on the button, although she hadn't expected to find any that were close to what she wanted.

My second example involves a student who wanted information on the "nonmilitary relations of the USSR with other countries." We quickly found the *LCSH* category "Soviet Union—Relations" (while also noting that the subdivisions "—Foreign relations" and "—Foreign economic relations" were not turning up what she wanted) and then discovered a host of other standardized search terms through cross-references and tracings, all combined with "Soviet Union":

Teachers, interchange of

Educational exchanges

Exchange of persons programs

Cultural relations

Exchanges, literary and scientific

Students, interchange of

As is evident, the deeper we got into it, the more the student decided to concentrate on educational exchanges, so I showed her the *Education Index,* too. This commercially published index also tends to use *LCSH* terminology (that is, all of the listed headings can be found in it); it quickly led to relevant journal articles that were not in the Library's computer catalog for books.

My third example, a professor who was the president of a classics association, and who had been teaching and writing in the field for twenty years, asked, "How would the Greeks and Romans have transcribed animal sounds?" That is, today we would write "quack" or "oink" or "ribbit," but how would the ancients have heard these sounds? Apart from some obvious sources (e.g., Aristophanes' *The Frogs*), he did not know where to look. Fortunately, the *LCSH* list provides a number of likely category terms for such information; and, not by chance, dozens of commercial indexes tend to use the same subject terms. "Animal sounds" did not turn up any good hits in LC's own computer or card catalogs; but it did turn up a promising article in the old *Social Sciences and Humanities Index* (which uses *LCSH*) on "Suetonius' catalogue of animal sounds." Yet another *LCSH* category, "Greek language—Onomatopoeic words," turned up a 439-page dictionary in Greek that hit the nail right on the head. And its Greek title, *Echopoietes lexeis kai rizes sten Hellenike,* is hardly something that would turn up in a "natural language" search by an English-speaker. Nevertheless, I could still find the work because, even though I do not know Greek, I do know how to use *LCSH;* and that ability usually gives any reference librarian the capability of finding sources in any language—sources that cannot be found even by full professors who have spent a lifetime of study in fields in which the librarians have no subject expertise whatever.

In this case, too, I had not known in advance that the subdivision "—Onomatopoeic words" existed; but, owing to the *precoordinated* display of subdivisions under the *LCSH* heading in the catalog, I could *recognize* its value when I saw it.

Let me digress a moment to explain a bit of library and information science jargon. *Precoordination* is the opposite of *postcoordination.* What these terms refer to is the method of combining two or more subjects in a single search. With a computer you can take two or more separate subject sets (e.g., "Women" and "Mass media") and cross them against each other to determine if any record includes both headings; this is known as postcoordination. A precoordinated heading, by contrast, is one that in effect has already done such a combination for you; it expresses in one predetermined phrase the overlap of two or more subjects, so that you do not have to combine them yourself through postcoordinating computer manipulations. Examples of precoordinated headings are "Women in television broadcasting—United States," "Smallpox in animals," "Minorities in medicine," and "Alphabet—Religious aspects—Islam."

To continue with a fourth example, I once received a "rush" inquiry concerning the date of construction of the memorial marking the millennium of the founding of Russia, in Novgorod. (The question came from the office of the Librarian of Congress. The Library was planning to present a picture of this memorial to Raisa Gorbachev, who would be touring the Library as part of a state visit.) I knew from past experience that a good way to find the date of any such memorial is first to find a guidebook to the city in question, and that such guides can be found predictably through the "—Description" subheading attached to the name of the city. In looking in the catalog under "Novgorod" with this subdivision, I found that the guidebooks themselves were clustered in the DK651 (Russia. Cities, towns, etc.) area of the stacks. Arriving there, I quickly went through about three shelves of books. I could tell from the illustrations that one booklet, in Russian, was precisely on the subject of the millennium memorial. Since I can't read Russian myself, I immediately took the booklet to a specialist in LC's European Division, who then quickly provided the date.

I checked later and found that the memorial booklet's cataloging record did not have the "[City]—Description" subject heading. Nevertheless, even though my catalog search had not shown me the record for that book to start with, I could still find the book anyway because the second system, the class scheme's arrangement of full texts, "kicked in" as a backup and revealed to me something I hadn't known enough about to specify in advance in the catalog. Both systems functioned together, in other words; the class scheme showed me the right book, but the subject heading in the catalog had first functioned as the index to the class scheme, directing me to the right area for subject browsing of the appropriate group of full texts with their crucial illustrations that enabled me to spot the relevant books. And because both systems functioned together, someone who knows nothing about Russian history, who cannot even read the language, and who had LC's 535 miles of bookshelves to search (the distance from Washington, D.C., to Charleston, South Carolina) could still find the answer to a question on a very obscure point within fifteen minutes of receiving the inquiry.

As a fifth example, for a scholar editing the diaries of Anna Whistler (mother of the artist James), I had to find biographical information on an obscure nineteenth-century stage performer whom Mrs. Whistler mentions having met in St. Petersburg, Russia, in the 1840s. His name was apparently "Risley" or "Rizley"; he was referred to as "The Professor"; and he had two sons of five and seven years of age. That was all that was known.

I thought the easiest way to start would be to browse the biographical reference books concerned with theatrical people; these are located around the PN2000+ area (Dramatic representation . . . Biography) in the LC system. I didn't know that precise class area in advance, but I did know that both literary and dramatic biographical works are in the general PN area of the biography alcove of the reading room's reference collection; and I could easily spot the theatrical cluster once I got there. This led to the quick discovery of J. P. Wearing's *American and British Theatrical Biography* at PN2285.W42; it is a 1,007-page cumulative index to about 170 old biographical directories and encyclopedias. It provided a reference for "RISLEY, Prof. (d. 1874) manager, athlete, musician" to the four-volume *Catalogue of Dramatic Portraits in the Theatre Collection of the Harvard College Library,* which was to be found at PN2205 in the stacks. This source gave Risley's full name, the names of his sons, and a description of part of their acrobatic act. And browsing in the books right nearby, I found numerous other references—in one a full paragraph, in another an engraving of the three Risleys doing their act—in the multivolume *Annals of the New York Stage* at PN2277. Additional information showed up in PN2256 in M. B. Leavitt's *Fifty Years in Theatrical Management* (1912), which gave details of Risley's managerial career, and also recorded the later-life activities of the two sons. (Note that all of this information lay concealed within the Library's full-text collections, but none of it was findable in the *catalog* of the collections, no matter how the catalog was searched.)

For a sixth and final example, in responding to a letter seeking photographs or drawings of an old private railroad car known as "Car 90," I first found, through the *LCSH* red books, that a likely subject heading would be "Railroads—United States—Private cars." This heading in the computer catalog turned up a citation to the American Association of Private Railroad Car Owners' *AAPRCO Roster of Private Railroad Cars,* at TF455 (Railroad equipment . . . Varieties of cars. Passenger cars); and this work listed a Car 90 as now being owned by the Illinois Railway Museum (with its address). Right nearby on the shelves was Lucas Beebe's *Mansions on Rails* (also in TF455), which provided photographs of the interior of a different Car 90, and which listed the plan number for still another 90 in its appendix, a copy of which could be obtained from the Pullman Technology Company.

In the first three examples, it was simply essential to have predictable category terms with systematic avenues of access (i.e., cross-references, tracings, and "browse" displays of precoordinated subject subdivisions) to find them. For the last three, a classification scheme that enabled me to search full texts in a systematic manner was indispensable. Additionally, in examples four and six, the index function of the precoordinated subject heading/subheading system in the catalog was essential for telling me which particular areas of full texts in the class scheme I needed to browse to find the very detailed information I was after.

Reference librarians who work in real libraries, rather than in academic departments or at personal workstations linked only to colleagues in the same subject discipline, receive hundreds of such inquiries every year. And this is the important point: *no* reference librarian can even begin to have subject expertise in all of the areas we are asked about. (Academics, in contrast, usually do not have either the occasion to ask or the requirement to answer so very extensive a variety of questions in subject areas outside their own.) But in the large majority of cases, librarians do not need subject expertise as long as we have predictable systems of access. And the vocabulary control of *LCSH* and the groupings of full texts brought about by the LC classification scheme *constitute* those systems. As long as we have good category terms to work with, predictable avenues of access to the category terms provided by cross-references, tracings, and "browse" displays of precoordinated subdivisions (either in printed or in electronic sources), full texts (not just brief catalog records) arranged by subject in a predictable and systematic manner, and a good index to the classification scheme (provided by the precoordinated headings with subdivisions in the catalog), then we have the crucial elements of a *system*. We have *predictability*, systematic *serendipity*, and *depth of access* to the knowledge records within it; and with these features we can usually do efficient subject searches even in areas in which we have no personal expertise.

Predictability

By *predictability* I mean, in general, the capability of a system to move searchers efficiently from whatever search strategy they think of themselves to the strategy that will produce the best results. In the matter of search vocabulary, for example, if readers want information on "Multinational corporations" in an *LCSH*-controlled catalog, they will not get the best results by looking under that term, which, admittedly, is the one that would occur to most people. The best *LCSH* term is "International business enterprises," which, even though a researcher might not think of it on his or her own, nevertheless can be easily found through *predictable* means: it can be determined either by consulting the cross-references in the *LCSH* books themselves, or by finding a record with the key words "Multinational corporations" in the title (or elsewhere) and then looking at the subject tracings for that record. In other words, we can *count* on having the means of moving *from* whatever term we think of *to* the best term(s).

Predictability is also a feature of the classified arrangement of full texts on the shelves: searchers will be able, through the catalog, to predetermine which areas of the stacks will best repay full-text browsing; and they will also be able reasonably to expect beforehand that such browsing will turn up a great deal more specific and detailed information on whatever their subject may be—information much too detailed to be included on any superficial surrogate records in the catalog. Being able to expect such things from a retrieval system gives one a great deal of power in doing research, especially the power to move about comfortably in the literature of unfamiliar subjects.

Indeed, the extent of predictability in a library structured according to *LCSH* and the LC classification scheme is much greater than most people realize. (The situation of most readers in a large research library is rather like that of the hiker in the woods who cannot see the forest for the trees.) Specifically, in such a configuration, librarians and researchers who perceive the structure can reasonably predict all of the following when dealing with a question in any subject area:

• That the principle of uniform heading will be effective—that is, that we won't have to think up all possible synonyms (For example, *capital punishment, death penalty, legal execution,*) or variant title key words (*A Life for a Life, To Kill and Be Killed, The Ultimate Coercive Sanc-*

tion) that may be scattered throughout the alphabet; rather, all of the variant forms will be grouped together for us under one approved *LCSH* term (Capital punishment).

• That the uniform English-language heading will include in its coverage all of the foreign-language books on that subject as well. (For example, *pena capitale, peine de mort, smertnaia kazn',* and *Todesstrafe,* will be grouped together under the very same heading [Capital punishment] that rounds up all of the English variant phrasings.)

• That the principle of specific entry will be effective—that is, given a choice of many possible search terms, it will be more helpful to use the specific rather than the more general headings (knowledge of this principle is a major advantage in systematic searching).

• That we can find the specific heading(s) by means of a systematic network of cross-references so we do not have to guess which terms to search under.

• That we can snag other relevant category terms that lie outside the cross-reference network through the subject tracings attached to the bottom of records discoverable through title or author searches. (Tracings, in other words, tell us to which categories any particular known item belongs.)

• That we can find still other category terms by their being alphabetically contiguous in the *LCSH* list. (For example, the heading ''Business intelligence'' is narrower than ''Business'' alone; but, nevertheless, it is not given a Narrower Term cross reference under the general heading, as might be expected. It can be spotted without the cross reference, however, simply by its appearance in a position alphabetically near the general term.)

• That in pursuing *focused* subject inquiries, browsing through precoordinated subdivisions of *LCSH* categories in the library's catalog can alert us to other search terms that we could not find either directly in the red books or through tracings. (For example, a researcher looking specifically for information on Thomas Jefferson's opinions on religious liberty could find the heading ''Jefferson, Thomas—Views on freedom of religion'' rather easily. In looking at either a computer catalog browse display, or a card catalog array of subdivisions under ''Jefferson,'' however, he could also easily notice ''Jefferson, Thomas—Quotations,'' which would lead to compilations of Jefferson's sayings on various matters, arranged by subject. The precoordination of the second [or third, or *n*th] element thus enables searchers to recognize relevant sources that they could not specify in advance—whereas in post-coordinate combinations, they would have to specify in advance all elements they wish to combine.)

• That we can sharpen questions that are *unfocused* or fuzzy to begin with—a frequent starting point for readers—by examining the array of precoordinated subdivisions under a heading that spell out and distinguish its various aspects in ways that we couldn't think of in advance; that is, the system will clarify our range of options for us, thereby enabling users to *ask better questions in the first place.* (For example, I have helped a few different readers who said they had to write their term papers on, simply, "Television." The precoordinated display of this subject's many aspects in *LCSH* [for example, "Television—Law and legislation," "—Production and direction," "—Vocational guidance," "Television actors and actresses," "Television and children," "Television in health education"] greatly assists such readers in narrowing their topics, by spelling out for them a wide array of options that they did not know they had.)

• That study of the list of possible standard subdivisions (*Free-Floating Subdivisions: An Alphabetical Index* [LC, revised irregularly]) can greatly aid reference librarians in helping readers as it gives us a foreknowledge of the types of questions that can readily be answered, over and above giving the readers an ability to recognize options that they did not know of in advance.

• That the catalog will usually not indicate the contents of individual chapters of books; and because of this we can have realistic expectations of what the catalog will *not* do, and turn instead to sources such as *Essay and General Literature Index, PsycBooks,* or *Index to Scientific Book Contents* for this kind of information—or to the classified array of full texts themselves.

• That we can bring directly to bear on a question a wide variety of types of literature (case studies, handbooks, concordances, pictorial works, textbooks, yearbooks), each designed to answer certain categories of questions, by quickly and easily identifying the "type" of reference sources through precoordinated form subdivisions in the catalog.

• That the standard form subdivisions "—Dictionaries" or "—Encyclopedias" are important aids in dealing with questions seeking specific factual data, as they lead directly to compilations of just such information.

• That the standard form subdivision "—Bibliography" is important in dealing with open-ended or in-depth research questions, since published bibliographies compiled by subject experts are often far superior to any computer-generated bibliographies.

• That many subject bibliographies can also be easily identified directly in the class scheme, even without reference to the catalog, because of their being clustered in the Z classes (that is, major bibliographies on individual people being arranged alphabetically by surname in the Z8000s, other subject bibliographies and indexes being arranged by continent/country in Z1201-4980 and alphabetically by subject category in Z5051-7999).

• That the standard form subdivision "—Directories" is important in leading researchers efficiently to information that is not to be found within the library itself.

• That established *LCSH* category terms can be used in scores of sources outside the library's catalog of books (commercially produced indexes, databases, catalogs, and bibliographies covering journal articles, speeches, government documents, special collections, etc.).

• That because so many commercial publishers "piggyback" on *LCSH,* and because we can plug the same term(s) into so many different disciplinary and format indexes, we can get an entire range of cross-disciplinary perspectives on the same subject with surprising ease. (For example, the *LCSH* term "Knowledge, Theory of" appears as a heading not just in *Humanities Index,* but also in *Social Sciences Index, Business Index, Magazine Index, Readers' Guide, Bibliographic Index,* the index to *Book Review Digest, Education Index, Applied Science & Technology Index, Biological & Agricultural Index, Essay and General Literature Index, Catholic Periodical and Literature Index, Art Index, InfoTrac, Legal Resource Index, Monthly Catalog of U.S. Government Publications.*)

• That postcoordinate Boolean search capabilities are rendered enormously more powerful when cataloger-assigned subdivisions can be searched for separately and used as sets themselves, for combination with other sets.

• That key word searching is also rendered much more powerful when we can search the component words of *LCSH* terms, which are "artificial" elements *added to* the records—not *transcribed from* the books—assigned by thinking professionals who notice and thereby define categories and relationships that are not defined by natural language title or note field words.

• That the scattering of the various aspects of a subject throughout the class scheme is corrected by the controlled-vocabulary subject headings in the library's catalog, which group together in one place the various aspects that are scattered on the shelves, and which display those aspects in a perceptible relationship, often through precoordinated subdivisions of headings.

• That because the *LCSH* headings (often with precoordinated subdivisions) group together in the catalog those subject aspects which are scattered in the stacks, the heading terms on records in the catalog function efficiently as the *index* to the class scheme; that is, they show that the same subject can appear in many different classes; they show the *full range* of classes that would be most promising for full-text browsing; and, through the distinctions pointed out by precoordinated subdivisions, they show *which* subject aspects are located in which areas of the stacks.

• That while a book can receive multiple subject headings in the catalog, it can receive only one classification number in the stacks; but that there is a functional linkage between the *first* subject heading given in the subject tracings on the catalog record and the book's class number. Because of this linkage, then, the first *LCSH* term on the catalog record will give the best indication of which subject aspect is emphasized in the corresponding class-number area of the stacks.

• That, in addition to grouping under *one subject heading* works on a subject that are scattered in many different classes, the catalog also provides *multiple access points* (by author, title, key words, subject headings, and cross-references) to each book in the class scheme, in which any work can appear in only one location. This, too, functionally makes the catalog an excellent index to the classification scheme.

• That extremely *specific* information—much too narrow to be included on any catalog records, even those with abstracts or added tables of contents—can still be found through the systematic examination and browsing of full texts, provided that the texts are arranged in predictable subject groups to begin with (rather than being shelved in simple accession-number order).

• That the classified arrangement of full texts will enable us to *recognize* useful information—*general* as well as *specific*—that we could not specify in advance through the catalog.

- That either of the two systems—*LCSH* in the catalog (not just in the red books) or full texts arranged in the LC class scheme—will enable us to recognize subject information that cannot be reached through the other system alone or through key word searches.
- That foreign-language books *in the stacks* are findable in the very same category groupings that hold the English books (just as the English-language subject groupings *in the catalog* also include foreign titles).
- That "introductory" or "overview" knowledge records, and general (rather than specialized) indexes to other knowledge records, can be found clustered at the beginning of the classification scheme in the A classes (general encyclopedias, *Readers' Guide,* newspaper indexes), while specialized and in-depth subject indexes are classed together at the end of the scheme, in the Z classes.
- That sets created by online retrieval which are too large—a frequent problem—can be cut down to more manageable size relatively efficiently by means of limit commands on fixed fields that aren't even displayed to users; limits can be done by language, by date of publication, by presence of a bibliography, by geographic area code, and so on.
- That in a large library, *millions* of full texts can be examined systematically in predictably narrow groups in the class scheme—much more full-text information than can be searched for in even the very largest full-text databases.
- That full texts in the class scheme can be searched systematically without the library or researcher having to pay stiff *copyright royalty or licensing fees* (NEXIS, by contrast, costs about $4.33 per minute to search in its "Omni" mode), and its contents are submicroscopic in extent compared to, for example, the 535 miles of texts in the Library of Congress.

In short, when a researcher can reasonably expect all of these features from a library's system of cataloging and classification, then he has enormous power to move around confidently and efficiently among knowledge records even in subject or language areas with which he has no a priori familiarity. This is what I mean by *predictability* being a crucial element of a retrieval system.

It is immediately noteworthy that all of this predictability is *lost* in a system represented by the extreme form of the Computer Workstation model, which would replace *LCSH* with natural language key word access and do away with classification entirely. With key words one has an *avenue* of access but not a *system,* precisely because there is no predictability to it. One cannot tell in advance *which* key words will work best, and if a searcher's specification is even slightly off, she will miss whole areas of records—perhaps even the large majority of works on her topic—without realizing that she's missed anything. Moreover, she must specify not only all the different synonyms and variant phrasings but also every form of each (singular, plural, possessive, adjectival) and in *all languages,* not just in English. (An avenue of access that does not retrieve foreign-language works just as readily as those in English would decimate the research potential of most large libraries. This is a fact that is frequently overlooked by overzealous Workstation advocates.)

Moreover, the Workstation model also tends routinely to ignore the fact that some questions can be answered *only* by the systematic browsing of printed full texts arranged in subject groupings (as in my earlier examples four through six). Legal, economic, preservation, and psychological reasons will prevent the digitization of anything more than a small fraction of a large library's full texts into computers (points to which I shall return). Most databases—even those with abstracts—will necessarily continue to hold only catalog surrogates that can contain merely a fraction of the information to be found in the corresponding printed full texts. Research libraries therefore continue to need predictable direct access to this deeper pool of information—not just to the superficial surrogates. And it is precisely the classification scheme that provides such systematic access to most full texts.

Serendipity

In addition to predictability, an efficient access system in a research library also requires *serendipity,* by which I mean the capability of a retrieval system to show researchers, in a systematic manner, many more sources relevant to their subject than they are able to specify in advance. It is the crucial element of a system that enables researchers to *recognize* sources from a display that shows them *more information than they had precisely asked for,* and that shows them such sources not merely haphazardly or by chance but *systematically.* The word "serendipity" in its usual sense has much more of a connotation of blind chance. In a library context, however, the "chance" involved in recognition and browsing is not by any means merely blind or random; *it is a deliberately designed structural property of the retrieval system.*

One aspect of the library retrieval system that promotes serendipity is the principle of *uniform heading* in *Library of Congress Subject Headings.* Thus, to return to a previous example, a searcher who specifies only "Capital punishment" will retrieve not just works with these two words in their titles but also an enormous variety of other relevant works that discuss the topic in quite different terms. In a natural language key word system, by contrast, the researcher would receive only those records containing the exact words "capital" and "punishment." In the Library of Congress's post-1968 computer catalog, for example, a search for these two words in title and note fields (i.e., data that can be simply transcribed verbatim from the book being cataloged) retrieves only 114 hits: but a search of the same words as an *LCSH* subject heading (i.e., a standardized category term added to the record by professional catalogers, rather than merely transcribed from preexisting data) retrieves 361 hits. The difference—247 relevant works—is an example of serendipity in an *LCSH*-controlled system that is not possible in a key word file.

Another aspect of the retrieval scheme that promotes systematic serendipity is the precoordination of subject heading strings. Thus, for example, I once helped a reader who wanted to find information on company intelligence (he was thinking of setting up a consulting business that would do this kind of research). It was easy enough to discover that the proper *LCSH* term is "Business intelligence"; and I also knew that "how to" information is often specifically findable through the form subdivision "—Handbooks, manuals, etc." So, in typing the precoordinated combination "Business intelligence—Handbooks, manuals, etc." into the computer, we immediately found two relevant hits (see Figure 9). But the "browse" display of other precoordinated subdivisions enabled us to recognize several categories of sources that looked very promising, specifically:

> Business intelligence—Bibliography
> —Case studies
> —Prevention
> —United States—Bibliography
> —United States—Case studies

```
B01+BUSINESS INTELLIGENCE//(INDX=71)
B02 BUSINESS INTELLIGENCE--ADDRESSES, ESSAYS,//(INDX=1)
B03 BUSINESS INTELLIGENCE--BELGIUM//(INDX=1)
B04 BUSINESS INTELLIGENCE--BELGIUM--CONGRESSE//(INDX=1)
B05 BUSINESS INTELLIGENCE--BIBLIOGRAPHY//(INDX=5)
B06 BUSINESS INTELLIGENCE--CALIFORNIA//(INDX=1)
B07 BUSINESS INTELLIGENCE--CASE STUDIES//(INDX=4)
B08 BUSINESS INTELLIGENCE--CONGRESSES//(INDX=2)
B09 BUSINESS INTELLIGENCE--EUROPE//(INDX=1)
B10 BUSINESS INTELLIGENCE--EUROPEAN ECONOMIC C//(INDX=1)
B11 BUSINESS INTELLIGENCE--GERMANY (WEST)//(INDX=2)
B12 BUSINESS INTELLIGENCE--GREAT BRITAIN//(INDX=1)
B13 BUSINESS INTELLIGENCE--HANDBOOKS, MANUALS,//(INDX=2)
B14 BUSINESS INTELLIGENCE--NORWAY//(INDX=1)
B15 BUSINESS INTELLIGENCE--NORWAY--CASE STUDI//(INDX=1)
B16 BUSINESS INTELLIGENCE--PREVENTION//(INDX=1)
B17 BUSINESS INTELLIGENCE--SOVIET UNION//(INDX=1)
B18 BUSINESS INTELLIGENCE--UNITED STATES//(INDX=10)
B19 BUSINESS INTELLIGENCE--UNITED STATES--BIB//(INDX=1)
B20 BUSINESS INTELLIGENCE--UNITED STATES--CAS//(INDX=2)
```

Figure 9

It had not occurred to me to specify these other categories in advance; I had thought only of "—Handbooks." Nevertheless, the precoordination of subdivisions effectively allowed us to see more options than we had asked for, and thus to retrieve many additional relevant sources while also excluding others of less relevance (e.g., "—Belgium," "—Norway"). While it is true that a Boolean postcoordination of any of these terms could have retrieved the same records, the problem is that neither the reader nor I had thought to specify terms such as "Case studies" or "Prevention" beforehand; and what may be obvious in hindsight nevertheless presents very real problems to readers in actual research situations who must struggle along with only imperfect foresight. Postcoordination gives you only what you know enough to ask for; precoordination shows you additional options that you didn't know you *should* ask for. A precoordinate system thus entails systematic serendipity as an integral structural property of its capability in a way that a purely postcoordinate system cannot match.

Depth of Access

In addition to predictability and serendipity, a retrieval system that offers both a catalog of surrogates for full texts and an array of subject-grouped full texts themselves provides much greater *depth* of access than one that allows only the brief surrogates to be searched. No catalog record—even with an abstract—can ever match the extent of information in the full text it represents. Thus, in my examples four through six discussed earlier, the desired information could not have been located through any catalog searches, whether by subject heading, key word, or class number. Only the systematic examination of the books themselves arrayed in predictably limited areas of the bookstacks could answer those questions. Moreover, the ability to browse full texts arrayed in subject groups adds not just depth of access but also an additional level of serendipity to the overall system: it, too, enables readers to *recognize* information—including pictorial illustrations—relevant to their interest that they could never have specified in advance through attempts at postcoordinating unpredictable text words in a computer search.

The importance of the classification scheme can be underscored by a thought experiment. Assume that there are two large research libraries with exactly the same collection. Assume, further, that each has an identical computer catalog that can be searched by author, title, key word, and class number, and that each can do postcoordinate Boolean combinations. Let us assume further that the table of contents of each nonfiction book had been scanned into the computer records, and can be searched as easily as the author and title information. (The full texts themselves have not been digitized for searching electronically; but the catalog records representing them are unusually detailed.) Assume, finally, one difference: that the volumes of Library A are physically arranged in subject-browsable groupings according to the LC classification scheme, whereas in Library B the volumes on the shelves are arranged only in random accession-number order. (The computer catalog of Library B attaches class numbers to the surrogate catalog records so that they may be searched for within the computer, but the books themselves are not arranged by class number on the shelves.)

The experiment, then, is simply to answer this question: Which library would you prefer to work in? Given identical computer systems for searching the catalog records, is there an additional and substantial advantage in being able to search the full texts themselves in subject-browsable groups?

I submit that anyone who actually has to do research, especially in unfamiliar subject areas or in languages in which he has little proficiency, would have a decided and fully justified preference for working in Library A. I further submit that those proponents of the Workstation model who would assert that Library B is just as good as Library A are probably spending too much time in ivory towers, and that they have too little experience of the range and nature of questions that people ask in real research libraries.

Digitized Research Libraries?

The objection raised by the Computer Workstation model advocates to the continuation of a classification scheme for printed books is that "eventually" whole libraries—not just isolated and carefuly limited subject collections—will be digitized, thus rendering unnecessary a scheme for physically arranging printed works in subject categories. And while it is certainly true that more and more full texts will indeed become digitized, it is equally true that entire research libraries will *never* become completely electronic—at least, not without substantially scaling down the definition of what constitutes a research library in the first place. At best, only small portions of the full range of research material that ought to be available to scholars will appear in full-text databases. There are four inescapable reasons for this.

Copyright Law

Copyright law continues stubbornly to resist change. Because of the networking, transmitting, broadcasting, and wholesale downloading capabilities of electronic formats, the digitization of texts is not a mere *copying* of them (as with microfilm); rather, it is much closer to *republication* of them, with all the attendant problems of intellectual property rights, fee requirements, licensing restrictions, and susceptibility to large lawsuits. If there is one bedrock fact in all of the studies of this problem, it is that they all agree that no substantial progress can be made toward digitizing libraries until "massive" and "unprecendented" changes are made in the copyright law. For example, *American Libraries* (December 1989), in reviewing the Library of Congress Network Advisory Committee's report *Intellectual Property Issues in the Library Network Context,* notes: "The overall conclusion of the committee is that the current intellectual property system must be substantially changed to meet current and future technological demands. Specific predictions include massive changes in the copyright law, perhaps even to the point of its replacement by contracts of adhesion . . ." (1093). And a major study prepared for Congress by the Office of Technology Assessment (Lynch, 1990), *Electronic Publishing, Electronic Libraries and the National Research and Education Network,* comes to a similar conclusion:

> The major impediment to large-scale conversion of paper collections to electronic form are two: cost and copyright. . . .
> The copyright problem is less tractable. While a great deal of material that is no longer protected by copyright is held by libraries . . . [t]he availability of this material will have a small effect on the perceived improvement in the quality of library service to the end user relative to the cost of converting it to electronic form since it is not typically heavily requested. For material protected by copyright, problems arise in two areas: The copyright holder may not permit the conversion of the material to electronic form and its subsequent storage, and may also argue that the transmission of electronic copies to end users is in violation of fair use (which is always a vexed issue between publishers and libraries even in the context of photocopying paper materials held by libraries). Large-scale conversion of collections to electronic form legally will require either unprecedented negotiations among participants in a proposed national conversion program and a large number of publishers holding copyright to this material, or a change to the copyright law to specifically permit such a conversion. (pp. 37–38)

If there is a second bedrock fact, it is that after decades of such diagnoses no one has been able to come up with a workable solution that will protect publishers from domestic and international piracy—and, be it noted, digitization greatly facilitates rather than impedes wholesale piracy—without also entailing exorbitant search costs that price the database access beyond the reach of the typical researcher.

I would suggest that the bedrock frustration of the Workstation proponents with the copyright law has to do with a fundamental misperception of the relation of human nature, private property, and technology (i.e., the means of production). Specifically, proponents of the Workstation model, in seeing massive changes to copyright law as "inevitable," seem actually to be basing their speculations on a Marxist model of economics. Such a model calls for the abolition of private property (in this case intellectual property protected by copyright law), the result of which will be a change in human nature itself—an overcoming of human divisiveness and a voluntary disregard of private advantage and exclusive ownership for the sake of the larger collective enterprise. According to Marxism, the equitable distribution of goods in such a system will be carried out voluntarily by the new, nonalienated citizenry, without the need for pricing mechanisms determined by market forces of supply and demand which reinforce capitalist class distinctions between haves and have-nots.

Whether the Marxist model is itself a valid perception of "economic man" is very much a relevant issue to the success of the Workstation model as the "library of the future." The events of 1989–1991 in eastern Europe, however, ought to give its proponents pause; and they ought to induce others to search actively for alternative models of the library of the future that are based on more workable assumptions. The burden of proof rests squarely on Workstation proponents to show that their program of making "everything" or "the entire Library of Congress" freely available through computers is at all compatible with a non-Marxist view of human nature. And until such a chimerical justification presents itself, we must ultimately recognize the unfashionable truth that copyright is not the *problem* it is represented to be by Workstation proponents; rather, copyright is precisely the *solution* to the more fundamental problem that human nature impels us to want compensation for the use of our own work and private property.

What is particularly interesting in this connection is that optimistic expectations of changes in the copyright law to accommodate new technology go back at least fifty years, to the time when microforms began to fill the cultural niche that personal computer workstations have now moved into. Back then, when the vision was one of having the entire Library of Congress available in a filing cabinet of microforms, rather than online through a computer, the visionary emphasis was also on the inexpensiveness of the technological medium. But then, too, the grandiose scheme of reproducing "everything" cheaply ran into the same brick wall of copyright restrictions, with the same result that only impotent and endlessly repeated speculations on the "possibility" that publishers "might be willing" to change their ways could be offered as a solution (see, for example, Rider, 1944: 170–73, 207–9).

Hindsight regarding microforms offers at least some important lessons of foresight regarding full-text databases: micropublishers of books wound up largely confining themselves to reprinting older, copyright-free works, which they could assemble and sell as prepackaged historical "libraries" on particular subjects (e.g., *Botany Li-*

brary on Microfiche, Early English Books, Landmarks of Science, Russian Revolutionary Literature, Goldsmiths'-Kress Library of Economic Literature). Such publishing projects found a viable niche in the market for two reasons: (1) they could supply many hard-to-find and out-of-print titles efficiently and at much less expense than it would take to assemble comparable paper collections; and (2) microfilm serves a definite preservation function, as (assuming proper storage conditions) it can last for centuries, unlike the acidic-paper printed volumes it replaces, which self-destruct in only decades.

Database vendors, too, are subject to the laws of supply and demand in the marketplace, a reality overlooked by the Marxist model, which assumes benevolent fairness in assigning compensation according to a "labor theory" of value, rather than pricing according to supply and demand as the mechanism of distribution; and the marketplace is inevitably driving them, too, into particular niches that are substantially different from the visionary "entire Library of Congress online" projections. The most supportable market for full texts online lies in the subject areas of business and law, whose practitioners can afford the very high online fees involved in searching current copyrighted materials. The market for digitizing the older, historical texts which are in the public domain is much softer. Market factors that stand in the way of digitizing (rather than microfilming) older books for which there is little current demand include *costs* and *preservation problems* with electronic formats.

Cost Factors

There are essentially two ways in which an existing print-format text can be electronically digitized: through raster scanning or OCR (optical character recognition) scanning. A third way, that of entirely rekeying the data rather than scanning it by machine, is so prohibitively expensive in its labor costs as to be simply out of the question in most contexts relevant to digitizing library collections. Raster scanning of a printed page in effect takes a "picture" of the page as a whole; and while this entire page image may then be stored and transmitted electronically, the individual component words appearing on the page cannot be directly searched. In other words, one cannot do *key word* searches of a raster-scanned text; the scanning process does not distinguish the individual words as such. (The process is also known as "bit mapping"; it requires an extraordinarily large amount of computer storage space.) OCR scanning, by contrast, does distinguish the individual words of the text in a way that allows for key word searching and Boolean combinations. The main problem with OCR scanning is that omnifont character recognition technology is simply not good enough to provide accurate texts that can be used immediately without prohibitively expensive human editing of the OCR product (Lynch, 1990: 36).

Raster scanning is thus less expensive, at least in "capturing" an image if not in storing it. Even so, it is still much more costly than microfilming documents. An indication of the difference is provided by the marketing manager of University Microfilms International (UMI), which is a leading company providing raster-scanned full texts of journals to libraries.

> The technology is available today to allow library vendors to put all of their holdings into CD-ROM image format. If we were to do that—and offer only CD-ROM editions—literally hundreds of libraries would be left without continuing access (beyond the life of existing paper copies) to all the materials we provide. Why? Because the CD-ROM editions would be too expensive. For example, the cost to UMI of converting every issue of 16,000 periodicals and 7,000 newspaper titles and over one million dissertations, from day one, is staggering—hundreds of millions of dollars. (Estimates for converting *one year* of the company's periodical holdings alone exceed $9 million.) In order to simply break even, the company would have to price the product at a level beyond the reach of most libraries. (Bamford, 1990: 59)

An indication of the even greater costs for OCR-scanning is provided by the executive director of the Law Library Microform Consortium, a cooperative microform publisher serving several hundred libraries.

> It would help immensely in this regard if librarians as a group would educate themselves and abandon their fantasies that the national preservation mission will be taken over by electronic media. There is no real possibility that the electronic media will supplant microforms as vehicles for widespread preservation efforts within the timeframe during which preservation is still an option.
>
> The reasons for this are simple economics and are worth reviewing once again. In order to enable preprinted text to be handled by any of the electronic media, it must be converted into digital format. That requires either manual keyboarding or conversion by [OCR] scanners with a human proofing component. The going rate for such conversion, when done

to an "error free" standard, hovers at, or a little above, $3 per page. That price has not been falling in recent years because, while the cost of scanning equipment has been going down, the labor costs for the required human component are rising and are now the major factor in the equation. This figure of $3 per page does not include the subsequent programming or premastering costs which would be incurred in massaging the data into the appropriate format for, say, publishing on CD-ROM. The $3 per page is assignable strictly to the data-capture function.

With microforms, on the other hand, data-capture costs for preprinted materials are amazingly lower. The organization for which I work, the Law Library Microform Consortium (LLMC), is a non-profit cooperative of over 800 libraries dedicated to the preservation and economical distribution of materials in the areas of law and government documents. We have been in business for 14 years, during which we have filmed over 50,000 volumes. In that time we have obtained a very accurate reading on all of the cost factors in microform publishing. While non-profit, we are not subsidized, and so we have to break even. In short, we don't give it away. So our current prices can serve as a fairly accurate index of the actual costs in the industry. We currently charge six cents per page for contract filming work, and we don't lose money on it. Three dollars versus six cents per page. This means that the costs for data-capture in the electronic media are at least fifty times those for microforms!

The difference in costs just for data-capture is the most dramatic example of why preservation work in the electronic media will always cost much more than it does with microforms. But there are many other costs in publishing—editorial, duplication, overhead, etc. It might make the case more clearly if I describe an actual publishing project.

The *United States Supreme Court Reports* is a large, multi-volume set, averaging 875 pages per volume, and currently numbering 478 volumes. We filmed this title long ago. But using present day costs for labor, equipment depreciation, materials, overhead, etc., it would cost LLMC just over $24,000 to bring an identically-sized title to market. For comparative purposes we recently bid out this same title to a CD-ROM publisher. Our request was for a quote to cover the creation of one CD-ROM master. We would supply the original data. The quotation we received back was for $1.25 million. That works out to 52 times the microform cost. (Dupont, 1990: 196)

An additional indication of the cost of searching full texts online in a format that allows key word searching and Boolean combinations is provided by Mead Data Central, Inc., which offers the NEXIS database. NEXIS includes the full text of about one thousand newspapers, magazines, newsletters, and wire services. (Most titles in it are represented by current years of coverage; there is little material in the database that is more than fifteen years old, and most does not go back even that far.) The 1991 undiscounted rate for searching NEXIS was $260 per hour, or $4.33 per minute; this does not include connect-time fees or offline printing costs.

By contrast, the Library of Congress currently receives over 50,000 magazines, journals, newspapers, and serials (not counting annuals); and it has over 800,000 other serials in its retrospective holdings. If LC's print-format database of just its current serials (a collection that is at least fifty times larger than that of NEXIS) were digitized, and the price were comparably fifty times larger, then it would be searchable at the rate of $216.50 *per minute*. And this, of course, would not include the retrospective serials, nor any of the Library's millions of books, nor its collection of audiovisual materials, maps, photographs, manuscripts, and so on. Given such a cost for searching *only* the current serials, it is absurd even to try to calculate the per-minute cost of searching LC's entire collection of 100 million items. And yet the chimera of doing just this continues to be held out as a goal by Workstation proponents.

Preservation Problems

A major study by the National Research Council (NRC) in 1986 came to the conclusion that none of the electronic media formats, including optical disks, is suitable for long-term archival preservation of knowledge records. This study, *Preservation of Historical Records* (National Research Council, 1986), tends to be overlooked by those proponents of the Computer Workstation model who are determined to envision a future when "everything" will be available electronically; and yet subsequent discussions in the professional literature have supported its conclusions (see the reference list at the end of this chapter).

The major problem associated with optical disks as archival media is not that the disks themselves are impermanent (claims of a disk lifespan of several decades are not uncommon); rather, the problem is with *the machines that are needed to read the disks* (not to mention the support documentation needed to operate the machines). The NRC reports that a twenty-year life is about the maximum that can be expected of a disk system before a new technology becomes dominant, at which point parts and service for the older machines will become difficult if not impossible to obtain (National Research Council, 1986: 74). As a result, data stored in such systems will have to be recopied every generation into a newer medium. While this is technologically possible, it is economically unfeasible for library budgets.[1]

The other problem is also related to economics rather than to technology. The mere creation of standards to ensure the ease of such generational transfers is not a panacea for the problem because, ultimately, *market forces rather than standards* will determine a medium's longevity. And while standards can certainly influence market forces, they cannot determine them. Indeed, market forces can cause *standards themselves to become obsolete* within a relatively short time. (An obvious example is eight-track tape players, which were manufactured compatibly by several different companies. The arrival of cassette tapes quickly made the eight-track format obsolete.)

One cannot look to electronic devices to solve preservation problems when it is in the very nature of such devices to cause the problems in the first place. Perhaps an analogy would be useful. Suppose a salesman from the XYZ Corporation were to tell us that it had created a photocopier that could make absolutely perfect copies of documents—that there would be no loss of data from one generation to another, that there would be no degradation in quality or increase in fuzziness in the copies, and that, in fact, the copies could even be cleaned up or improved through the suppression of stains and dirt marks. But suppose, too, that the company added one caveat: the process could work only by using acid-based paper. In other words, the copies would not last for more than a few decades without becoming brittle, and so would have to be recopied, say, every twenty years while the paper was still strong enough. But, the salesman assures us, the copies would be absolutely perfect, even after a hundred generations, and their perfection from one generation to another is absolutely guaranteed.

Most people who were not suffering from an extreme case of technological infatuation would, I suspect, point out the obvious to the salesman: that if we have to keep recopying the data every generation, then he simply has no business touting such an impermanent system as a preservation medium in the first place. And the need to recopy data from one generation of optical disk to the next—*just as with an acidic-paper system*—renders it unsuitable for archival preservation purposes. (Note that I am referring very specifically to the preservation of printed texts, that is, those that would normally be microfilmed or mass deacidified for preservation purposes if the optical disk alternative were forgone. *Machine manipulability* of such data is not an issue. The vast bulk of any research library's holdings was never intended or designed for such manipulability; and so a requirement to store it in a manipulable format is a very expensive irrelevancy.)

In preservation, then, legal and economic considerations are just as much realities within the storage-system universe as are technological concerns. And grandiose visions of the Computer Workstation model as encompassing "everything" are simply and dangerously unrealistic when they focus exclusively on the technology. Moreover, even within the technical arena itself, the issues of *image-quality* retention from one generation of copy to the next, and of *machine manipulability* of data (as opposed to simple machine readability) are largely side issues, as neither is directly relevant to the *permanence* of any system needed to store nonmanipulable data such as is found in printed books and journals.

Psychological Problems

A classic paper by George Miller, "The Magical Number Seven, Plus or Minus Two: Some Limits on Our Capacity for Processing Information" (1956), has been widely referred to in the literature of human-factor design in information processing (see, e.g., Schneiderman [1980], Burns [1985], Horton [1990]). While the number of information units that one's short-term memory can process efficiently is debatable—and is certainly variable according to experience and training—a basic truth remains that most people cannot keep too much information in short-term memory. Displays that provide too many options, or too many levels of choice within any one option, therefore tend severely to impede users' efficiency in navigating the system. With computers, specifically, there is a tendency under such conditions for users to become "lost in hyperspace" (or simply "menu-space"). One must therefore, once again, take with a large grain of salt the facile projections that "everything" or "the entire Library of Congress" can be made available online at a computer workstation. Even assuming that the legal, copyright, economic, and preservation problems were completely solvable—a more than questionable assumption—one would still be left with the task of navigating, simultaneously, all possible subjects in all formats in all languages, and doing it in a way that does not overload one's perceptions, or one's ability to sort through a massive retrieval in which the desired search terms may appear more often than not in the wrong contexts. Of course, this task would be made even more difficult if, as some proponents of the Workstation model assert, the intellectual structure of categorizations provided by *LCSH* and the LC class scheme can be abandoned, with raw computer retrieval power applied to unstructured data being substituted instead. And the "solution" of programmed artificial intelligence seems always, alas, just beyond the horizon. Moreover, even if it did work outside very narrow disciplinary bounds, it still could not handle multilingual collections of knowledge records.

In a nutshell, then, the unfashionable truth is that entire research libraries *cannot* be reduced to the Computer Workstation model because of the combination of essentially unbudgeable legal, economic, preservation, and psychological impediments. The computer model at best can offer only a small fraction of the resources that ought to be available to serious scholars for in-depth research in a real library—a *place* containing physical, printed knowledge records in addition to electronic sources. (The analogy to microforms is again relevant. While many large collections of knowledge records have been sold as prepackaged microform "libraries," the larger reality is that such sets themselves form only a small part of the resources available in the real libraries in which they are held.) It may provide an excellent supplement to the three components of the Library Science model, but the Workstation replaces none of them. And if it is represented as replacing them, a skeptic can legitimately wonder if the Workstation proponents have any real idea how much access to the written (and other) records of humanity is being completely lost or overlooked.

The Continuing Need for Subject-Grouped Full Texts and Precoordinated, Controlled-Vocabulary Subject Headings

One of the facts that remains after all of the dust has settled is that many researchers' inquiries can be answered *only* by the systematic browsing of printed full texts arranged in predictably findable subject groupings. For the reasons given earlier, most texts *cannot* be digitized; and furthermore, the brief catalog records representing the texts that *can* be digitized are necessarily and inherently much less informative than the actual works for which they serve as markers. (Again, examples four through six at the beginning of this chapter could never have been answered on the basis of a search that looked only at catalog records rather than directly at classified full texts themselves.)

The classification scheme component of the Library Science model cannot be superseded as a means for answering *some* types of questions. It is of course foolish to believe that the class scheme can encompass the entire universe of knowledge records; but no such claim is being made. The point is that it is equally foolish to view the Computer Workstation model as encompassing that universe. The comparison is a two-way street. (One important feature of the class scheme that is almost routinely overlooked is that it provides direct access to full texts in predictably limited subject groupings in a way that entirely circumvents the need to pay copyright royalty or licensing fees.) Each approach does something that the other *cannot* do. Therefore neither is sufficient, and both are necessary components of a still larger model of the information storage and retrieval universe. (The larger model must have additional components as well; see chapter 11.)

For the classification scheme component to work properly, however—that is, for researchers to be able to find which classes of full texts would most efficiently repay systematic browsing—a good index to the scheme is required. And here, too, the key word search capability of the Computer model proves to be inadequate. The catalog of the research library's collection—which *is* the index to the class scheme, in addition to serving as a valuable access system in itself, even apart from its functional link to the classified bookstacks—must have the properties of both vocabulary control and precoordination to serve as the needed index. I have already given examples of how the precoordinated combination of *LCSH* headings and subdivisions function in this capacity; let me add another.

The *LCSH* term "Alphabet" has many different precoordinated subdivisions in a large library's catalog; at the Library of Congress itself, some of the subdivisions are:

Alphabet—Caricatures and cartoons

   —Fiction

   —History

   —Religious aspects—Islam

   —Religious aspects—Sufism

What is important is that each of these subdivisions steers readers to a different area of the bookstacks. Thus the subdivision "—Caricatures and cartoons" refers readers to a book in NC1639.M28 (Caricature. Pictorial humor and satire). The subdivision "—Fiction" refers readers to a group of seven books in PZ7 (General juvenile belles lettres); the subdivision "—History" refers them to nineteen books clustered in P211 ("Comparative grammar" within "Language/Science of language"). The subdivision "—Religious aspects—Islam" refers them to a book in NK3636.5 (Islamic alphabet/calligraphy), while the quite different subdivision "—Religious aspects—Sufism" refers them to an entirely different class area, BP189.65.A47 ("Alphabet" as a special topic within "Sufi practice").

In other words, the precoordinated subdivisions tell readers, in effect, that if you want to browse through *subject-grouped full texts,* which are much more informative than catalog records and which contain all sorts of detailed information and illustrations not indicated by the superficial catalog records, then go to the NC area for the "Caricature" aspect of "Alphabet." Avoid all of the PZ7 books if you want nonfiction. Go to P211 for more information on the "History" aspect, to the NK area for the "Islamic" aspect, and to the very different BP area of the stacks for the "Sufi" aspect.

If these subdivisions were not spelled out as precoordinated terms, the reader would simply retrieve a confused jumble of records under "Alphabet" in general, and would not know *which specific areas of the stacks* to browse (or avoid) for further information on particular aspects of "Alphabet." Nor would undecipherable foreign-language titles make up for the loss of *English-language* subdivisions under the *LCSH* heading in clarifying which aspects are treated in which areas of the class scheme. Furthermore, if the information displayed in an array of subdivisions were no longer so displayed (as on a "browse" screen), and could be found only through postcoordinate Boolean combinations, then readers would have to specify in advance all possible combinations that would indicate the range of scattering of the subject. Thus, a reader who combined "Alphabet" and "Islam" alone would miss the "Sufism" aspect entirely, although she might very well have been interested in seeing the latter, additional religious aspect if it had been brought to her attention when it did not occur to her to specify "Sufism" in advance. The same reader, similarly, might have been interested in the "Caricature" or "History" aspects. The precoordination of the aspects through a display of subdivisions thus spells out in the catalog a range of subject options that could not be noticed in the bookstacks, which scatter the various aspects of the subject without providing cross-references among them. Moreover, even in the computer catalog itself, readers could not recognize such an array of distinct aspects simply from examining nonexpressive or confusing foreign-language titles collocated under "Alphabet" without such a range of English-language subdivisions.

In spelling out the full extent of subject aspects available on a topic—which could never be efficiently specified in advance, and which also could never be noticed in the bookstacks themselves—and in efficiently directing readers to browse one area of the class scheme rather than another, the precoordinated *LCSH* terms and subdivisions thereby serve as the index to the classified bookstacks.

A Computer Workstation model that would substitute key word access rather than *LCSH,* or postcoordination rather than precoordination, would thus do serious harm to the retrieval *structure* of a research library. The point needs emphasis because some theorists seem to think that the retention of precoordination in *LCSH* is "merely" an unthought-out carryover from a manual card catalog system into the online age. The fact, however, is that even with a catalog that is capable of doing postcoordinate Boolean combinations, *the human beings who use the catalog* still require an indexing system that enables them to *recognize* research options that they could never specify in advance. And the larger the library's collection is, and the more obscure the subject areas and languages it contains, all the more necessary are those components of the cataloging structure that give the retrieval system predictability and serendipity, that enable reference librarians and researchers to move with confidence and efficiency among knowledge records in subject areas and even languages in which they have no expertise. And it is the standardized intellectual gridwork of vocabulary-controlled, precoordinated, authority-networked, cross-referenced, and scope-note–defined *cataloging* that provides these features. Predictability and serendipity, in other words, are much more features of the *intellectual content* of the catalog records and cross-references than they are of the computer's software.

The need for precoordination in a research library's catalog also needs emphasis because some theorists assert that *LSCH* is ultimately not generically different from any other controlled-vocabulary list, such as the *ERIC* thesaurus for educational literature or the *Thesaurus of Psy-*

chological Index Terms. A major difference nevertheless exists, in spite of the theorists' apparent inexperience in exploiting it. Neither the *ERIC* nor the psychological thesaurus has to serve as the index to a classified subject array of printed full texts. These thesauri serve to index microfiche reports that are unbrowsable to begin with, and so are arrayed in an accession-number order that makes no pretense at subject-category distinctions; or they index journal articles scattered in thousands of periodicals, articles that also cannot possibly be shelved in subject groups in the way that monographic books are in the LC scheme. Neither thesaurus, in other words, is called on to serve as the index to a class scheme of contiguously browsable full texts; *LCSH,* in contrast, does have to serve this function. And there is no way that the full range of different class areas for various aspects of the same subject can be brought to a researcher's attention without the precoordination of a heading plus the particular aspect represented by a subdivision or other precoordinated secondary term.

The ability of researchers to recognize aspects of a subject that they could not specify in advance—even in the catalog itself, apart from any tie to a classification scheme—is also fostered by *LCSH* in a way that neither the *ERIC* nor the psychological thesaurus can match. This is especially important in a system that seeks to provide access to the entire range of human knowledge, or at least that major segment of it contained in printed books, in all subject areas and in all languages; such a system must frequently deal with users who are not experts in the subjects they wish to research. An omnidisciplinary and omnilanguage collection of documents, in other words, needs precoordination in its indexing terms much more than does a collection of documents focused on only one discipline, and primarily in one language to boot. Researchers will necessarily have more trouble doing subject searches in the former collection; and so they simply require more help to enable them to recognize what they cannot specify in advance. Precoordination supplies just this help.

Proponents of the Workstation model may object at this point that I am misrepresenting their position regarding the desirability of natural language key-word searching *replacing* LC subject headings. What they are actually calling for, they may assert, is a *combination* of natural language searching *plus* artificial intelligence (AI) computer programming that would eliminate the "noise" level of natural language words retrieved in irrelevant contexts. Two difficulties arise here, however.

The first is that many Workstation proponents are indeed advocating the replacement of *LCSH* by key word searching without any AI programming, as is happening in some quarters of the Library of Congress itself. There, an increased emphasis on publishing and distributing the substantive content of the Library in digitized form has been paralleled by a decrease in the priority of doing full cataloging of printed books in the Library's backlog. Specifically, an increased emphasis on minimal-level cataloging (MLC)—which adds neither *LCSH* terms nor LC class numbers to books—is being embraced as the solution to the problem. Furthermore, any book that remains in the backlog for three years is automatically assigned to the MLC track. Key word searching of transcribed natural language terms in the computer catalog provides the *only* access to these books—or, more precisely, to their catalog records. The books themselves are being shelved in simple accession-number order, outside the Library's classified collections, and are therefore entirely outside the normal retrieval systems of *LCSH* and the class scheme.

The second difficulty is with AI itself. The problem is suggested by Theodore Roszak in *The Cult of Information:*

> After talking to several experts and enthusiasts—some academic, some in industry—I realized I had a problem. When it came to the power of computers, nearly everybody I met was prone to vastly optimistic exaggeration. Machine translation . . . conversation in ordinary language . . . total mastery of chess . . . face and voice recognition . . . creative writing . . . legal decision making—there was nothing these machines could not do, or would not soon be able to do. How "soon," I would ask. The answer was never too clear. Possibly next year, almost certainly in another two or three, for absolute sure by the end of the decade. In any case *sooner* than you might think. . . . For, *in principle* (this phrase comes to be repeated on all sides like a liturgical response) nothing is impossible.
>
> It soon became clear to me what the source of this optimism was and why I was having such trouble pinning down realistic predictions about the future of computers. All these people—the academicians as well as the industrial experts—were part of the information economy. . . .
>
> In short, the experts were *selling*. They were in the habit of extrapolating astonishing "megatrends" for the press, the public, the funding agencies. It was only when I applied persistent skeptical pressure—say, with respect to machine translation, or the ability of computers to "read" and "summarize" a book, a story, a lecture [an aspect of AI necessary in

wished-for library applications]—that I might finally evince an honest admission of how deucedly difficult such problems really were and how far off a solution might be. (pp. 30–31)

The real difficulty with such predictions, specifically in the research library context, is that *they skew administrative priorities*.[2] A vision of efficient natural language searching being "just around the corner" has a way of translating into decisions *right now* that it is unnecessary to continue assigning *LCSH* terms and LC class designations in the meantime. Key word access—with or without AI programming—is seen as a way of reducing the high costs of labor-intensive cataloging. (The costs of AI programming are problematic themselves; it is by no means "given" that the maintenance of such a system would be *less* expensive than continuing LC subject cataloging.)

It is certainly a fact that key word searching *can* retrieve knowledge records that are blind spots to a controlled vocabulary. And while this is understandably—and wonderfully—true, it simply does not follow that the vocabulary control (including precoordination) of *LCSH* is no longer of critical importance. Such an assumption is literally a non sequitur. Perhaps the fallaciousness of the assumption would be clearer by analogy. We now have, owing to the good offices of the Institute for Scientific Information in Philadelphia, the capability of doing citation searches in all subject areas; and this method of inquiry (i.e., tracing the citation or footnoting of any knowledge record in subsequent journal articles) enables us to see all sorts of subject connections and linkages in the various subject literatures that are blind spots to key word searching (i.e., work A may cite work B in an important way without the works' having any title key words in common).

Does it follow, then, that citation searching should *replace* key word searching? Of course not. The fact is that each method of searching reveals something important in the literature of a subject that cannot be revealed efficiently—or even at all—by the other. Research libraries therefore need both, and must allocate resources accordingly.

But exactly the same relationship obtains between key word searching and controlled-vocabulary inquiries. It is just as much, and as serious, a mistake to say that key word searching can "replace" *LCSH* as it is to say that citation searching can "replace" key word searching. Each of the three search methods enables us to see something quite different in the literature of whatever subject we're pursuing. Each has strengths and weaknesses. And the strength of each compensates for the blind spots in the others.

In this light it is a mistake to regard key word and vocabulary-control searching as lying along the same continuum. In other words, there is an unarticulated assumption in much of the information science literature that if one simply adds more key words to a catalog record (say, through including tables of contents or chapter headings), then one gradually gets so close to the retrieval provided by *LCSH* that the subject headings become unnecessary. I submit that this is a categorical mistake. Key word searching is essentially different *in kind* from vocabulary-controlled searching, just as both are themselves different in kind from citation searching. We are not looking at one piece of fruit at different stages of ripeness; we are, rather, comparing apples to oranges to pears. They do not subtly merge into, or asymptotically approach, each other along the same continuum; rather, there is a large precipice between each pair of the three search methods.

The assumption that key words can replace *LCSH* also entirely overlooks the function of the subject heading system in indexing the classification scheme. But since an arrangement of printed books on actual library shelves does not fit into the Procrustean bed of the Computer Workstation model to begin with, the need for such an index never seems to occur to Workstation proponents.

It would seem that theorists who have too little experience with the weaknesses of postcoordinate key word searching—and perhaps, too, not enough firsthand experience with the strengths of *LCSH* (in uniformity of heading *and* cross-referencing *and* precoordination)—have unjustifiably monopolized the center stage of library and information science in recent years. The reason is not hard to find: postcoordinate key word searching fits the Computer Workstation model more economically than does the maintenance of *LCSH*. And yet, as I have tried to show in this chapter, the Computer Workstation model itself cannot be realistically regarded, either at present or in the future, as encompassing the entire universe of knowledge records that ought to be available to researchers. Certainly it must be an integral part of a larger model; but it cannot be the entire larger model itself, if only for the fact that it is the *intellectual structure* of cataloging, *much more than any software,* which determines the predictability, serendipity, and overall depth of a research library's access systems to books.

What, then, are the other components that must supplement the computer and its distinctive contribution of postcoordinate key word searching in a still larger model of the information universe? We shall see in the next chapter.

Reference List

Bourke, Thomas A. "To Archive or Not to Archive: Is That Really the Question?" *Library Journal*, 114, 17 (October 15, 1989), 52–54.

Calmes, Alan. "New Confidence in Microfilm." *Library Journal*, 111, 15 (September 15, 1986), 38–42.

———. "To Archive and Preserve: A Media Primer." *Inform: The Magazine of Information Storage and Management*, 1, 5 (May 1987), 1–17, 33.

Channing, Rhoda K. "Looking Back at the Twentieth Century: Implications of Our Format Choices on Libraries and the Preservation of Information." In *Information Literacies for the Twenty-First Century*, 447–56. Edited by Virgil P. Blake and Renee Tjoumas. Boston: G. K. Hall, 1990.

Crawford, Walt. *Current Technologies in the Library*. Boston: G. K. Hall, 1988. (See pp. 10, 11, 281–82.)

Cribbs, Margaret A. "The Invisible Drip . . . How Data Seeps Away in Various Ways." *Online* (March 1987), 15–26.

"Don't Throw Away That Microfilm Yet, Because Compact Disks for Data May Not Be Forever!" *Micrographics Newsletter*, 23, 11 (November 1991), 5–6.

Dupont, Jerry. "CD-ROM in Law Libraries: Machines in Search of a Mission." *Microform Review*, 18, 4 (Fall 1989), 235–40.

———. "De-Romancing the Book: The Pyrrhic Victory of Microforms." *Microform Review*, 19, 4 (Fall 1990), 192–97.

Harriman, Robert. "The World's Biggest Paper Drive." *Inform* (October 1991), 20–24.

Herther, Nancy. "Between a Rock and a Hard Place: Preservation and Optical Media." *Database*, 10, 2 (April 1987), 122–24.

———. "THOR-CD, and Other New Optical Storage Media: A Troubled Future for Optical Storage?" *Database*, 11, 5 (October 1988), 115–16.

Landau, Herbert B. "Microform vs. CD-ROM: Is There a Difference?" *Library Journal*, 115, 16 (October 1990), 56–59.

Lawton, Stephen. "Being There: How Well Will Optical Disks Last? What Do Accelerated Aging Tests Tell Us?" *Inform* (October 1991), 25–27.

Machrone, Bill. "Unreasonable Expectations? (Technical Support for Older Equipment)." *PC*, 10, 9 (May 14, 1991), 75.

Mallinson, John C. "Preserving Machine-Readable Archival Records for the Millennia." *Archivaria*, 22 (Summer 1986), 147–52.

———. "On the Preservation of Human-Readable and Machine-Readable Records." *Information Technology and Libraries*, 7, 1 (1988), 19–23.

National Archives and Records Service. Committee on Preservation. Subcommittee C. *White Paper: Strategic Considerations Relative to the Preservation and Storage of Human and Machine Readable Records.* July 1984.

National Archives and Records Administration. NARA Bulletin no. 88-8. "Use of Optical Disk Systems to Store Permanent Federal Records." September 19, 1988.

———. "A National Archives Strategy for Development of Standards for the Creation, Transfer, Access, and Long-Term Storage of Electronic Records of the Federal Government." National Archives Technical Information Paper no. 8. National Archives and Records Administration, Archival Research and Evaluation Staff, June 1990.

National Research Council. Commission on Physical Science, Mathematics, and Applications. Computer Science and Technology Board. System Security Study Committee. *Computers at Risk.* Washington, D.C.: National Academy Press, 1990.

Neavill, Gordon B. "Electronic Publishing, Libraries, and the Survival of Information." *Library Resources & Technical Services* (January/March, 1984), 76–89.

Saffady, William. *Optical Disks vs. Micrographics as Document Storage & Retrieval Techniques.* Westport, Conn.: Meckler, 1988. (See esp. pp. 60–61.)

Swan, John. "Micropermanence and Electronic Evanescence." *Microform Review*, 20, 2 (Spring 1991), 80–83.

Swora, Tamara, and Merrily Smith. "Preservation Work Module Action Plan." Draft Revised April 20, 1989. Library of Congress internal document. (P. 14: "Optical storage media . . . are currently not considered to be archival.")

Tenner, Edward. "The Paradoxical Proliferation of Paper." *Harvard Magazine* (March-April, 1988), 23–26.

Woodcock, Roderick, and Marc Wielage. "Laser Rot." *Video* (April 1987), 49–52.

U.S. House of Representatives. Committee on Education and Labor. Subcommittee on Post-Secondary Education. *Oversight Hearing on the Problem of "Brittle Books" in Our Nation's Libraries*. March 3, 1987. Washington, D.C.: U.S. Government Printing Office, 1987. (See pp. 7, 69.)

Yerburgh, Mark. "Studying All Those 'Tiny Little Tea Leaves': The Future of Microforms in a Complex Technological Environment." *Microform Review*, 16, 1 (Winter 1987), 14–20.

11

The Methods-of-Searching Model

The discussion of the several different conceptual and physical models for arranging the universe of knowledge records has indicated that no one of them by itself is adequately comprehensive. An overall problem is that each model imposes too restrictive a frame on the vision of the researcher (or librarian); each in practice closes off as many options as it opens, forgoes as many alternatives as it pursues, and limits as much as it liberates. The following are some of the specific problems that now exist and that need to be addressed by a new model.

The Subject Model (as embodied either in a printed list of specific sources given to students by a teacher, or in a classification scheme designed for displaying books in a subject-grouped arrangement) blinds its adherents to sources outside the confines of its particular subject or disciplinary purview; it gives researchers no power to predict the existence of likely sources, nor systematic means to retrieve them, in disciplines outside the scope of the resource list or subject array at hand.

The classification scheme—which is mistakenly but nevertheless usually perceived as the entirety of the Library Science model—biases research toward printed monographs, to the comparative neglect of journal articles, unclassified research reports, newspapers, microforms, government documents, photographs and prints, sound recordings, online databases and CD-ROMs, manuscripts, motion pictures, maps, and other nonbook formats that do not lend themselves to arrangement in browsable groups with books.

The classification scheme, even at its best (i.e., when considered as an arrangement primarily or even exclusively for books), still scatters

151

many different aspects of the same subject in many different classes. And in providing no cross-references within the bookshelf arrangement of printed texts (which is all that most people perceive of the class scheme in the first place), it effectively undercuts cross-disciplinary research and encourages insular disciplinary perspectives.

The Actual-Practice model makes it very difficult for readers to achieve an overview of the range of resources available on any subject. Its reliance on unsystematic browsing in the class scheme (divorced from efficient use of the library catalog's subject heading system as an index) blinds its adherents to the subject's scattered aspects; its disregard for journal indexes blinds researchers to vast areas of relevant material; and its reliance on footnote chasing (which leads only to earlier sources) similarly disregards the option of citation searching (which leads to subsequent sources).

The Actual-Practice model also leads researchers to put inordinate trust in computer searches, often with little or no critical thought as to which databases ought to be searched or which terms should be used as search elements. Indeed, there is often a noticeable lack of any critical thought as to whether a database—rather than, say, a published bibliography—ought to be used in the first place.

Another variant of the Actual-Practice model leads researchers to rely too heavily on simply talking to colleagues ("the invisible college") to the virtual neglect of library or print resources. While such a research technique can often be very useful, it is not without dangers, particularly when one's colleagues are themselves innocent of contact with library resources. (And the growth of bulletin-board networks accessible by means of computer terminals will undoutedly magnify both the strengths and the weaknesses of this research approach.)

The class scheme and the Actual-Practice model share the same weakness of blinding researchers to the existence of journal indexes (especially paper-format journal indexes, which often contain significant subject coverage not found in computer databases).

The class scheme and the Actual-Practice model also both tend to blind researchers to the existence of published bibliographies. Readers who are unaware of the index function of the library catalog in providing systematic entry into the class scheme usually miss bibliographies in the bookstacks because bibliographies are not shelved with monographs on their respective subjects but are grouped by themselves in the Z classes in the LC system. They are thus overlooked by shelf browsers. They also tend to be missed in library catalogs because most readers are unaware of the technicalities of the LCSH system; they therefore usually miss the *subdivision* "Bibliography"—which is easily found by those versed in *LCSH* use—because they fail to determine the proper (and specific rather than general) subject *heading* in the first place.

The Type-of-Literature model—which, with the Subject Model, is the one most frequently taught in schools—simply fails to "take" readily among students. The difficulty they have in absorbing the Type model seems to arise from three factors.

• There are scores of different types of literature (e.g., dictionaries, handbooks, union lists, case studies), simply too many to be readily remembered (see Appendix 2).

• Students are not usually taught the use of the precoordinated *LCSH* system, whose form subdivisions enable students to recognize the various types of literature available to them in any subject area. Rather, students are usually given simple lists of sources to study—lists that are highly selective and quickly outdated to begin with.

• The Type-of-Literature model does not match the actual arrangement of sources on library shelves; thus students must remember dozens of categories they cannot simply recognize in front of them.

The Computer Workstation model biases research heavily toward recent literature, entailing in its use the concealed (and erroneous) proposition either that the older literature is simply unimportant or that it is always fully recapitulated within the most recent sources. The full-text component of the Workstation model also biases research in two ways. First, it creates a bias toward only those texts for which copyright clearances can be secured for digitization, a subset of sources that remains microscopic in proportion to the full range of texts that are actually published. The result is that proponents of this model tend, right from the start, to have a severely restricted view of what constitutes the "everything" that should be available to researchers. Second, when it does include copyrighted material, the Computer Workstation model tends to bias its own availability to relatively—or even decidedly—affluent researchers who can afford to pay the high per-minute search costs that are necessarily entailed in the most inclusive version of the model.

The Computer model also has a curious way of blinding its adherents to the very possibility of full-text subject browsing in a classified array of printed sources. Extreme proponents of the model tend unconsciously to assume that if text-word searching cannot be done directly and immediately by computers, then it cannot be done *at all,* even by a systematic browsing method that has demonstrated its utility for centuries.

The Computer model also tends to blind its proponents to the problems of the long-term archival preservation of electronic records. This is more of an immediate problem for librarians than it is for researchers; still, if librarians assume the unconcern of the researchers, the effect will eventually tell on both groups.

While proponents of the Computer Workstation model have tended to criticize the Library Science model for "privileging" certain formats of knowledge records (i.e., printed-book texts over audiovisual formats such as movies, sound recordings, and pictures or photographs), the criticism is actually a two-edged sword. Since the A/V formats lend themselves readily to digitization and workstation playback, and since readers tend not to like the tedium of reading long printed texts in screen-format displays (as has been amply demonstrated with microfiche), it can reasonably be said that the Computer model "privileges" the audiovisual formats at the expense of book-length texts. A further reasonable question then arises as to whether a "universe" of knowledge records that is sloped toward educing passive, aesthetic, or emotional responses to "visual experiences" at the expense of extended intellectual, ethical, and verbal analyses is entirely a boon to the civilization it seeks to represent.[1]

The Computer model, with its new capability of key word searching, tends also to blind users to the advantages of controlled-vocabulary cataloging; that is, in usually presenting researchers with *some* results no matter what terms they search with, the computer tends to hide from them the magnitude of the array of sources they are not getting, but ought to be.

Both the Computer model and the Subject model (as taught from a list of specific sources) make it difficult for researchers to retrieve sources they cannot specify clearly in advance.

Both the Computer and Subject models tend to limit searchers' range of awareness of sources to the one list, class area, or database that they start with; neither makes it easy to envision sources beyond the starting point, or teaches how to find them in a systematic manner.

The full potential of both the catalog component of the Library Science model and the entire Computer Workstation model tends to be undercut by the simple but persistent failure of librarians to teach students the important difference between natural language key word searching and controlled-vocabulary subject heading searching (e.g., *LCSH*). This critical distinction is entirely overlooked by the Subject and the Type-of-Literature models of bibliographic instruction, which are usually taught instead.

The full potential of the Library Science model tends also to be overlooked even by librarians themselves. There seem to be three reasons for this.

• First, library schools tend to train new reference librarians according to the Type-of-Literature model, and cataloging courses apparently fail to inculcate a full understanding of *LCSH* (especially insofar as, unlike conventional thesauri, it must serve as the index to a classified array of full texts, and also provide, through precoordination of terms, *recognition* capabilities in thousands of subject areas and hundreds of languages in which its users have no prior subject expertise).

• Second, library schools also tend not to emphasize the importance of subject bibliographies (as opposed to computer printouts); they especially neglect to teach the structural embodiment of that emphasis contained in the classification scheme (the Z classes).

• Third, there is a fashion in library schools to seek greater social legitimacy by distancing librarians as a group from what is perceived to be an old-fashioned model, and to embrace instead what is perceived to be "cutting edge": high technology. This technology then tends to set its own agenda as to what is intellectually important. Thus the fashionable emphasis on "information science" at the expense of "library science." (The former, in practice, tends within this context toward simple synonymy with "computerization.") In other words, the one profession that is intellectually in the best position to correct and compensate for the inadequacies of the Computer Workstation model is, for social reasons, often apparently unwilling to do so for fear of appearing old-fashioned or outdated.[2]

All models except the Actual-Practice model tend to bias researchers toward printed (or electronic) sources at the expense of talking to knowledgeable people.

All of the various models tend to overlook the citation and related-record searching capabilities that exist in all subject areas.

All of the various models lend insufficient emphasis to the means of finding special collections, government documents, and microforms, whose existence is often missed by standard catalogs and databases. Finally, the undeniable reality of the Principle of Least Effort ensures a situation in which most researchers will simply settle for any easily obtained results derived from any of the various models, regardless of the superficiality or incompleteness of such results.

While it is true that each of the different gestalts for organizing the universe of knowledge records—whether the Subject, tripartite Library Science, Type-of-Literature, Actual-Practice, or Computer Workstation model—has weaknesses and blind spots, it is also true that each has peculiar strengths and areas of particular efficiency. What is required of a new model, then, is a balance of the existing models against one another so that a weakness in any one may be compensated for by a strength in another.

A Methods-of-Searching model may be best at meeting this requirement. Just as with the others, it can exist as both a conceptual scheme (i.e., a mental model usable regardless of the physical arrangement of research resources in an actual library) and a physical model by which the library—or at least a reference collection within a library—can actually categorize its resources.

A Methods model categorizes the universe of knowledge records according to the ways in which they are searched. At the outset of this discussion, however, let me emphasize that such a model embraces and includes the existing subject classification scheme virtually in its entirety, as the embodiment of one of its component methods of searching, and requires no change in standard library processes. As a conceptual model, of course, a Methods scheme can exist independently of any actual physical arrangement of knowledge records. As a physical model, however, it would require some small adjustments only to the arrangement of a research library's reference collection—and only to a small portion of that, in order to give greater prominence to certain sources whose importance is more concealed than revealed by conventional subject classification, or even Z-class, arrangement.

The Methods model distinguishes, at present, eight different methods of searching the universe of knowledge records.

1. Controlled-vocabulary searches in manual or printed sources.
2. Key word searches in manual or printed sources.

3. Citation searches in printed sources.
4. Searches through published bibliographies (including sets of footnotes in relevant subject documents).
5. Searches through people sources (whether by verbal contact, E-mail, electronic bulletin board, letters, etc.).
6. Computer searches—which can be done by subject heading, classification number, key word, or citation, but which add the possibility of postcoordinate Boolean combinations while often at the same time excluding earlier time periods of coverage and also forcing more precise specification of search elements at the expense of easier browsing and simpler recognition.
7. Related-record searches (available only through three particular CD-ROM databases).
8. Systematic browsing, especially of full-text sources arranged in predictable subject groupings.

Note that virtually all of the elements of the other models are included in this scheme (Type-of-Literature excepted, a point to which I shall return), but they are given an explicitness of distinction and a parallelism of emphasis in importance not found in the other models. The basic concepts of the Methods model are:

• Each of these eight ways of searching is applicable in any subject area.

• None of the eight is confined exclusively to English-language sources.

• Each has both strengths and weaknesses, advantages and disadvantages.

• The weaknesses or blind spots within any one method are corrected or balanced by the strengths of the others.

• The strength of each is precisely that it is capable of turning up information or knowledge records that cannot be found efficiently—or often even at all—by any of the others.

In regard to the overall scheme as a conceptual model, these points hold true regardless of how the various library resources embodying the search methods may be physically arranged. Considered as a physical model, the Methods scheme entails a further point:

• Each of the eight categories allows for a reasonably distinct physical grouping of actual library reference sources, so that the eight groups can be displayed (and recognized) both in relation and in contradistinction to one another.

I mentioned that the Methods model includes the existing classification scheme already in place in research libraries. Actually, it includes all three components of the Library Science model, for it incorporates the vocabulary-controlled catalog (within elements 1 and 6) and published bibliographies (element 4) as well as the class scheme (element 8). An important point is that the Methods model also incorporates the Computer Workstation model in its entirety, in a combination of elements 6 and 7. One of the major advantages of a Methods model, however, is that it places the Workstation within a larger context of other resources that lie beyond the computer's reach; moreover, it is a larger context that is reasonably specific and definable in its components. The elements that are lacking in *both* the Traditional Library Science and the Computer Workstation models are thus readily perceptible when the existing models are regridded within this larger intellectual framework. And the larger framework itself, having only eight elements, is such that it can be readily taught, and remembered, as an outline of the universe of research possibilities that ought to be perceptible in any inquiry. A Methods model, in other words, makes it easier for researchers to achieve a sense of *closure* in their projects. It spells out more clearly than the other models the full range of options available for research, regardless of the subject area.

It remains to consider the content of each of the eight elements, particularly if viewed as a model for the physical arrangement of a research library's reference collection. (A more detailed discussion of the scheme as a conceptual model may be found in my earlier book, *A Guide to Library Research Methods* [Oxford, 1987].)[3]

Controlled-Vocabulary Sources in Manual or Printed Formats

A major problem with all existing research models is that journal indexes do not readily fit into them. A single index, even though ostensibly devoted to a particular subject or discipline, nevertheless covers an amazing range of topics. Thus, for example, a recent annual volume of *Business Periodicals Index* has entries not only on "Banks and banking," "Employee stock options," "House buying," "Personnel management," and "Real estate business," but also on:

Abortion

Adult education

Aesthetics

Bashfulness

Capital punishment

Detective and mystery stories

Eastern Europe—Social conditions

Freedom of speech

Genetic code

Heart diseases

Historic houses

Homosexuality

Ideology

Infertility

Japan—Race problems

Knowledge

Listening

Literacy education

Medical ethics

Minerals in nutrition

Nonverbal communication

Opera

Oriental rugs

Paintings

Philosophy of science

Quantum theory

Radar—Countermeasures

Rape

Religion

Right to die

Sex differences (Psychology)

Shakespeare

Teachers—Tenure

Television broadcasting—Moral aspects

Theory of numbers

Urbanization—Developing countries

Violence in sports

Walesa, Lech

Women—History

X-rays

Yachts and yachting

Zoos

Comparable subject "scatters" can be found in almost any other index that is ostensibly devoted to a single subject area (e.g., *Art Index, General Science Index, Education Index, Social Sciences Index*). The important but usually overlooked point is that disciplinary indexes cover not only their "own" subjects but also an amazing range of other subjects from the perspective of their discipline. Thus, any topic of a certain critical mass may show up in a surprisingly wide variety of journal indexes—precisely as the same topic in books may have many different aspects that appear in a wide variety of classification areas. And just as the class scheme for books hides the scattering of subject aspects, so the shelving of journal indexes according to their overall "major" subject or discipline (or their geographic association in the Z1200–Z4999 range) hides the real variety of subjects that they cover.

The Methods model would compensate for this scattering by grouping the basic journal indexes—not *all* journal indexes, just the basic ones—in all subject areas together, and arranging them in groups not according to their "subject" but rather according to their method of searching (e.g., controlled-vocabulary, key word, citation). The full theoretical implications of such a scheme will, I hope, become clear after a consideration of specific examples.

The first physical grouping of reference sources within a Methods model would comprise basic indexes in all subject areas that have in common the use of *Library of Congress Subject Headings* for the fundamental structuring of their categories. Two qualifications need to be stated immediately. First, by "basic" indexes of the controlled-vocabulary type I mean essentially those from the H. W. Wilson and Information Access Corporation (listed later in this chapter), plus a few others. Thus, this first group would include *Social Sciences Index* but not the much larger and more specialized *Psychological Abstracts* or *Sociological Abstracts; Education Index* but not the larger *ERIC* indexes; the *Applied Science and Technology Index* but not the larger *Engineering Index;* and so on. Second, while these basic indexes lean heavily on *LCSH* for their category terms, they do not use that list exclusively. New topics tend to show up in journal articles before they appear in books, and it is only at the latter stage that the LC (and other) librarian catalogers seek to standardize the vocabulary of subject headings that appear in *LCSH*. Nevertheless, even when the Wilson or Information Access index does use a different term, it tends to supply a cross-reference from the *LCSH* heading, and so researchers can still frequently use *LCSH* terms as initial entry points in these variant controlled vocabularies.

The following indexes, then, would be grouped physically together in section 1 (the collocating principle being not their subjects but rather their tendency to use *LCSH* category terms):

Nineteenth-Century Readers' Guide

Readers' Guide to Periodical Literature

Essay and General Literature Index

International Index

Social Sciences and Humanities Index

Social Sciences Index

Humanities Index

Art Index

Industrial Arts Index

Business Periodicals Index

Applied Science and Technology Index

General Science Index

Biological and Agricultural Index

Education Index

Index to Legal Periodicals

Access (a supplement to *Readers' Guide*)

Public Affairs Information Service (P.A.I.S)

P.A.I.S. International

Bibliographic Guide to Government Publications—United States

Monthly Catalog of U.S. Government Publications five-year cumulative indexes (Oryx Press)

Index to U.S. Government Periodicals

Magazine Index (microfilm version)

Business Index (microfilm version)

National Newspaper Index (microfilm version)

Legal Resource Index (microfilm version)

I would also include four other vocabulary-controlled indexes that use a different set of category terms, but which are in general internally consistent among themselves in their subject headings:

CIS Congressional Index

American Statistics Index

Statistical Reference Index

Index to International Statistics

This entire group, then, extends beyond *Library of Congress Subject Headings;* but in its general outline it is still immediately teachable and, with some point-of-use instruction, recognizable as a "vocabulary-controlled" group that is categorically different from key word or other index groups.

There are several advantages to such an array. First of all, it would enable researchers simply to *recognize* that they have many more search options than just the *Readers' Guide,* and this alone would be a major plus. (Conventionally these indexes are rather widely scattered when shelved according to LC class numbers.)

Second, such a grouping would greatly facilitate *point-of-use instruction* by reference librarians, especially if the array were visibly distinct from other arrays of key word and citation indexes. A librarian could then say: "Here is your *LCSH* term. After you've searched for it in the catalog for books, then try using the same term in *this, this,* and *this* index in section 1 over here. That way, you'll be covering not just books but also journal articles, anthologies, newspapers, government documents, and microforms on your subject.''

A third advantage is immediately apparent: such a grouping would very efficiently facilitate both *cross-disciplinary* and *cross-format* research, which is tedious to do otherwise. While a reader looks for ''The Aged'' as a heading in the *Social Sciences Index,* for example, the librarian could pull out volumes of the *Humanities Index, Education Index, Index to U.S. Government Periodicals, Business Periodicals Index* (with its cross-reference to ''The Elderly'')—or virtually any of the other titles—or set up microfilm-screen displays of ''Aged'' in *Magazine Index* right next to *Business Index* and *Legal Resource Index.* If we can put such sources right under the readers' noses and show how easy it is to come at the same subject from multidisciplinary perspectives, then more readers would follow that path. Paved roads create traffic. Such instruction by librarians and recognition by researchers, however, is virtually impossible when these same indexes are arranged in a conventional manner in the LC class scheme. Under such a condition of scattering, the Principle of Least Effort ensures that their *aggregate power* will be entirely dissipated.

Key Word and Key Word/Citation Sources in Print Formats

The second and third physical groupings of reference sources in a Methods model would be those of key word and key word/citation indexes. Section 2 (key word indexes) would include sources such as:

> *Combined Retrospective Index to Journals in History, 1838–1974*
>
> *Combined Retrospective Index to Journals in Political Science, 1886–1974*
>
> *Combined Retrospective Index to Journals in Sociology, 1895–1974*
>
> *ISSHP: Index to Social Sciences & Humanities Proceedings*
>
> *ISTP: Index to Scientific and Technical Proceedings*
>
> *ISR: Index to Scientific Reviews*
>
> *ISBC: Index to Scientific Book Contents*

> *Comprehensive Dissertation Index* (not *Abstracts*)
>
> *Publications Reference File* (*GPO*)
>
> *Government Reports Announcements & Index*
>
> *NTIS Title Index on Microfiche*
>
> *Transdex* (an index to translations)

Section 3 (key word/citation) indexes would include:

> *Arts & Humanities Citation Index*
>
> *Social Sciences Citation Index*
>
> *Science Citation Index* (or its abridged version)

Since the three citation indexes are also major key word sources, they need to be shelved next to the other key word indexes; and yet their citation search capability must also be segregated for special emphasis.

With such a configuration, reference librarians would finally be able to emphasize concretely a distinction that most researchers routinely blur: that key word searching is not the same thing as controlled-vocabulary searching. Librarians could say, in effect: "If there is no *LCSH* term that corresponds to the subject you want, we can still pursue the topic efficiently. After you've done a computer key word search for books in the online catalog (or used the CD-ROM databases), then come back here and search for the same key words in sections 2 and 3. These sources, in aggregate, cover over six thousand journals, plus conference proceedings, doctoral dissertations, state-of-the-art review articles, translations, report literature, and government documents, and also provide decades of retrospective coverage that are blind spots to corresponding online databases and CD-ROMs. The three key word/citation indexes in section 3 are especially good for cross-disciplinary research." Once again, in-depth research across both disciplines and formats would be greatly facilitated in a way that cannot be matched by a conventional arrangement of the same indexes in the LC class scheme. (The latter, for instance, classes the *Arts & Humanities Citation Index* in AI3 while putting the *Social Sciences Citation Index* in Z7161.)

The particular emphasis given to the citation search method in section 3 would be especially helpful in bringing this technique to readers' attention in the first place. It usually tends to be overlooked entirely when its indexes are simply buried in the A and Z classes with everything else. When the indexes are grouped together according to the principle of the method by which they are searched, however (rather than according to their "subject"—which is much broader, more diverse, and more scattered than any single index title would indicate), then both point-of-use instruction by librarians and recognition by readers are greatly facilitated. The arrangement of materials can significantly reduce the burden for both of having to specify in advance a listing of which sources would be most useful in any particular inquiry.

Indexes to Published Bibliographies and Special Collections

Although a large percentage of the reference collection of any research library will be Z-class material, it is neither possible nor desirable for every reference source classed from Z1200 or above (see chapter 5) to be shelved in the reference area rather than in the regular bookstacks. Moreover, even the subset of available Z material that is selected for more prominent shelving in a reference collection is so voluminous that it cannot readily be grasped as a whole or noticed as a definable collection of sources in the same way as sections 1, 2, and 3. This is not to say that such material should not be present (see the discussion of section 8). For recognition purposes, however, a related alternative is desirable. Section 4 in a Methods scheme, then, would consist of a grouping not of the library's bibliographies themselves but rather of a more manageable collection of *indexes to* and *listings of* the bibliographies. It would contain, at a minimum:

Bibliographic Index (1937–)

World Bibliography of Bibliographies by Theodore Besterman

World Bibliography of Bibliographies, 1964–1974, by Alice Toomey

Subject Bibliographies of Government Publications (Detroit: Omnigraphics)

Guide to Published Library Catalogs by Bonnie Nelson

First Stop: The Master Index to Subject Encyclopedias by Joe Ryan (useful in locating brief, *selected* bibliographies at the ends of encyclopedia articles)

Bibliographische Berichte (1959–)

A slight expansion in the scope of section 4 would enable librarians to solve an additional problem as well: that special collections and micro-forms tend to be overlooked by researchers. Overview guides to such materials could themselves reasonably be included here, since, concep-tually, having the means of identifying a special collection on a particu-lar topic is much like having the means to identify a bibliography on the subject: a citation pointing to either one would lead a researcher to a whole aggregate of relevant sources. To some extent such collections would already be signaled by some of the sources already listed (e.g., the *Government Publications* and *Library Catalogs* sources); but other could be included, too, such as:

> *Microform Research Collections* by Suzanne Dodson
>
> *Index to Microform Collections* by Ann Niles
>
> *Subject Collections* by Lee Ash
>
> *Special Collections in College and University Libraries* (Collier Macmillan, 1989)
>
> *World Guide to Special Libraries* (K. G. Saur, latest edition)

Such general listings could then easily be supplemented as appropri-ate by local area sources (e.g., in the Washington area, *Special Collec-tions in the Library of Congress, Library and Reference Facilities in the Area of the District of Columbia,* and so on). The grouping together of such sources would thus facilitate the recognition and use of sources—bibliographies and special collections, including microforms—that oth-erwise too often get overlooked because readers cannot notice them by browsing in the regular classified bookstacks. Segregation of these sources in section 4 would be a means of emphasizing that, as an aggregate, they are both different from and equal in importance to the sources that are more readily noticeable in the classified bookstacks (section 8) or in computer databases (sections 6 and 7).

People Sources

Often the best way to find information on a subject is to go beyond print or database sources and talk to knowledgeable people. This option, however, seems not to occur to large numbers of researchers who come into libraries. And yet libraries have wonderful means of connecting researchers with experts in all subject areas. The creation of a separate section 5, of equal status with the others as indicated by comparable placement and parallel signage, would go a long way toward bringing the "people" option to researchers' attention whether or not they were looking for it. It would also, once again, facilitate point-of-use instruction by librarians. We would no longer have to say, "Let me make a list of several different directories in several different class areas that you should consult"; rather, we could simply say, "Look through this section here, and especially *this, this,* and *this* directory."

Section 5, then, should include sources such as:

> *Encyclopedia of Associations* (including International and local volumes)
>
> *Directories in Print*
>
> *National Directory of Bulletin Board Systems*
>
> *Washington Information Directory*
>
> *Who Knows: A Guide to Washington Experts*
>
> *Federal Yellow Book*
>
> *State Yellow Book*
>
> Carroll Publishing Company directories (*Federal Executive Directory, State Executive Directory, County Executive Directory, Municipal Executive Directory*)
>
> Washington Researchers directories (*How to Find Information About Companies, . . . About Private Companies, . . . About Japanese Companies, . . . About Service Companies*)
>
> *Yellow Pages* and other local directories

In a conventional library arrangement, these sources would be scattered all over the classification scheme; and yet any one of them can be useful in identifying and locating knowledgeable people in a truly surprising range of subject areas.

One additional point should be noted about people sources: reference librarians themselves should be considered an integral part of the configuration I am advocating. While I would not have them wear tags that say "I'm part of section 5," I would nevertheless insist that any bibliographic instruction given to explain the Methods model ought to emphasize explicitly that readers should talk to the librarians. It is standard practice in many library instruction classes—especially when they are taught by nonlibrarian professors in graduate schools—to tell students: "You're no scholar if you can't find what you want on your own. You shouldn't have to ask for help from the librarians." This is *very* bad advice, especially since most of the professors who insist on it are ignorant of how much material they themselves have been missing over the years in following the Actual-Practice model.

Computer Sources

In exactly the same way that printed indexes to journals (e.g., *Social Sciences Index, Business Periodicals Index*) cover much more than just a limited range of topics within one discipline—any index can cover any subject from "Abortion" to "Zoology"—so, too, each of the various CD-ROM databases that are now so popular is also surprisingly multi-disciplinary in its actual coverage. Rather than hiding the cross-disciplinary coverage of these sources by physically scattering them, it would make more sense to group them together in a section 6. (Whether each CD-ROM appears on its own terminal or all are networked to appear on any terminal is irrelevant here. The point is that there should be a grouping *of the terminals themselves*).[4] What would be distinctive, of course, would be not their subject coverage—which is the same in its omni-disciplinary extent as all the other sections—but rather the method of searching that computers allow. The electronic formats enable researchers to do key word searches that cannot be done in most print indexes; and they especially allow searches to be done through postcoordinate combinations of various elements. (Their noticeable weaknesses in diminishing browsing and simple recognition capabilities, and in covering only recent literature, are counterbalanced by the other sections.) Section 6 would thus group together, as a physically separate aggregate, all of the library's computer-search potential, both in-house (e.g., in online catalogs and commercially produced CD-ROMs) and externally tappable (e.g., Internet or NREN connections to electronic bulletin boards). Finally librarians would have not only an easy way of conveying to readers the range of available computer sources but also, by pointing to the other sections, a simple means of indicating the range of *other* library resources that are *not* in the computers.

In such a context, point-of-use instruction would be much more effective. Librarians could say: "After you've used the computers over there, then come back to section 1 (or 2) for coverage of other sources on the same subject. Look at section 4 for bibliographies that have already been compiled; then you might try section 3 to see if someone has cited any of the sources you've found—especially the better sources—in the other sections; or try section 5 if you need to find someone to talk to''; and so on. Researchers could thus see more of the *whole* library's resources than the computers alone reveal to them.

Related-Record-Search CD–ROMs

Section 7 calls for a distinction to be made within the grouping of computer terminals that form the Computer Workstation portion of a reference collection. (The distinction here between sections 6 and 7 is analogous to that between sections 2 and 3. There, the key word/citation print-format indexes had to be physically next to the other key word indexes, but also distinguished from them because of their additional and distinctive search capability.) Specifically, three CD-ROM databases, all from the Institute for Scientific Information (ISI), provide an additional and different way to do subject searches. The three are the CD-ROM versions of the *Science Citation Index,* the *Social Sciences Citation Index,* and the *Arts & Humanities Citation Index.*

Their "related record" search capability assumes that a researcher has already found a good starting-point article within any of the databases' disks through either key word or citation searching. Once such a starting point is found, one can then find any other article within the same computer disk that has footnotes in common with it. In other words, the records found in this way will be related to the first article in that all of them cite the same sources in footnotes. The important thing to note is that articles that are closely related in that they cite the same sources may nevertheless have *entirely different key words in their titles,* and so could not be found together by key word searches.

Once researchers have found an initial set of related records, they can then search *their* related records, which will lead to a second level, and so on. Up to five levels of footnote-related articles can be generated in this way.

Usually, related-record searching can be done only in single-year disks, although in the *Social Sciences* and *Arts* databases it is possible to search some multiyear retrospective disks as well.

Since this method of searching is of such importance, it needs special emphasis to bring it to the reader's attention in the first place. I would recommend that even within the aggregation of computer terminals brought about by the creation of section 6, those terminals offering the ISI disk sets should be physically separated from the other terminals and labeled section 7. In other words, if this related-record search capability is to be given noticeable emphasis, it would be better to segregate the terminals capable of providing it rather than simply to network the ISI CD-ROMs into other terminals in a way that would blur their distinctive feature. Ideally, a mini-network of just these three databases would be offered in a physically distinct grouping of their own terminals.

Classified Bookstacks for Systematic Browsing of Full Texts

In a Methods-of-Searching configuration, the vast majority of a research library's reference collection would remain just as it has always been, in a conventional subject-classified arrangement. The general bookstacks beyond the reference collection would also remain in similar classified order, just as they have always been. Moreover, most of the library's collection of printed bibliographies and in-depth indexes (e.g., *Current Index to Journals in Education* rather the *Education Index*) would remain in their regular Z-class positions rather than being in section 1, closer to the reference desk.

What would change in a Methods configuration would be the way that readers are taught by librarians to perceive the class scheme as a whole. Instead of representing it as containing "everything," we would emphasize that even in its entirety it still constitutes only *one* avenue of access to *some* of the library's resources. As an aggregate of resources on all subjects, then, it should be perceived as *one* such aggregate among seven other comparable aggregates, each covering *all* subject areas, but each providing a "window" on the full spectrum that enables a researcher to see different parts of any subject. Such a perception of the class scheme as a whole is impossible in a conventional library configuration, as there is nothing perceptibly "outside" it—save for computer terminals—to which it may readily be compared and contrasted. A

Methods scheme, however, finally solves this problem: it enables researchers to see more than just "browsing" and "computers" as the main components of library research.

A Methods model, in a sense, turns a conventional perception of library structure inside out, as in Figures 10 and 11. Figure 10 represents a conventional understanding of the array of resources in a library; here, these resources are divided by subject, and the researcher, in moving in one subject direction rather than another, is thereby led to focus narrowly on his topic to the exclusion of seeing other subjects, or the scatter of his own subject's many aspects in many different class groupings. Figure 11, in contrast, shows a Methods scheme. Here, the researcher moves from one method of searching to another—or, in the physical model, from one aggregate of sources to another, each aggregate embodying a different method of searching—and each method/aggregate is capable of showing him not just a particular topic but all topics, and also cross-disciplinary relationships to all other topics. Each method functions as a window that enables anyone to see the range of all subjects and their interconnections; and yet no one method can disclose the full depth of that range. Each window allows the perception of something that is a blind spot to the other windows, regardless of the subject sought.

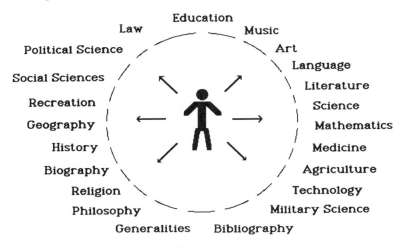

Figure 10

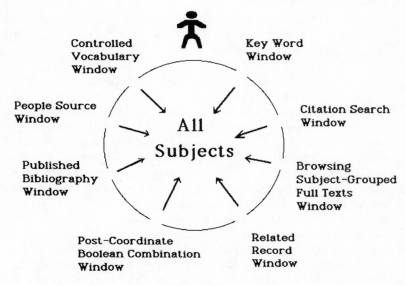

Controlled
Vocabulary
Window

Key Word
Window

People Source
Window

All
Subjects

Citation Search
Window

Published
Bibliography
Window

Browsing
Subject-Grouped
Full Texts
Window

Post-Coordinate
Boolean Combination
Window

Related
Record
Window

Figure 11

Relation Between the Methods and the Type-of-Literature Models

I mentioned earlier that such a Methods model, while completely integrating most of the other models (especially the Library Science and the Computer Workstation configurations), does not fully absorb the Type-of-Literature model. A number of points are relevant here.

First, it does incorporate much, though not all, of the Type model. Its insistence on an *LCSH* vocabulary-controlled catalog—and not just a key word–searchable file—ensures that the form subdivisions that identify the various types of literature (e.g., [*LCSH* heading]—Bibliography,—Directories,—Chronology) will still be present and searchable; and it is this system of precoordinated subdivisions in *LCSH* that provides the major avenue of access to the types of literature. Additionally, the Methods model places an increased emphasis on the use of published bibliographies, which are often themselves internally arranged by types of literature. Indeed, by placing such extra emphasis on bibliographies (section 4), the model thereby lends added weight to the importance of *that type* of literature itself; and, similarly, it also lends particular emphasis to several other unusually important types: directories (section 5), indexes (sections 1–3), and computer databases (sections 6 and 7).

It does not, however, lend any particular emphasis to the scores of other types of literature that could be similarly distinguished by physical segregation into distinct groupings. To do so, of course—to create hundreds of aggregates rather than just eight—would be to create an overall scheme that is just as confusing and as mentally unabsorbable (to most researchers, anyway) as the existing subject classification in its full extent from A through Z.

In one important sense, then, the Type-of-Literature model does not fit completely into the Methods model, at least when considered as a *physical* scheme of arranging actual library resources. There is a way to handle this problem, however; but its solution, I think, is a *mental* configuration that reference librarians alone—as opposed to general researchers or academics with subject specialties—will be able to work with comfortably. I say this because most others who are taught the Type model simply do not absorb it for lack of extensive experience in actually using it in a habitual manner. Most people, if they remember it at all, focus on only a very few of the many scores of literature types that make up the full model (see Appendix 2 for a partial indication of its extent). In contrast, librarians who work with large reference collections, and who must deal with thousands of questions in areas where they have no personal subject expertise find that, after one has considerable experience in using it in unfamiliar subject areas, the Type model is absorbable in ways that more desultory researchers, or those confined to particular topic areas, cannot readily appreciate. The Type of Literature model, then, has something to offer reference librarians over and above—or, rather, off to the side of—what a Methods model provides. The relationship of the two may be broadly indicated if we first recognize an important distinction.

The distinction is between what may be labeled "reference" questions and "research" questions. The former may be described as those inquiries seeking specific factual data (e.g., "What is the mailing address of the Department of Education?" "Who won the Oscar for best supporting actor in 1954?" "What is the distance between Chicago and Atlanta?"). Such questions have a "correct" answer that is determinable. Research questions, by contrast, may be described as open-ended inquiries that do not have a simple "correct" answer (e.g., "What information do you have on Chinese snuff bottles?'' ''I'm interested in U.S.-Israeli relations right after the Six-Day War. What can I read about that?'' ''How do I go about setting up a small business?'').

If, for purposes of this discussion, we distinguish between reference and research questions, we can see how the Type-of-Literature model and the Methods-of-Searching model relate to each other. At the risk of some oversimplification, we can say that the Type model works best for most reference questions and the Methods model works best for most research questions. This is not to say that the two are mutually exclusive, or that there won't be considerable overlap for some particular questions. But the distinction points up the major strengths of each model.

In a sense, one could simply expand the Methods model itself to include the Type model as its ninth component part. And this can easily be done if the Methods scheme is regarded simply as a conceptual configuration. It won't work, however, if it is regarded as a physical model for actually arranging real library resources on shelves: one cannot have a developed Type-of-Literature section (i.e., a section 9) that does justice to the full range of forms and is also manageable in size. Indeed, one of the existing components—section 8 (the classification scheme)—is itself already so large that most people will not be able to perceive it in its entirety. But this is not terribly important in this particular case, for most people can indeed grasp how the scheme ''works'' for the one subject they're interested in. And, more important, the overall Methods model tells people, in effect, that no matter how well or how badly they perceive the class scheme as a whole, that scheme in its entirety is only *one* way to search *some* of the library's holdings; that is, it is not the entire universe of available options but rather only one component of a larger universe.

I find it more practically useful, in actually doing reference work, to keep the Type-of-Literature model off to the side. I think it is especially useful to do this in bibliographic instruction classes. The eight components of the Methods model are much more readily teachable, and absorbable, without the Type model thrown in, too. And most students don't function well with the latter anyway. (Reference librarians, in contrast, must continue to be thoroughly familiar with it.)

In actual practice, then, the first question I ask myself in responding to a searcher's inquiry is: ''Is this a reference question or a research question?'' By far, most of the inquiries I get as a reference librarian are in the latter category, and so the Methods model is most useful most of the time as the basic conceptual framework. Once the question is categorized as an open-ended ''research'' inquiry, then the next question to ask is *not:* ''Which sources cover this particular *subject?*''—for there will always be many sources that cover any research subject—but rather: ''Is there an LC subject heading that corresponds to this subject?'' If there is a good category term to start with, then it can be plugged into a wide variety of sources, each of which solves the major problem of vocabulary control of synonyms and variant phrasings. If there is not a good subject heading, then the next question is: ''Which of the other methods of searching would be most appropriate to start with?'' (The Principle of Least Effort makes the choice of starting point for a researcher unusually important, for most readers are not persistent in moving beyond their initial efforts.)

If, however, the first ''cut'' determines that the question is a reference rather than an open-ended research inquiry, then frequently the first choice among options becomes: ''Which type of literature—dictionary, encyclopedia, chronology, directory, atlas—would zero in fastest on the type of fact that is being sought?''

The line between the Type-of-Literature and the Methods models becomes somewhat blurred when the Type model crosses over, in its inclusiveness, into kinds of literature (indexes, bibliographies, computer databases) that are appropriate for research (as opposed to reference) questions. But it is precisely at that line, I believe, that the Methods scheme should take over to provide a more efficient framework of organization for dealing with resources appropriate to the research questions. The Methods model makes finer distinctions among types of indexes (controlled vocabulary, key word, citation) that are all lumped together indiscriminately within the form subdivision ''—Indexes'' in the Type model. Moreover, the Methods scheme adds another method of indexing (i.e., related-record) that would be missed entirely by form subdivisions in *LCSH* because this additional method does not exist in a printed-paper format. Also, the Methods model makes explicit use of the overall classification scheme itself, which is a most appropriate source in dealing with some research questions, but which is entirely outside the purview of the Type model.

Summary of Overall Benefits

A reference collection—that is, not an entire library but just the reference collection portion of it—arranged according to the Methods-of-Searching model would help solve several persistent problems.

• It would greatly facilitate point-of-use instruction by librarians, as it would enlist researchers' ability to *recognize* options displayed and distinguished right in front of them, rather than overload their memory for complicated verbal instructions. Moreover, it calls on readers to perceive only eight basic options, a number within easy grasp of short-term memory.

• It would enable librarians and researchers to pursue cross-disciplinary inquiries in an easy and systematic fashion. This has not been possible with a subject-classified scheme of resource arrangement. The grouping together of the major controlled-vocabulary indexes in all subject areas, however, would permit readers to plug the same search term into a variety of different disciplinary indexes, and thereby to achieve cross-disciplinary coverage that cannot be obtained when the indexes are scattered. And the groupings brought about by each of the other methods of searching would similarly facilitate the easy crossing of disciplinary lines.

• It would similarly enable researchers to do cross-format searches (i.e., searches for information not just in books but also in journals, essays, newspapers, reports, conference papers, bibliographies, special collections, microforms, government documents, computer databases, people sources, and so on). A spin-off benefit here is that the Methods arrangement would also alert researchers more easily and systematically to recognize the relevant holdings of libraries other than the one in which they are working.

• It would enable librarians and researchers more easily to *exclude* whole groups of sources that, while apparently relevant ''by subject,'' are actually a waste of time because of inappropriate indexing. Thus, for example, the student researching ''Managing sociotechnical change'' encountered nothing but frustration in using the *Business Index* and *Business Periodicals Index,* both of which used controlled-vocabulary subject headings that do not have a category term appropriate to that topic. Had the student been referred directly to key word sources (both print and computerized), she would have saved time and avoided frustration. A categorization of sources by method of searching rather than by subject would solve many such problems.

• It would more easily enable librarians to teach the crucial distinction between controlled-vocabulary and key word searching, which is blurred by most researchers. Physically distinct groupings of the two types of sources would aid in reinforcing the recognition of the difference.

• It would finally give librarians a meaningful way to convey to readers the fact that searching computers alone will not give them "everything," and, similarly, that browsing in the bookstacks alone is not the best way to research most questions. A Methods arrangement would allow librarians to point out definite alternative aggregates of sources in any subject area—beyond *just* the computer or *just* the classification scheme—aggregates that would indicate in a very definite way precisely what is the larger whole of which the computers and class scheme are only parts.

• It would enable librarians to get researchers into *older* knowledge records with much greater facility, and thereby to correct the strong bias of computers toward recent sources.

• It would be much more teachable, and memorable, than a Subject model, which can never cover all subjects, and which therefore leaves students narrowly constricted in their views of what a library can offer them. Similarly, it would be much more teachable than a Type-of-Literature model, which, in its full extent, is too large to be teachable to nonexperts, and which, even in a scaled-down version, is not readily absorbable by readers who lack considerable research experience.

• More than any other model, it would permit researchers to achieve a sense of "closure" in their research by enabling them to see the full range of search options available to them, and to see which avenues remain to be explored if their first attempts do not yield satisfactory results.

Now, it may be objected, first, that a scheme which calls for a library's computer terminals to be grouped adjacent to one another undercuts a major advantage of computerization in the first place, which is that computers can provide the same access to sources no matter whether the terminals are within the library or outside it. A moment's reflection, however, will indicate a solution to this apparent problem. First, the creation of a physical grouping of terminals in one major reference area within the library need not preclude the positioning of terminals in other areas as well, both inside and outside the library building. The creation of the main grouping, however, simply solves a problem for those researchers in the major area that is intended to serve as the "introduction" to the collection, a difficulty that cannot be solved without such a central grouping. This is the problem of users' assuming that "everything" they need is available through their computer workstations. To the extent that researchers at noncentral workstations make this assumption, they are arbitrarily and severely reducing the size of the universe of knowledge records that they perceive as searchable in the first place; and this will remain a persistent problem for users at physically remote workstations. Within the library building itself, however, there is a way to correct the mistaken assumption: by positioning the aggregate of workstation sources close to the several other aggregates of sources (including reference librarians!) that are not in the computers, and never will be.

The Methods scheme, then, does not preclude remote access to the library's resources—or, rather, to just some (not all) of them. It simply leaves those searchers at remote workstations within an overall universe of sources that is microscopic in comparison with the universe inhabited by researchers in the central reference area of the research library *as a physical place*. This cannot be singled out as a problem peculiar to the Methods model, however; it will exist in *any* model that can be devised.

A second possible objection to the Methods arrangement concerns the removal of several print-format indexes (especially those from the H. W. Wilson Company and the Institute for Scientific Information) from the conventional A through Z classification scheme, and shelving them in separate groups. Again, however, a bit of common sense would indicate a justification. It must be remembered that the Library of Congress classification scheme was created in the earliest years of the twentieth century, and at that time journal indexes *did not even exist* (with only scant exceptions such as *Poole's Index* and the very early years of the *Readers' Guide*). The class scheme was designed to arrange monographs in subject-browsable groups, and it has always had trouble with the positioning of polytopical sources, for the assignment of a collective work to one area automatically precludes its being placed in any other subject areas, even though it "covers" those subjects too. Multisubject indexes, par excellence, point out a major weakness of the scheme. Thus, for example, monographs on the social sciences tend to be grouped in the various H classes; but browsers in this area will then necessarily overlook the *Social Sciences Index* (in AI3), the *Bibliographic Index* (in Z1002), and the *Social Sciences Citation Index* (in Z7161), all of which are excellent sources for social science topics. In other words, there have been some major changes in the library field within the last century, and we can now see weaknesses in the class scheme—and ways to correct them—that were not apparent to its original designers. While the Methods scheme insists on the overall retention and continuation of the class scheme, its call to reposition only a handful of key indexes—probably less than 2 percent of any large library's reference collection, which is itself only a tiny fraction of the library's whole collection—is simply an overdue accommodation to the reality of these changes. To ignore the need for such an accommodation while hewing, instead, to the letter of a system designed a hundred years ago is to ignore the *principles* of library science: it is to misunderstand what the subject classification scheme was designed to do, and to overlook what it was not designed to do.

Indeed, a strict adherence to the logic of the class scheme would theoretically preclude even the separating out of a distinct ready-reference collection, which points up yet another problem: not only does the straight class-order arrangement fail to deal adequately with multi-topical works, but it also fails to distinguish the relative *importance* of works. And if there is one thing that is undeniably a matter of common sense to reference librarians, it is that some reference sources are simply more important than others, and that they need to be pulled out into special ready-reference areas to prevent their being buried in the class scheme as a whole. The Methods model provides a formal mechanism for subarranging a part of this ready-reference collection to provide the greater emphasis that some sources require.

The objections to a Methods of Searching model, then, do not seem to be insuperable, and the advantages remain strong. There are still other implications to be addressed, however.

12

Implications of the Methods-of-Searching Model

The adoption of a Methods-of-Searching model has important implications for both the researchers who use libraries and the librarians who create and maintain those libraries. The main implication for researchers who use it as a mental roadmap is that it gives them more predictive power in exploiting large research collections; it enables them to move around easily, with much greater confidence and facility, within the knowledge records of subject areas that are unfamiliar to them. And, most important, a Methods model lets them ask better questions in the first place. If the only avenue of subject approach a scholar consciously expects to find in a library is a classified arrangement of texts, then she will tend to frame her questions in the first place only in general terms ("Where are your books on English literature?" rather than "Where can I find sources on the 'dark tower' theme in nineteenth-century English poetry?").

A Methods model will also help solve another problem for researchers: not only will it enable them to ask better questions in the first place, but it will also introduce them more efficiently to a larger range of resources capable of answering those questions. What happens all too often is that students or other researchers who cannot find the information they want give up the search because they cannot think of alternative approaches beyond a few obvious ones (general browsing, talking to colleagues, using any computer database at hand), and they then change the focus of their research to *write around* the hole they cannot fill. In other words, instead of answering their own question, they simply write a different paper in which that question does not come up in the first place. And the quality of their very *thinking,* not just of their research, suffers as a result.

A researcher who is conversant with the Methods model will not be stuck in such a situation. Someone who knows in advance that there are definite ways to find proper subject category terms will be able to do better research than someone who doesn't. Someone who understands the radical differences between vocabulary-controlled indexes and databases on the one hand and key word sources on the other will be able to get farther into the literature of a subject than someone who does not grasp the distinction. A researcher who knows in advance that he can find *previous sources* through footnote chasing and *subsequent sources* through citation searching will be able to find information more efficiently than someone who does not see the second alternative. Someone who knows that published bibliographies will fill holes not covered by computer printouts—and who knows that such bibliographies will not be found simply by browsing among monographs in the bookstacks—has a decided advantage. Someone who perceives talking to people as a viable research option will have many more chances to answer his questions than someone who cannot see beyond print sources. And so on. A Methods model gives researchers the best overview of *the full range of options* available within any subject area.

Cardinal Newman made the point, in *The Idea of a University,* that if any subject within the full circle of knowledge is not taught in a university program, the void it leaves will tend to be filled in, within students' perceptions, by the other disciplines—with less than satisfactory results. He was arguing, ultimately, for the place of theology in the curriculum; but his larger point applies to any subject. By analogy, one could say the same about the various methods and models of searching that have been the subject of this book. If vocabulary-controlled searching isn't taught, then people will mistakenly perceive key word searching as "covering" that void. If the use of published bibliographies isn't taught separately, then people will mistakenly perceive computer searching as filling that need. If talking to people isn't emphasized, then students will try to overinflate the use of print or electronic sources to try to cover that lack. The point is this: people will generally not allow themselves to perceive a gap in their knowledge; what they will do instead is to inflate the part they do grasp to take the place of the whole that they do not see. And if they get any results at all from the part, they will then "satisfice" with the results. Furthermore, they will mistakenly conclude that they have tried "everything" when in fact they've exhausted only the few avenues they do perceive—all the while missing much more than they find, but not being aware of it because they have indeed searched "everything" in the knowledge universe *as they perceive it.* A Methods model, more than any other, would correct this problem for researchers. It would give them the best map of the *whole* of the research universe that ought to be available to them.

The model has important implications for librarians, too. Perhaps the key contribution here would lie in its restoring a certain intellectual coherence to librarianship. The basic principle of this scheme—that the way one searches for a subject changes what one sees within the subject—has a certain affinity with the mental sets of other disciplines. Moreover, a Methods model enables us to solve problems that are intractable within the alternative models. For example, reference librarians often notice the course of researchers' work being skewed in any of three directions: (1) overemphasis on computer searches, to the neglect of a vast array of sources that are not and cannot be computerized; (2) overemphasis on browsing in the classified array of books, particularly inefficient browsing that fails to note the scattering of the many aspects of a subject and that also entirely overlooks journal indexes and subject bibliographies; and (3) overemphasis on talking to colleagues ("the invisible college") to the outright neglect of a wealth of print sources that are more on target. These problems cannot be solved within, respectively, the Computer Workstation model, the classification scheme (which, again, is usually perceived as the entirety of the Library Science model), or the Actual-Practice model, precisely because it is the limitation of each of these models that is *causing* the skewing problems in the first place. That is, when adherents of each model cannot see "outside" it, they mistakenly conclude that whatever they happen to see within it constitutes "everything" that is available. The problem is solved, however, if we begin to view each of these smaller "universes" as one *part* of a still larger universe.

This insight suggests a clarification of the role of librarians, in two areas. First, there is a perennial debate within the profession as to whether librarians should, on the one hand, simply point readers to appropriate sources for their needs, or, on the other, actually do the research for them. A Methods model would suggest that this dichotomy is too simple to do justice to the problem, and that there is another area in between that needs greater conscious attention. Specifically, librarians have a responsibility to regulate the slope of the gameboard on which the research activity takes place. To return to a previous analogy I offered in discussing the Principle of Least Effort, one may look at library research as being similar to a pinball game. The skill of the players in manipulating the ball is essential to success. But there is another factor that is equally important: the slope of the gameboard itself. If the playing surface is tilted more steeply downward and to the left, then inevitably more of the balls will wind up in the lower left corner *regardless of the skill of the players.*

Librarians have the responsibility of determining what the slope of the library gameboard will be—of regulating its contours and making some aggregates of sources rather than others easy to perceive as the *first* avenue of attack, depending on the nature of the question. Perhaps I may profitably switch analogies at this point and repeat the saying "Paved roads create traffic." To the extent, then, that librarians pave certain avenues of access, those roads will be used. And to the extent that they leave others unpaved or obscured in uncleared underbrush and obstructions, then those avenues will not be used.

What, specifically, *are* the roads that need to be paved? And how many of them are there? The Methods model indicates that there are eight avenues of access—not just two or three—that must be deliberately and consciously paved if researchers are to have efficient access to the full range of resources available to them.

1. The avenue of controlled-vocabulary subject heading sources.

    a. Library catalogs of surrogate records (primarily for books), either computerized or manual.

    b. Printed indexes or databases (primarily for nonbook records) created by commercial companies.

2. The avenue of a classified array of subject-grouped printed full texts.

3. The avenue of printed key word indexes (which have substantial coverage not in computer formats).

4. The avenue of printed citation indexes (which also have substantial coverage not found in computer databases).

5. The avenue of published bibliographies (again, providing wide-ranging and deep coverage not duplicated by computers).

6. The avenue of computer sources beyond those in avenues 1 and 7 (including CD-ROM, dial-up or in-house; also encompassing bibliographic-citation, full-text, network, and bulletin-board forms—the whole range).

7. The avenue of related-record CD-ROMs.

8. The avenue of people sources.

The goal of reference librarians, then, should be to get readers first of all on the *best* road—that is, on the one that is most likely to repay their efforts with on-target results, given the nature of the question. And in this context one can much more clearly understand what the nebulous concept of "best" means in the first place if one considers it to be definable, for reference purposes, in terms of the various advantages of each of the eight methods of searching.

There will always be many individual sources relevant to any subject inquiry, and the positive value of the content of each cannot readily be determined in advance by either librarians or researchers. And yet, using the Methods criteria, one can at least steer researchers initially, with some efficiency, *away* from whole groups of sources that would probably waste their time. Thus, when no good controlled-vocabulary category term exists for their subject, the *LCSH* sources should be passed over in favor of key word sources; or when a broad overview of a subject is sought, an annotated bibliography or review article should be pursued rather than a key word computer search or a print-format citation search; and so on.

It therefore becomes the function of libraries to see to it that the gameboard on which researchers operate does not encourage *only* computer searching (primarily avenue 6, along with 7 and part of 1) and browsing in the stacks (avenue 2), for example. What librarians must have readily available is a gameboard arranged so that *all* of the several alternative paths of searching are just as easily perceptible and pursuable as are these two. (A spinoff benefit of paving several roads, not just the two mentioned, would be economic: libraries could greatly increase the efficiency of access to their collections simply by reconfiguring their *existing* resources into different aggregates, entirely apart from having to spend more money for additional sources.) Librarians are thus responsible for the overall system design of the library so as to integrate the computer and the class scheme into a larger whole—and make this larger whole easily teachable to, and perceptible by, readers.

A second clarification of the role of librarians would also follow. If we consider the development of the computer workstation (avenues 6 and 7, with part of 1) to be the concern of those who call themselves information scientists (often deliberately to set themselves apart from librarians), then it is apparent that librarians must do what information science tends to neglect: that is, librarians must *create* avenues 1a and 2, but must *also make accessible*—and in a *systematic* manner—*the entire range* from 1 through 8. No group except librarians is attending to *both* of these tasks. Commercial companies create better avenues of access to nonbook sources, but they do not create better or even comparable avenues of access to *books*. Moreover, within the entire field of library and information science, it falls uniquely to librarians to make the entire range of sources available to researchers—both those avenues which the librarians create *and those they do not create themselves*. No one else assumes the latter responsibilities to the comprehensive extent that librarians do.

In other words, the distinctive elements that librarians *create* within the overall enterprise are, first, the classification scheme for arranging printed full texts so that their entire contents can be systematically browsed without incurring copyright royalty or licensing fees, and second, the controlled-vocabulary catalog that indexes the class scheme. Without the vocabulary control provided by *LCSH* and name-authority work in the library's catalog, the class scheme in the bookstacks has no effective index. Mere key word searching of transcribed titles, especially if they are in many languages, simply does not suffice to provide the predictability, serendipity, and depth of access that are necessary for the efficient use of large research libraries.

Furthermore, it is librarians who, virtually alone, have the responsibility to point out to researchers the enormous range of subject coverage provided by *printed* indexes and published bibliographies, and by the *classified array of full texts itself,* which cannot be duplicated by computer databases, either those that now exist or any that are even projected to exist within the ultimately controlling constraints of copyright law, economics, and preservation realities. Of course, librarians are *also* the strongest advocates of the full utilization of computerized sources; but it is an advocacy tempered by an apparently unique understanding of the limits as well as the strengths of the databases.

Perhaps it needs to be pointed out, too, that librarians have the duty to *acquire* knowledge records in the first place, and that in this respect, too, they are quite different from those information scientists who concern themselves only with *tapping into* databases that are mounted elsewhere. Librarians, of course, must also provide the means of tapping into such resources; but they must do other things too: they must acquire and make available printed and other sources (microforms, maps, etc.) that cannot be dialed up remotely. And librarians must also discharge their duty of *preserving* knowledge records in realistic ways—a duty that is not discharged, be it noted, by the naive belief that the "transportability of digitized data" from one generation of machine to another is a consideration sufficient to actually solve the problem.

These four things, then, are the distinctive responsibilities of librarians:

1. Acquiring knowledge records (not just "tapping into" them remotely, although doing that too).
2. Cataloging knowledge records (i.e., doing the *intellectual work* of creating standardized and predictable *categorizations* for them). Not all records, however, are worth the expense of full cataloging; librarians must therefore focus primarily on books for full treatment, while providing partial catalog records for other formats, and relying on ready-made report or accession numbers for others.
3. Making the full range of resources accessible in a *systematic* manner (i.e., not just the traditional Library Science components, and also not just the Computer Workstation components; rather, all eight avenues of access must be presented, and in a way that relates them to one another in perceptible and understandable categorizations).
4. Preserving knowledge records.

Inherent in this program is the recognition that librarians cannot do everything by themselves but must rely on private industry for some things. Specifically, librarians cannot afford to create the journal indexes (either printed or electronic) or the majority of published bibliographies that provide detailed access to their library's own collections in ways that the librarian-created catalog and class scheme do not provide. Nor can librarians create all of the databases and networks that allow researchers to see some of what is available in other physical locations, or indeed within the electronic networks themselves.

Equally inherent in this program, however, is the recognition that nonlibrarians are not doing and cannot do what librarians are doing: they

are not providing access to *books* in predictable, serendipitous, and deep
ways as librarians are; and those who do create "tappable" sources are
merely supplementing (rather than duplicating or replacing) the coverage of remote—and even local—knowledge sources that is supplied by
published bibliographies and printed indexes and directories, to which
researchers also need access.

When the role of librarians is clarified—when one sees what they
must create themselves, and what they must rely on others to create but
on themselves to acquire, to present systematically to researchers, and to
preserve—there is a further implication. Specifically, it becomes clear
that it is simply not the business of *librarians* to enter the arena of
creating full-text databases that publish the actual contents of their libraries in electronic form. While librarians must make such industry-
created full-text sources *accessible,* it is not librarians' business to *create* them. To do so would be to enter an extraordinarily expensive arena
in a way that would only divert scarce funds from the four tasks for
which librarians already have a unique responsibility. Furthermore, if
librarians ever came to regard electronic digitization of printed sources
as a substitute for microfilming them, they would directly and seriously
undercut their own responsibilities for the long-term preservation of
their collections. Tax-supported research libraries and those with limited
private endowments simply cannot afford to put themselves in competi-
tion with private industry, and to consider the electronic publishing of
full texts as a fifth responsibility for librarians, for this would inevitably
undercut the funding of the other four.

What I am mainly suggesting, then, is that there is a continuing and
distinctive contribution that librarians must make to the field of information storage and retrieval, and that this contribution is not reducible to
the Computer Workstation model. Research libraries simply cannot be
forced onto this Procrustean bed without disastrous consequences, specifically in a radical diminution of the basic understanding of what ought
to constitute the full "universe" of available knowledge records.

Unfortunately, it is not fashionable to assert this nowadays, even—or
sometimes especially—within the library profession itself, which has so
lost its own compass that it is uncritically buying into the Computer
Workstation model almost by default, as a means of supplying the status
that no longer attaches to the Library Science model. And equally unfortunately, the higher social status of the newer model is blinding many
librarians to the false trails it leads them to follow. The list of these

concealed but erroneous propositions is, in a way, a summary of the concerns of much of this book.

• It is a mistake to think that a vocabulary-controlled system of subject category terms can be replaced (rather than supplemented) by key word searching.

• It is a mistake to think that *LCSH* headings are merely a carryover from a manual system to an online age, and that precoordinated, multi-word strings of terms can be replaced (rather than supplemented) by postcoordinate computer manipulations of single terms.

• It is a mistake to think that browsing access to printed full-texts arranged in subject groups is no longer necessary for scholars in research libraries, or that scholars of the twenty-first century won't need it.

• It is an equally bad, and related, mistake to think that the ability to search superficial catalog records grouped by class number in an online catalog renders unnecessary the practice of making full texts themselves searchable in classified subject groupings.

• It is a mistake to think that information that cannot be searched for directly and immediately by computer therefore cannot be retrieved *systematically,* or worse, that it cannot be searched for, or found, *at all.*

• It is a mistake to think that ''access'' can replace (rather than merely supplement) acquisition.

• It is a mistake to think that the mere acquisition of books without proper cataloging renders them accessible (the false assumption is that software enhancements such as word proximity or Boolean search capabilities can replace rather than supplement the intellectual work of categorization and standardization.)

• It is a mistake for librarians to believe that the work of cataloging can be abandoned in the expectation of the imminent arrival of expert-system or artificial intelligence programs, which will probably never be successful when applied outside very narrow disciplinary bounds, and which will also not work outside the confines of one language. (Do librarians need to be reminded that their catalogs must cover all disciplines and also a wide variety of languages?)

• It is a mistake to believe that the mere *existence* of information ensures *access* to it. While the Documentation movement provided a major advance for information science by insisting that the content of a knowledge record could be freed from its original physical container, the movement also made a correspondingly large mistake in failing to attach sufficient weight to the fact that changing the *format* of a knowledge record also radically changes *access* to it. If access to a high-quality record becomes more difficult (e.g., a microfilm capture of the contents of a large card catalog), then the Principle of Least Effort will bring about a marked drop-off in actual use. Similarly, if a notably superficial index is presented in an attractive CD-ROM format, the same principle will ensure an increase in its use, in spite of its low quality, with users "satisficing" with any results they get from it and disregarding better sources in less attractive formats.

• It is a mistake to think that the copyright law will magically change in a radical way to make "everything" freely available online.

• It is a mistake to think that the "transportability of digitized data" is sufficient to transform electronic formats into preservation media.

• It is a mistake for librarians themselves to think that their own traditional model is reducible to a classification scheme plus controlled-vocabulary catalog *alone*. This view overlooks the existence, and the function, of bibliographies and indexes in providing the very same kind of "access" that overzealous Workstation advocates are now claiming to have invented afresh, ex nihilo.

A reexamination of this unfortunate collection of errors is long overdue in the literature of librarianship; and I hope that a Methods model will contribute to providing a framework for such a reconsideration. Only such a scheme clarifies the differences, and the importance of the differences, that librarians make to information retrieval which are not reducible to or replaceable by better computers, larger electronic networks, or improved scanning devices and softwares.

As a reference librarian myself, I think that the most important of the distinctive contributions that librarians make lies in creating, maintaining, extending, and stocking the standardized intellectual gridwork that makes the literature of the world—in all subject areas and in all languages—identifiable and retrievable in a systematic manner even by people who are not already experts in the subject they wish to research. Part of this gridwork is created by the intellectual work of cataloging (categorizing and standardizing, as opposed to merely transcribing existing natural language words), which is done to make research more predictable, to increase the serendipity of the search, and to improve the depth of access to knowledge records. The other aspect of this intellectual gridwork—for not all knowledge records fit into the cataloged parts of it—can only be created in the future, I believe, by presenting the work of cataloging itself within a larger but still definable intellectual framework, a new framework of categorizations that it has been the purpose of this book to outline. Such a model would, I believe, have an even greater effect in extending the predictability, serendipity, and depth of access that must charaterize the research process.

In any consideration of library research models, both researchers and librarians must be careful not to lose the benefits of our existing systems of access to knowledge records in exchange for unfulfillable promises. At the same time, while preserving the best of the past, we must not be limited by it, but must instead add to it and go beyond it. And librarians especially must not lose sight of the fact that what is at stake in choosing any overall model of library research is nothing less than the ability of the human race to retrieve and remember its past. We must therefore choose our model carefully.

APPENDIX 1

Class Z:
Arrangement of Bibliographies

I. National Bibliography: Z1200s–Z4900s

North America	Z1201–1595
South America	Z1601–1946
Europe	Z2000–2959
Asia	Z3001–3499
Africa	Z3501–3975
Australia and Oceania	Z4001–4980

(Antartica is included under "Polar regions" within "Geography" at Z6005.P7.)

II. Subject Bibliography   Z5000s–Z7900s

(Numbers listed are often starting points of extended ranges; the "Criminology" and "Fiction" categories are spelled out as just two of many possible examples. Most such subdividing ranges are not given here in order to keep this list at the level of a general overview. "Fine arts" and "Political and social sciences" are instances that would each require several pages of further breakdowns.)

Z5051	Academies
Z5056	Aerospace technology
Z5069	Aesthetics
Z5071	Agriculture
Z5095	Almanacs

Z5111	Anthropology and ethnology
Z5119	Archaeology
Z5151	Astronomy
Z5158	Atmospheric radioactivity
Z5165	Authorship (General)
Z5167	Automation
Z5170	Automobiles
Z5180	Bacteriology and microbiology
Z5256	Bees and bee culture
Z5275	Bells
Z5301	Biography. Genealogy. Heraldry
Z5320	Biology
Z5331	Birds
Z5346	The Blind
Z5351	Botany
Z5440	Calendars
Z5451	Canals
Z5481	Cards and card playing
Z5491	Cats
Z5521	Chemistry
Z5541	Chess
Z5579	Civilization
	.2 Ancient
	.5 Medieval
	.6 Modern
Z5601	Coffee
Z5615	Collectors and collecting
Z5630	Communication. Mass media
Z5640	Computer science
Z5680	Cosmic physics
Z5691	Costume
Z5701	Cotton

Z5703 Criminology
       Z5703.4 Special topics, A–Z
       .A75   Arson
       .C36   Capital punishment
       .C62   Commercial crime
       .C65   Corrections
       .C7   Crime prevention
       .C72   Criminal anthropology
       .C728 Criminal investigation
       .C73   Criminal justice administration
       .D48   Deviant behavior
       .E38   Education of prisoners
       .E46   Embezzlement
       .E93   Ex-convicts
       .F35   Family violence
       .G35   Gangs
       .G85   Gun control
       .H35   Halfway houses
       .J87   Juvenile corrections
       .J88   Juvenile delinquency
       .M33   Mafia
       .M46   Mentally handicapped and crime
       .M87   Murder
       .O35   Offenses against the person
       .O7   Organized crime
       .P37   Parole
       .P74   Prison furlough
       .P75   Prisons
       .P76   Probation
       .P8   Psychology
       .R35   Rape
       .R42   Recidivists
       .R45   Reparation
       .R87   Rural crimes
       .S45   Sex crimes
       .S5   Shoplifting
       .S8   Statistics
       .T47   Terrorism
       .V36   Vandalism

.W53   Wife abuse
.W66   Work release

Z5705   Curiosities and wonders

Z5706   Dairying

Z5710   Days. Holidays. Festivals

Z5721   Deaf-mutes

Z5725   Death

Z5761   Devil

Z5771   Directories

Z5772   Disasters

Z5775   Domestic economy. Home economics

Z5781   Education

Z5831   Electricity

Z5836   Electronics

Z5841   Emblems

Z5848   Encyclopedias

Z5851   Engineering

Z5856   Entomology

Z5861   Environment

Z5865   Erotic literature

Z5873   Ethics

Z5877   Etiquette

Z5883   Exhibitions

Z5885   Explosives

Z5895   Fables

Z5906   Fencing and dueling

Z5916   Fiction

Z5917 Special topics, A–Z
.A39   Adventure stories
.A7   Artists and authors in fiction
.B8   Business fiction
.D5   Detective stories

.F3	Fantastic fiction
.G45	Ghost stories
.G66	Gothic revival
.H6	Historical fiction
.J4	Jewish fiction
.L2	Labor and laboring class fiction
.L3	Legal novels
.M6	Moral and religious fiction
.N83	Nuclear warfare
.O25	Occupations in fiction
.P3	Paperback editions
.P5	Picaresque literature
.S34	Schools in fiction
.S36	Science fiction
.S4	Sea stories
.S44	Sequels
.S45	Sequence novel
.S454	Sexual perversion in fiction
.S5	Short stories
.S69	Spy stories
.T7	Translations
.W33	War stories
.W6	Women authors

Z5931   Fine arts (Visual arts). The Arts (General) (including Architecture Z5941–; Painting Z5946–; Sculpture Z5951–; Special topics [A–Z], Z5956–)

Z5970   Fish culture

Z5971   Fishing and fisheries

Z5979   Flagellants and flagellation

Z5980   Flags

Z5981   Folklore

Z5986   Food service

Z5990   Forecasting

Z5991   Forestry

Z5993   Freemasons

Z5994   Funeral customs

Z5994.6	Fur
Z5995	Furniture
Z5996	Gardening. Horticulture. Landscape
Z5998	Gems
Z6000	Geodesy
Z6001	Geography and travels. Maps. Cartography
Z6031	Geology. Mineralogy. Paleontology
Z6041	Geophysics
Z6046	Glass
Z6055	Gold and silversmiths' work
Z6075	Graffiti
Z6081	Graphology
Z6121	Gymnastics
Z6122	The Handicapped
Z6151	Handicraft
Z6201	History
Z6240	The Horse. Horsemanship
Z6250	Hotels
Z6260	Human engineering
Z6265	Humanities
Z6270	Ice cream
Z6293	Indexes. Abstracts
Z6297	India rubber. Rubber
Z6331	Iron and steel
Z6366	Jews
Z6461	International law and relations
Z6490	Letters
Z6511	Literature
Z6601	Manuscripts
Z6651	Mathematics
Z6658	Medicine

Z6677	Mental retardation
Z6678	Metals. Metallurgy
Z6681	Meteorology
Z6704	Microscopy
Z6721	Military science
Z6736	Mines and mining
Z6827	Nature
Z6831	Naval science
Z6837	Navigation
Z6866	Numismatics
Z6876	Occult sciences
Z6900	Parasitology
Z6905	Parks
Z6915	Peat
Z6935	Performing arts
Z6940	Periodicals, newspapers, and other serials
Z6972	Petroleum
Z6980	Pets
Z7001	Philology and linguistics
Z7125	Philosophy
Z7134	Photography
Z7141	Physics
Z7155	Poetry
Z7161	Political and social sciences
Z7179	Pottery
Z7191	Proverbs
Z7201	Psychology
Z7215	Radar
Z7221	Radio
Z7231	Railroads
Z7254	Rehabilitation

Z7291	Riddles
Z7295	Roads. Highways
Z7335	Salt
Z7401	Science. Natural history
Z7421	Seals
Z7511	Sports
Z7536	Stammering
Z7551	Statistics
Z7609	Sugar
Z7615	Suicide
Z7631	Swimming
Z7660	Symbolism (General works)
Z7671	System analysis
Z7711	Television
Z7721	Temperature
Z7751	Theology and religion
Z7876	Time and timekeepers
Z7882	Tobacco. Smoking
Z7890	Toxicology
Z7893	Toys
Z7911	Useful arts and applied science. Technology
Z7925	Vocational rehabilitation
Z7935	Water supply
Z7951	Wine and wine making
Z7961	Women
Z7971	Wool
Z7991	Zoology

III. Personal Bibliography: Z8000s

(Arranged alphabetically by the surname of the subject of the bibliography.)

APPENDIX 2

Form Subdivisions Within the Library of Congress Subject Headings *System*

(Note: The following list is neither complete nor "official"; many of the headings given here can be used only within very narrowly defined contexts. The list is offered simply to show something of the range of possible options that are available when one wishes to search by type of literature.)

Form Subdivisions

—2-piano scores

—Abbreviations

—Abbreviations of titles

—Abridgments

—Abstracts

—Acronyms

—Adaptations

—Aerial photographs

—Aerial views

—Almanacs

—Amateurs' manuals

—Anecdotes

—Apologetic works

—Archival resources

—Archives

—Art

—Art and the war [revolution, etc.]

—Artificers' handbooks

—Atlases

—Audiotape catalogs

—Autographs

—Bibliography

—Bibliography—Catalogs

—Bibliography—Early

—Bibliography—Exhibitions

—Bibliography—First editions

—Bibliography—Graded lists

—Bibliography—Folios

—Bibliography—Microform catalogs

—Bibliography—Quartos

—Bibliography—Union lists

—Bio-bibliography

—Biography

—Biography—Dictionaries

—Book reviews

—Breeding—Selection indexes

—By-laws

—Calendars

—Caricatures and cartoons

—Case studies

—Cases

—Catalogs

—Catalogs, Manufacturers'

—Catalogs and collections (*May Subd Geog*)

—Catalogues raisonnés
—Catechisms
—Catechisms—English [French, German, etc.]
—Census
—Census, [date]
—Chapel exercises
—Charters
—Charters, grants, privileges
—Charts, diagrams, etc.
—Children's sermons
—Chord diagrams
—Chorus scores with piano
—Chorus scores without accompaniment
—Chronology
—Claims
—Claims against
—Claims vs.
—Code numbers
—Code words
—Comic books, strips, etc.
—Commercial treaties
—Commentaries
—Committees—Rules and practice
—Compact disc catalogs
—Comparative studies
—Composition and exercises
—Computer programs
—Concordances
—Concordances, English
—Concordances, French [German, etc.]
—Congresses

—Constitution

—Constitution—Amendments

—Constitution—Amendments—1st [2nd, 3rd, etc.]

—Controversial literature

—Conversation and phrase books

—Conversation and phrase books—English

—Conversation and phrase books—French [Italian, etc.]

—Conversation and phrase books—Polyglot

—Conversation and phrase books (for air pilots)

—Conversation and phrase books (for bank employees)

—Conversation and phrase books (for clergy, etc.)

—Conversation and phrase books (for construction industry employees)

—Conversation and phrase books (for domestics)

—Conversation and phrase books (for farmers)

—Conversation and phrase books (for fishers)

—Conversation and phrase books (for flight attendants)

—Conversation and phrase books (for gardeners)

—Conversation and phrase books (for geologists)

—Conversation and phrase books (for gourmets)

—Conversation and phrase books (for lawyers)

—Conversation and phrase books (for mathematicians)

—Conversation and phrase books (for medical personnel)

—Conversation and phrase books (for merchants)

—Conversation and phrase books (for meteorologists)

—Conversation and phrase books (for musicians, musicologists, etc.)

—Conversation and phrase books (for petroleum workers)

—Conversation and phrase books (for police)

—Conversation and phrase books (for professionals)

—Conversation and phrase books (for restaurant and hotel personnel)

—Conversation and phrase books (for school employees)

—Conversation and phrase books (for seamen)

—Conversation and phrase books (for secretaries)
—Conversation and phrase books (for social workers)
—Conversation and phrase books (for soldiers, etc.)
—Correspondence
—Credit ratings
—Creeds
—Criminal provisions
—Cross-cultural studies
—Curricula
—Data bases
—Data tape catalogs
—Description and travel
—Designs and plans
—Devotional literature
—Diaries
—Dictionaries
—Dictionaries—Early works to 1700
—Dictionaries—French [Italian, etc.]
—Dictionaries—Polyglot
—Dictionaries, Juvenile
—Dictionaries, Juvenile—Hebrew [Italian, etc.]
—Diet therapy—Recipes
—Digests
—Directories
—Discography
—Drama
—Drawings
—Drill manuals
—Early works to 1800
—Econometric models
—Encyclopedias

—Encyclopedias, Juvenile

—Entrance examinations—Study guides

—Examinations—Study guides

—Examinations, questions, etc.

—Excerpts

—Excerpts, Arranged

—Exercises for dictation

—Experiments

—Exhibitions

—Facsimiles

—Fiction

—Film catalogs

—Films for foreign speakers

—Films for French [Spanish, etc.] speakers

—Folklore

—Forms

—Gazetteers

—Genealogy

—Gift books

—Glossaries, vocabularies, etc.

—Glossaries, vocabularies, etc.—Polyglot

—Guidebooks

—Handbooks, manuals, etc.

—Harmonies

—Harmonies, English [French, German, etc.]

—History—Chronology

—History—Sources

—History Bibles

—Humor

—Hymns

—Hymns—Texts

—Illustrations

—Imprints

—Index maps

—Indexes

—Instruction and study (*May Subd Geog*)

—Instruction and study—Fingering

—Instruction and study—Juvenile

—Instruction and study—Pedaling

—Instructive editions

—Instrumental settings

—Interlinear translations

—Interlinear translations, English [French, etc.]

—Interviews

—Introductions

—Inventories

—Job descriptions

—Juvenile

—Juvenile—Instruction and study (*May Subd Geog*)

—Juvenile drama

—Juvenile fiction

—Juvenile films

—Juvenile humor

—Juvenile literature

—Juvenile poetry

—Juvenile software

—Juvenile sound recordings

—Laboratory manuals

—Language—Glossaries, etc.

—Languages—Texts

—Law and legislation (*May Subd Geog*)

—Legal status, laws, etc. (*May Subd Geog*)

—Legends

—Library—Catalogs

—Library—Marginal notes

—Library—Microform catalogs

—Library resources

—Librettos

—Life skills guides

—Linear programming

—Lists of vessels

—Literary collections

—Liturgical lessons, Dutch [English, etc.]

—Liturgy—Texts

—Longitudinal studies

—Manuscripts

—Maps

—Maps—Bibliography

—Maps—Symbols

—Maps—To 1800

—Maps, Comparative

—Maps, Manuscript

—Maps, Mental

—Maps, Outline and base

—Maps, Physical

—Maps, Pictorial

—Maps, Topographic

—Maps, Tourist

—Maps for the blind

—Maps for the visually handicapped

—Marginal readings

—Mathematical models

—Medicine—Formulae, receipts, prescriptions

—Meditations

—Methods

—Methods—Group instruction

—Methods—Juvenile

—Methods—Self-instruction

—Methods (Jazz [Rock, Bluegrass, etc.])

—Microform catalogs

—Miscellanea

—Music

—Musical settings

—Necrology

—Newspapers

—Nomenclature

—Nomenclature (Popular)

—Nomograms

—Non-commissioned officers' handbooks

—Notation

—Notebooks, sketchbooks, etc.

—Obituaries

—Observations

—Observers' manuals

—Officers' handbooks

—Orchestra studies

—Order-books

—Outlines, syllabi, etc.

—Pamphlets

—Papal documents

—Parallel versions, English [French, etc.]

—Paraphrases

—Paraphrases, English [French, German, etc.]

—Parodies, imitations, etc.

—Parts

—Parts (solo)

—Pastoral letters and charges

—Patents

—Pedigrees

—Periodicals

—Periodicals—Abbreviations of titles

—Personal narratives

—Personal narratives, American [French, etc.]

—Personal narratives, Confederate

—Personal narratives, Jewish

—Petty officers' handbooks

—Photo maps

—Photographs

—Photographs from space

—Piano scores

—Piano scores (4 hands)

—Pictorial works

—Picture Bibles

—Poetry

—Popular works

—Portraits

—Posters

—Prayer-books and devotions

—Prayer-books and devotions, English [French, German, etc.]

—Prayers

—Prefaces

—Private bills

—Problems, exercises, etc.

—Proclamations

—Programmed instruction

—Programs
—Quotations
—Quotations, Early
—Quotations in rabbinical literature
—Quotations in the New Testament
—Quotations, maxims, etc.
—Readers
—Readers—[topic]
—Readers for new literates
—Records and correspondence
—Reference editions
—Regimental histories
—Registers
—Registers of dead
—Regulations
—Relief models
—Resolutions
—Reverse indexes
—Reviews
—Rituals—Texts
—Road maps
—Romances
—Rules
—Rules and practice
—Safety regulations (*May Subd Geog*)
—Scenarios
—Scholia
—Scores
—Scores and parts
—Scores and parts (solo)
—Seamen's handbooks

—Sections, columns, etc.

—Sections, columns, etc.—Advice

—Sections, columns, etc.—Arts

—Sections, columns, etc.—Comics

—Sections, columns, etc.—Corrections

—Sections, columns, etc.—Editorials

—Sections, columns, etc.—Fashion

—Sections, columns, etc.—Fiction

—Sections, columns, etc.—Finance

—Sections, columns, etc.—Food

—Sections, columns, etc.—Genealogy

—Sections, columns, etc.—Letters to the editor

—Sections, columns, etc.—Op-ed pages

—Sections, columns, etc.—Reviews

—Sections, columns, etc.—Sports

—Sections, columns, etc.—Women

—Self-instruction

—Self-portraits

—Sermons

—Simplified editions

—Slides

—Social registers

—Software

—Solo with harpsichord

—Solo with harpsichord and piano

—Solo with keyboard instrument

—Solo with organ

—Solo with piano

—Solos with organ

—Solos with piano

—Songs and music

—Sound recordings for foreign speakers

—Sound recordings for French [Spanish, etc.] speakers

—Sources

—Specifications (*May Subd Geog*)

—Specimens

—Speeches in Congress

—Spurious and doubtful works

—Stage guides

—Statistics

—Statistics, Medical

—Statistics, Vital

—Stories, plots, etc.

—Students—Yearbooks

—Studies and exercises

—Studies and exercises—Fingering

—Studies and exercises—Juvenile

—Studies and exercises—Pedaling

—Studies and exercises (Jazz [Rock, Bluegrass, etc.])

—Study guides

—Surveys

—Tables

—Teaching pieces

—Telephone directories

—Telephone directories—Yellow pages

—Terminology

—Terms and phrases

—Textbooks

—Textbooks for English [French, etc.] speakers

—Textbooks for foreign speakers

—Textbooks for foreign speakers—English

—Textbooks for foreign speakers—German [Italian, etc.]

—Texts

—Thematic catalogs

—Thumb Bibles

—Tours

—Trademarks

—Translations

—Translations, French [German, etc.]

—Translations into French [German, etc.]

—Travel regulations

—Treaties

—Treaties, [date]

—Trials, litigation, etc.

—Union lists

—Video catalogs

—Voting registers

—Zoning maps

Notes

Chapter 3

1. A number of other library subject-classification systems exist besides LCC and DDC. These include the Universal Decimal Classification, S. R. Ranganathan's Colon Classification, H. E. Bliss's Bibliographic Classification, and the Bibliotechno-Bibliographischeskaia Klassifikatsiia used in the former Soviet Union. My emphasis in this book will be on the Library of Congress Classification, which is used by most large research libraries in the United States. (The Dewey system is more suitable for smaller collections, and so is widely used in public libraries.) One of the reasons for the widespread use of LCC is that a system of controlled-vocabulary subject category terms, the *Library of Congress Subject Headings* (*LCSH*) list, was created in conjunction with it, and catalogs using the *LCSH* terms function as a very good index to the classification scheme. The other systems do not have such good indexes for directing researchers to particular subcategories. (For a discussion of this indexing function, see chapter 4.) Also, the fact that the Library of Congress catalogs so many books from all over the world in its system—more than any other library—and distributes its records so widely through several computer systems makes LC cataloging the system of choice for economic reasons, for libraries can obtain many records "already done," and can thus avoid expensive duplication of effort.

2. Full-text databases are discussed in chapters 9 and 10. To anticipate a few points to be made there, such databases do not and cannot provide systematic access to all or even most full texts in a library. Economic, legal, and even psychological restrictions severely limit the range of texts that can be entered into the database in the first place, and that can be readily discovered by researchers. The important point is that in the full information-delivery system,

nonengineering factors are just as much realities as the technological factor of the computer's storage capacity.

3. Note that changes in subject headings in the library's catalog can be made with much less trouble and expense. In this case only the surrogate records need to be changed; and if the library has computerized "global update" capabilities in its software, a large number of records can be changed simultaneously without the labor-intensive work of handling each record. With books in the classification scheme, however, the class-number labels attached to their spines cannot be changed by any computer manipulation. Such changes would entail the very expensive labor of physically removing old call number labels and typing and applying new ones to each book. The ensuing reshelving of the books—and, likely, the reshifting of the existing collection in the new class area to accommodate them—would add a further labor expense. Since such costs are so high, books tend to keep their existing class numbers even when subject headings referring to them are changed in the catalog.

Chapter 5

1. Discipline-specific indexes that include abstracts of articles are usually an exception; these are cataloged within the subject classes for the monographs rather than in the Z classes.

2. The advantage of a "faceted" classification system such as that devised by S. R. Ranganathan is that it enables those who understand its components to go directly to the right area of the stacks (or of the catalog using this system); its arrangement of subject relationships and subordinations is much more systematic and predictable than is the LC arrangement. Even experienced reference librarians using the LC system need an external index to it—and the vocabulary-controlled catalog *is* that index. (Ranganathan's overall model is singularly deficient in this regard. It may be a theoretically better classification scheme, but it does not work as well in the real world because it is not linked to as good an index as that which the catalog provides in the LC model.)

3. See my own *Guide to Library Research Methods* (Oxford, 1987), chap. 8.

4. Related-record searching begins with a particular citation to a journal article. With such a starting point in hand, a related-record search enables one to locate any other journal articles written within the same year (or, sometimes, a multiyear period) that have any footnotes in common with the starting-point article.

5. Of course it is also important for librarians to acquire and preserve knowledge records (see chapter 12).

Chapter 7

1. An overview of several of these studies is provided by Stephen K. Stoan in "Research and Library Skills: An Analysis and Interpretation," *College and Research Libraries,* 45, 2 (March 1984), 99–109. There he concludes: "In fact, the Hernon, Stieg, Wood, Styvendale, Stenstrom and McBride, and Bath University Studies together indicate that footnotes, personal recommendations from other scholars, serendipitous discovery, browsing, personal bibliographic files, and other such techniques that involve no formal use of access tools account for the great majority of citations obtained by scholars" (p. 101). Stoan goes on to suggest, however, that this aggregate of practices, which I call the Actual-Practice model, is just fine, and that attempts by librarians to bring about improvements in scholars' research techniques are futile. If, however, the only possible improvements are perceived as those held out by a garbled Type-of-Literature model, which Stoan seems to see as the sole alternative, then this suggestion is inadequate. In addition to these (and other) sources cited by Stoan, see: Robert J. Greene, "The Effectiveness of Browsing," *College and Research Libraries,* 38, 4 (July 1977), 313–16; Melvin J. Voigt, *Scientists' Approaches to Information,* ACRL Monograph 24 (Chicago: American Library Association, 1961); Mary Ellen Soper, "Characteristics and Use of Personal Collections," *Library Quarterly,* 46, 4 (October 1976), 397–415; Harry B. Back, "What Information Dissemination Studies Imply Concerning Design of On-Line Reference Retrieval Systems," *Journal of the American Society for Information Science,* 2, 3 (1972), 160; Human Interaction Institute, *Putting Knowledge to Use* (Los Angeles: The Institute, 1976), pp. 53–54; Herbert Menzel, "Information Needs and Uses in Science and Technology," *Annual Review of Information Science and Technology,* 1 (1966), 54; National Enquiry into Scholarly Communication, *Scholarly Communication* (Baltimore: Johns Hopkins University Press, 1979), 133, 135; L. Uytterschaut, "Literature Searching Methods in Social Sciences Research: A Pilot Inquiry," *American Behavioral Scientist,* 9, 9 (May 1966), 14–26; H. C. Morton and Anne J. Price, *The ACLS Survey of Scholars* (Washington, D.C.: American Council of Learned Societies, 1989), 49, 52, 121; and Patricia McCandless et al., *The Invisible User: User Needs Assessment for Library Public Services* (Urbana: University of Illinois Library, 1985), ERIC report ED 255 227.

2. I do not mean to criticize the whole of *The Modern Researcher* by pointing out this one lapse. It is a wonderful book which I highly recommend.

3. The Library of Congress's commercially available catalog records for published bibliographies actually supply two different class numbers for each bibliography; the first is always in the Zs, while the second is an alternative number appropriate to the specific subject. For example, the call number for K. F. Harrell's *Corporal Punishment in Public Schools: A Selected Bibliogra-*

phy (Vance, 1985) is given the designation "Z5814.D49 H37 1983 (Alternate class LB3025)." (LB is the class for works on the theory and practice of education.) The individual library that uses this record may choose either class number. The noteworthy point is that the Z number is always fully extended by a "Cutter number," which subdivides the class and designates exactly where *within* the Z5814.D49 subject group the book is to be shelved, whereas the alternate class is never given a subdividing Cutter number. Libraries that choose the alternate class, in other words, have to take an extra step to add that part of the call number themselves; and every extra step slows down the cataloging process and costs extra money in expensive staff time. There is thus an economic inducement for libraries simply to accept the full Z number as is; and since libraries usually suffer chronic underfunding, this economic inducement to "go with the Z" rather than the incomplete alternate class number is very strong.

4. Not all of these indexes always use *LCSH* exactly; see my *Guide to Library Research Methods* (New York: Oxford University Press, 1987), chap. 4, for qualifications.

5. See my *Guide to Library Research Methods,* chap. 6.

Chapter 10

1. A complicating factor in making any data transfer from one generation of media to the next is the matter of copyright royalty fees. Again, the capture of data in a new electronic format is not simply a matter of recopying it; because of the transmission, broadcasting, networking, and downloading capabilities of the electronic formats, such a generational transfer can be looked at as a republication of the data. An example of the problem may be found in the attempts of medical libraries to convert three-quarter-inch instructional videotapes to the newer half-inch format; some libraries have discovered that videotape producers charge large copyright fees for the generational transfer, and so they converted only the free and small-fee tapes (*American Libraries* [March 1990], 194–95). The International Publishers Association and the International Group of Scientific, Technical, and Medical Publishers have also mounted an international campaign for intellectual property rights that would assure publishers of the right to demand payments from libraries and others that convert print data into electronic formats ("The Price of Rights," *Library Journal,* October 15, 1989, p. 4).

2. A typical example of such predictions may be found in Herbert C. Morton and Anne J. Price, *The ACLS Survey of Scholars: Final Report of Views on Publications, Computers, and Libraries* (Washington, D.C.: Office of Scholarly Communication and Technology, American Council of Learned Societies,

1989), pp. 106–7: "In a provocative essay appearing in the January 1987 issue of *Library Resources and Technical Services*, Jay David Bolter suggests that the electronic storage and transmission of information is a landmark in the communication of human thought, ranking with the invention of the papyrus, the codex, and the printing press. He suggests that the ways in which we think of and combine information will be transformed to exploit the potential of the electronic medium. The most obvious advantage is the ease with which an entire text can be searched to find words, or word combinations of interest. The library of 25 years from now will support a different kind of access to a different kind of knowledge. For the humanist, primary texts in Greek and French are becoming available in this form. The technical problems of retrospectively storing and indexing a printed book in computer format are probably solvable within the decade."

Chapter 11

1. The musings of Mario Vargas Llosa are relevant in this connection. In "Books, Gadgets, and Freedom," *Wilson Quarterly*, 11, 2 (Spring 1987), 86–95, he writes, concerning the waning influence of books: "Together with books, and their writers and readers, something else will vanish: the culture of freedom.

"My pessimism is based on two certainties. First, audio-visual culture is infinitely more easily controlled, manipulated, and degraded by power than is the written word. Because of the solitude in which it is born, the speed at which it can be reproduced and circulated, and its lasting mark on people's conscience, the written word has put up a stubborn resistance against being enslaved. With its demise, the submission of minds to power—to the powers—could be total.

"Second, the audio-visual product tends to limit imagination, to dull sensibility, and to create passive minds. I am not retrograde, allergic to audio-visual culture. On the contrary. After literature I love nothing more than the cinema, and I deeply enjoy a good TV program. But even in the few countries such as England where TV has reached a high level of artistic creativity, the average TV program, that which sets the pattern, attempts to embrace the widest possible audience by appealing to the lowest common denominator."

Regarding the power of the audio-visual culture, perhaps one could meditate on this question: which will "play" better, and attract more attention, in an electronic workstation environment: Oliver Stone's movie *JFK* or the twenty-six volumes of the Warren Commission's findings?

2. An excellent analysis of the persistent defensiveness of librarians in this regard may be found in George E. Bennett's *Librarians in Search of Science and Identity: The Elusive Profession* (Metuchen, N.J.: Scarecrow Press, 1988).

3. That book discusses seven of the eight methods of searching. The eighth, related-record searching, became possible after the book's publication. I hope eventually to cover this new method in a revised edition. In the meantime, however, I outline it here in this book.

4. Such a grouping of terminals in a ready-reference area, of course, would not preclude other terminals on the same network from appearing elsewhere within, or outside, the library.

Bibliography

Allen, Thomas J. "Performance of Information Channels in the Transfer of Technology." *Industrial Management Review,* 8, 1 (Fall 1966), 87–98. Notes the dismaying but nonetheless real human frailty in the process of information seeking; one of his principal conclusions is that "[t]here is a serious discrepancy between the quality of the ideas generated through the channels studied, and the frequency with which these channels are used by engineers" (p. 98). Earlier he observes: "The most important aspect of this data . . . is that the channels used with the greatest frequency are not the ones which provide the greatest number of acceptable ideas" (p. 92).

————. *Managing the Flow of Technology.* Cambridge, Mass.: MIT Press, 1977.
"[C]hannel accessibility appears as the dominant criterion upon which selection is based. . . . In the selection of information channels, the engineers in the study certainly appeared to be governed by a principle closely related to Zipf's law. . . . [E]ngineers do attempt to minimize effort by turning first and more frequently to more accessible sources of information" (p. 184).
"THE DECISION TO USE A CHANNEL. Looking at the influence of cost on channel selection, we find a strong relation between channel accessibility and frequency of use. . . .
[P]erceptions of quality and accessibility are themselves slightly correlated, and the first-order relation between quality and frequency of use is illusory and appears only as a result of the mutual relation with the third variable, accessibility" (p. 184).

Allen, Thomas J., and Peter G. Gerstberger. *Criteria for Selection of an Information Source.* Cambridge, Mass.: MIT Press, 1967.

Atherton, Pauline. *Putting Knowledge to Work: An American View of Ranganathan's Five Laws of Library Science.* Delhi: Vikas, 1973.
See pp. 122–23 for a discussion of the "principle of least action."

―――. "Catalog Users' Access from the Reseacher's Viewpoint: Past and Present Research Which Could Affect Library Catalog Design." In *Closing the Catalog: Proceedings of the 1978 and 1979 Library and Information Technology Institutes,* edited by D. Kaye Gapen and Bonnie Juergens, 105–22. Phoenix: Oryx Press, 1980.
"Findings about Catalog Users" . . . "Most people do not persevere very long in catalog searches. More than 50 percent will look up only one entry and then stop, regardless of whether or not they have found what they are looking for. Most subject searches are attempted under a single subject heading" (p. 115).
"Findings about Subject Searches" . . . "Proportion of subject searches declined markedly with 'increased' seniority of the searcher" (p. 116).

Back, Harry B. "What Information Dissemination Studies Imply Concerning the Design of On-Line Reference Retrieval Systems." *Journal of the American Society for Information Science,* 2, 3 (1972), 156–63.

Bamford, Carol M. "Allocating Resources for CD-ROM: A Vendor Perspective." *Library Journal,* 115, 2 (February 1, 1990), 58–59.

Bates, Marcia J. "Subject Access in Online Catalogs: A Decision Model." *Journal of the American Society for Information Science,* 37, 6 (November 1986), 357–76.
"We also know from information seeking research, however, that people have a powerful prejudice for information easily acquired and will bypass information sources that are known to have good information if they are perceived as the least bit difficult to use" (p. 374).

Beckman, Margaret. "A Compromise—Until Fifth Generation Computers Arrive." *American Libraries,* 15, 4 (April 1984), 252.

Benbasat, Izak, and Ronald N. Taylor. "Behavioral Aspects of Information Processing for the Design of Management Information Systems." *IEEE Transactions on Systems, Man, and Cybernetics,* 12, 4 (July/August 1982), 439–50.
"A major research conclusion is that the decision processes typically used in making judgments are very simple ones" (p. 440).
"Subjects [i.e., decision makers] generally seem to prefer strategies that are relatively simple . . . and that are easy for the subjects to understand and to justify to other people. Slovic [1975], for example, found that when faced with two alternatives of equal value subjects tended to

choose the alternative that was better on the most important dimension—
an easily used and logically defensible strategy'' (p. 440).

Bennett, George E. *Librarians in Search of Science and Identity: The Elusive Profession.* Metuchen, N.J.: Scarecrow Press, 1988.

Bettman, James R., and Pradeep Kakaar. ''Effects of Information Presentation Format on Consumer Information Acquisition Strategies.'' *Journal of Consumer Research,* 3, 3 (March 1977), 233–40.

Bierbaum, Esther G. ''A Paradigm for the '90s.'' *American Libraries* (January 1990), 18–19.

Buckland, Michael K. ''Ten Years Progress in Quantitative Research in Libraries.'' *Socio-Economic Planning Sciences,* 12, 6 (1978), 333–39.
''It is known that *accessibility* is a dominant factor in information-gathering behavior. People are likely to choose a source that is convenient rather than a source that is particularly likely to provide the information sought. . . . Improving physical ambience (as when a library is opened), reducing travel effort, and increasing the probability of finding what users seek are all known to increase library usage. Financial charges are unusual in libraries. When instituted they decrease demand'' (p. 336).

Burns, Christopher. ''Three Mile Island: The Information Meltdown.'' *Information Management Reviews,* 1, 1 (Summer 1985), 19–25.

Clark, Katherine E., and Joni Gomez. ''Faculty Use of Databases at Texas A&M University.'' *RQ,* 30, 2 (Winter 1990), 241–48.

Coates, E. J. *Subject Catalogues.* London: Library Association, 1960.

Columbia University Bureau of Applied Social Research (project leader, Herbert Menzel). *Formal and Informal Satisfaction of the Information Requirements of Chemists.* Interim Report. August 1966. Grant NSF-GN-185.

Committee on Scientific and Technical Communication of the National Academy of Sciences–National Academy of Engineering. *Scientific and Technical Communication.* Washington, D.C.: National Academy of Sciences, 1969.
''Very often, however, user response to new, even good services is characteristically slow; therefore, a greater marketing effort must be mounted. Probably scientists and scholars are slow to acquaint themselves with existing library and information services simply because society tends to reward originality rather than thorough literature searching. Yet, it is hard to believe that this state of affairs will continue when it becomes widely apparent that much rediscovery of what is already known is taking place. Though the process may be slow and cumber-

some, it seems clear that a readjustment of the habits of the scientific community is necessary. A different balance must be struck between the allocation of time for original research and the time spent searching, assimilating, reviewing, and consolidating the literature.

"In view of this obligation of the scientific community, it is imperative that library services be made more responsive" (p. 60).

"Another aspect of the operation of the communication network which we need to understand more fully is the sluggishness with which individual working habits respond to new opportunities or challenges. There is evidence that not only individuals but whole blocs of scientists or technologists often will get into a rut and for years fail to take advantage of information tools that could help their work significantly. Allen [1966] has found with some consistency that the channels used with the greatest frequency are not the ones providing the greatest number of acceptable responses. . . . A better understanding of these aspects of communication behavior is necessary before we can effectively design and promote the use of communication techniques and media" (p. 103).

"The application of external testing techniques to the determination of the information habits of scientists and technologists is complicated by the likelihood that the experiment itself may distort the phenomenon under study, a situation further aggravated by the aforementioned unreliability of user reports and user adherence to firmly entrenched patterns of behavior" (p. 103).

"The use (or nonuse) of abstracting and indexing services, whether in printed form or in an on-line system, depends in large part on their responsiveness to so-called 'human factors.' Data from recent studies suggest that when users select information channels, they often act in a manner which minimizes effort rather than maximizing gain. . . . In some studies accessibility—not technical quality—was the single most important determinant of the extent of a channel's use, though familiarity and experience with a service also were major determinants of channel selection" (p. 172).

Culnan, Mary J. "The Dimensions of Perceived Accessibility to Information: Implications for the Delivery of Information-Systems and Services." *Journal of the American Society for Information Science,* 36, 5 (September 1985), 302–8.

"According to Mooers' Law [Mooers, 1960], an information source or system will tend not to be used whenever it is more painful or troublesome for the customer to have the information than it is not to have it. . . . While the same information may be available from a number of sources, the perceived accessibility or expected level of effort required to use a particular information source will influence an individual to select a particular source from among a range of alternative sources'' (p. 302). ''For the providers of information services, the challenge is to develop systems that not only meet user needs for information, but that are also perceived as accessible'' (p. 302).

''Prior research in organizational communication has reported a strong positive relationship between perceived accessibility and the selection of a particular information source over alternative sources'' (pp. 302–3; citing Allen [1977], Gerstberger and Allen [1968], O'Reilly [1982]).

''Three studies reported that the use of a single information system was positively related to its perceived accessibility'' (p. 303; citing Lucas [1978], Maish [1979], and Pearson [1977]).

''Prior research has shown that perceived accessibility plays an important role in influencing an individual to select one information source from among available alternative sources'' (p. 307).

Dervin, Brenda, and Michael Nilan. ''Information Needs and Uses.'' *Annual Review of Information Science and Technology,* 21 (1986), 3–33.
''[A] host of authors decry the low use of virtually every kind of information system'' (p. 6).

Dolan, Donna R. ''What Databases Cannot Do.'' *Database,* 2, 3 (September 1979), 85–87.

Dougherty, Richard M. ''The Evaluation of Campus Library Document Delivery Service.'' *College & Research Libraries,* 34, 1 (January 1973), 29–39.
''In general, researchers secure information from the sources most convenient to them. In 1963 Slater found that the distance from a researcher's office to his technical library influenced his use of that library. Allen and Rosenberg found that information channels are selected on the basis of ease of use and accessibility rather than on the amount of information those channels are expected to generate'' (p. 29).

Dupont, Jerry. ''De-Romancing the Book: The Pyrrhic Victory of Microforms.'' *Microform Review,* 19, 4 (Fall 1990), 192–97.

Dwyer, James R. ''Public Response to an Academic Library Microcatalog.'' *Journal of Academic Librarianship,* 5, 3 (1979), 132–41.
Refers to the ''principle of least effort in information gathering'' (p. 132) and the ''principle of information processing parsimony'' (p. 134).
''People cannot be expected to look in supplements if they can get a few citations from a basic file. . . . One respondent noted, 'I do not trust its [the basic catalog's] contents thoroughly' yet that same person had never used the supplements'' (p. 137).

————. ''The Effect of Closed Catalogs on Public Access.'' *Library Resources & Technical Services,* 25, 2 (April/June 1981), 186–95.

Cites "principle of least effort," "Mooers' Law," and "Zipf's Law";
"Mooers would not be surprised to read the following [comment] elic-
ited during the University of Oregon survey: . . . 'The fiche [catalog]
is one of the few work saving devices I've used. After using it once it
cures you of all desire to use it again, thus decreasing the amount of work
you do.'" "In a library, 'more than fifty percent . . . will look up only
one entry and then stop—REGARDLESS of whether or not they have found
what they are looking for'" (p. 189).

Elcheson, Dennis R. "Cost-Effectiveness Comparison of Manual and On-Line
Retrospective Bibliographic Searching." *Journal of the American Society for Information Science,* 29, 2 (March 1978), 56–66.

Etzioni, Amitai. "Socio-Economics: Humanizing the Dismal Science." *Washington Post,* January 11, 1987, C3.
Reports that "Herbert Simon of Carnegie Mellon got a Nobel Prize in
economics in 1978 for showing (among other things) that people do not
think through most questions. Long before they reach the maximal solution, they stop collecting information and processing what they have.
They often grab the first satisfactory solution that pops up. (Not just
consumers and investors; governments do the same.)"

Faibisoff, S. G., and D. P. Ely. "Information and Information Needs." In *Key
Papers in the Design and Evaluation of Information Systems,* edited by
Donald W. King, 270–84. White Plains, N.Y.: Knowledge Industry,
1978.
Cited by King and Baker (1987) as a "general review" indicating that
researchers do not use secondary and tertiary library tools and that people
"satisfice" with poor-quality sources.

Fairthorne, Robert A. "Empirical Hyperbolic Distributions (Bradford-Zipf-
Mandelbrot) for Bibliometric Description and Prediction." *Journal of
Documentation,* 25, 4 (December 1969), 319–49.

Fine, Sara. "Research and the Psychology of Information Use." *Library
Trends,* 32, 4 (Spring 1984), 441–60.
"In general, asking people what they want is not the answer; people are
limited in their ability to respond by their own potential for imagination
and by their preconceptions about and experiences with the library" (p.
449).

Folster, Mary B. "A Study of the Use of Information Sources by Social Science
Researchers." *Journal of Academic Librarianship,* 15, 1 (March 1989),
7–11.
Indicates that researchers do not use indexes; they rely on colleagues and
footnote chasing.

Gerstberger, Peter G., and Thomas J. Allen. "Criteria Used by Research and Development Engineers in the Selection of an Information Source." *Journal of Applied Psychology,* 52, 4 (August 1968), 272–79.

"Accessibility is definitely the dominant cost criterion determining the relative frequency with which information channels are used" (p. 275).

"Apparently, in the minds of the [subject], there is some relationship between the perception of technical quality and channel accessibility, but it is the accessibility component which almost exclusively determines frequency of use" (pp. 275–76).

"Here again accessibility appears as the dominant criterion upon which selection is based. Engineers turn first to the channel which is most accessible; perceived technical quality influences this decision only to a minor extent" (p. 276).

"The only way to increased use is through increased accessibility" (p. 278).

"Accessibility is the single most important determinant of the overall extent to which an information channel is used" (p. 279).

Goodrum, Charles A., and Helen W. Dalrymple. *The Library of Congress.* 2nd ed. Boulder, Colo.: Westview Press, 1982.

Gore, Daniel. "Teaching Bibliography to College Freshmen." *Education Forum,* 34 (November 1969), 111–17.

Greene, Robert J. "The Effects of Browsing." *College & Research Libraries,* (July 1977), 313–16.

"[B]rowsing is the most important method used by faculty to learn about library books they borrow. However, . . . browsing ranks last among all of the methods of learning about books when the usefulness of the books discovered by the various methods is considered" (p. 316).

Gupta, M. S. "Information Retrieval Techniques in Engineering Curriculum." *IEEE Transactions on Education,* 19, 4 (1976), 165–68.

"These surveys indicate that the preference for a given method of information gathering reflects the estimated ease of use of the method rather than the amount of information expected. Users find it natural to rely on the most accessible and familiar sources rather than to experiment with new ones that may require a greater initial investment of effort. . . . [U]sers of scientific and technical information are slow to change their habits, usually learned in their formative years. As a consequence, there are strong tendencies toward 'in a rut' behavior and toward apathetic responses to new and more effective services" (p. 165).

228   *Bibliography*

Haines, George H. "Process Models of Consumer Decision Making." In *Buyer/ Consumer Information Processing*. Chapel Hill: University of North Carolina Press, 1974.
See pp. 96–97 for a "principle of information processing parsimony."

Harter, Stephen P., and Susan M. Jackson. "Optical Disc Systems in Libraries: Problems and Issues." *RQ*, 27, 4 (Summer 1988), 516–27.
"Studies of *InfoTrac*, for instance, have shown that often users will choose to search this system, which is convenient, quick, and provides a printed record, even when the databases covered are inappropriate to the search, rather than undertaking laborious searches of more relevant print sources. . . . But reference librarians are obligated to ensure that users are given the opportunity to retrieve, either independently or with the help of a librarian, relevant and high quality information related to their needs. We cannot abdicate this responsibility even though, at times, users may opt for convenience because of their lack of knowledge about the art of the possible. . . . Our goal should be to provide access to high quality information services" (p. 525).

Herner, Saul, and Mary Herner. "Information Needs and Uses in Science and Technology." *Annual Review of Information Science and Technology*, 2 (1967), 1–34.
Citing Rosenberg (1966): "The results, perhaps predictable, but also quite sobering, were that there was a high significant correlation between the preference rankings in the first question [regarding methods or media of information gathering] and the ratings of ease of use in the second, while there was no significant correlation between preferences and expected amounts of information. From this, Rosenberg validly concludes that 'the ease of use of an information-gathering method is more important than the amount of information expected . . .'" (p. 21).

Horton, William K. *Designing and Writing Online Documentation*. New York: John Wiley, 1990.

Huber, George P. "The Nature and Design of Post-Industrial Organizations." *Management Science*, 30, 8 (August 1984), 928–51.
"[T]he attractiveness of informal information sources is largely a function of their ready accessibility" (p. 936).

Information Seeking and Communicating Behavior of Scientists and Engineers. Edited by Cynthia Steinke. New York: Haworth Press, 1991.

Jenell, Carol Ann. "The Reorganization of a Monographic Reference Collection." *Medical Library Association Bulletin*, 64, 3 (July 1976), 293–98.

Johnston, Susan M. "Choosing Between Manual and On-Line Searching." *Aslib Proceedings (U.K.)*, 30 (October/November 1978), 383–93.

Johnston, Susan M., and D. E. Gray. "Comparison of Manual and Online Retrospective Searching for Agricultural Subjects." *Aslib Proceedings* (*U.K.*), 29 (July 1977), 253–58.

Jordan, Robert T. "The 'Complete Package' College Library." *College & Research Libraries*, 23, 5 (September 1962), 405–9, 421.

Kenney, Donald J. "Library Instruction in the 1980s: Where Has It Been and Where Is It Going?" In *Bibliographic Instruction: The Second Generation*, edited by Constance A. Mellon, 191–97. Littleton, Colo.: Libraries Unlimited, 1987.
"With the advent of online retrieval and information systems, instructional responsibilities will increase. These new sources cannot be expected to decrease the questions, problems, and indeed laziness of library users. Much of the same ineptness that users display as they encounter the traditional card catalog and printed indexes will be duplicated as they approach computer-generated or computer-managed systems. In many ways, these new information technologies will increase user problems and frustrations. The paramount misconception concerning automated catalogs and information sources is that they are a panacea for those with information needs. Some users are under the impression that the problems they encounter with a manual catalog will automatically vanish with the advent of technology. Information, they believe, will be forthcoming for all seekers who push the right button or give the right command. Discounting these misconceptions can be considered one of the main objectives of bibliographic instruction for the next decade. Users need to realize the vast potential of online information systems and automated catalogs but at the same time they need to have realistic expectations and to understand that systems are only as good as the information they contain" (p. 196).

Kenney, Larraine. "The Implications of the Needs of Users for the Design of a Catalogue." *Journal of Documentation*, 22 (September 1966), 195–202.

King, David, and Betsy Baker. "Human Aspects of Library Technology: Implications for Academic Library User Education." In *Bibliographic Instruction: The Second Generation*, edited by Constance A. Mellon, 85–107. Littleton, Colo.: Libraries Unlimited, 1987.
"One of the principal events governing information seeking is accessibility, particularly among library clientele who place great value on their time. Librarians have long been aware that users may be satisfied with a readily accessible source, even of dubious quality, rather than invest more time or effort to obtain a source that might be superior" (p. 95).
"In contrast, more advanced students, faculty, and researchers, who in

the past relied heavily on information-seeking and information management techniques that exploited the self-indexing nature of the primary literature, are finding it increasingly difficult to maintain those practices. The explosive growth in volume of the literature in many disciplines has disrupted methods that a decade ago were reliable and efficient'' (p. 101).

Kremer, Jeannette Marguerite. "Information Flow Among Engineers in a Design Company." Ph.D. diss., University of Illinois at Urbana-Champaign, 1980. AAD80-17965. *DAI* 41/02A, p. 445-A.
From the abstract: "Accessibility and ease of use are perceived by these engineers to be greatly similar to each other. . . . Evaluation of the location of sources of information by the engineers seems to follow Zipf's principle of least effort, since they rank higher those locations which present highest physical and psychological accessibility . . ." (p. 445-A).

Krikelas, James. "Information-Seeking Behavior: Patterns and Concepts." *Drexel Library Quarterly,* 19, 2 (Spring 1983), 5–20.
"The importance of the interpersonal, informal channels of communication has already been documented among scientists, engineers, and social scientists. Similar results have shown up among some of the recent, large-scale surveys of general publics" (p. 15).
"Why do individuals prefer certain sources over others? . . . [U]nder normal circumstances, convenience seems to outweigh accuracy" (p.16).

Lancaster, F. W. *Evaluation of the MEDLARS Demand Search Service.* Washington, D.C.: National Library of Medicine, 1968.
"The quality of an entry vocabulary can substantially affect the recall performance of an information retrieval system" (p. 49; see also p. 48 on the need for cross-references).

————. *The Measurement and Evaluation of Library Services.* Arlington, Va.: Information Resources Press, 1977.
For findings that "[m]ost people do not persevere in catalog searches," see pp. 69–70.

Large, Peter. *The Micro Revolution Revisited.* Totowa, N.J.: Rowman & Allenheld, 1984.

Leisener, James W. "Learning at Risk." In *Libraries and the Learning Society: Papers in Response to 'A Nation at Risk.'* Chicago: American Library Association, 1984. ERIC document ED246920.

Lucas, Henry C., Jr. "The Use of an Interactive Information Storage and Retrieval System in Medical Research." *Communications of the ACM,* 21, 3 (March 1978), 197–205.

Lynch, Clifford A. *Electronic Publishing, Electronic Libraries and the National Research and Education Network: Policy and Technology Issues.* OTA Contractor Report. Washington, D.C.: Office of Technology Assessment, U.S. Congress, April 1990.

McArthur, Tom. *Worlds of Reference: Lexicography, Learning, and Language from the Clay Tablet to the Computer.* Cambridge: Cambridge University Press, 1986.
"[I]nformation as such can only exist as a usable resource *if* it is properly accessible, and it is only properly accessible *if* all the appropriate procedures of the secondary media are in place: numbers, letters, alphabetization, thematization, contents lists, correspondences between indexes and locations of data, and so forth. Without these vital 'secondary' procedures, 'primary' material, however valuable in itself, may be rendered functionally worthless" (p. 11).

McBride, Ruth B., and Patricia Stenstrom. "Psychology Journal Use." *Behavioral and Social Sciences Librarian,* 2 (Fall 1982), 2–3.

Machlup, Fritz. *Knowledge: Its Creation, Distribution, and Economic Significance.* Vol. 2. *The Branches of Learning.* Princeton, N.J.: Princeton University Press, 1982.

McLaughlin, C. P., R. S. Rosenbloom, and F. W. Wolek. *Technology Transfer and the Flow of Technical Information in a Large Industrial Corporation.* Cambridge, Mass.: Harvard University, School of Business Administration, 1965.
"We believe that the behavior of engineers seeking information to meet specific needs is largely *programmed* in the sense that specific patterns of behavior, relatively stable over time, are invoked under such circumstances. . . . We believe that a major factor behind this implicit strategy is the perceived cost of information seeking. . . . [V]alue [in the sources] must be in line with the average cost of using them" (p. 29).

Maish, A. M. "A User's Behavior Towards His MIS." *MIS Quarterly,* 3, 1 (1979), 39–52.

Mann, Thomas. *A Guide to Library Research Methods.* New York: Oxford University Press, 1987.

———. *Cataloging Quality, LC Priorities, and Models of the Library's Future.* Washington, D.C.: Cataloging Forum, Library of Congress, 1991.

Menzel, Herbert. "Information Needs and Uses in Science and Technology." *Annual Review of Science and Technology,* 1 (1966), 41–69.

Menzel, Herbert, and Elihu Katz. "Social Relations in Innovation in the Medical Profession." *Public Opinion Quarterly,* 19 (1955), 337–52.

"Microbooks—A Future Revolution in Printing." *Graphic Arts Monthly*, 36 (September 1964), 216–17.

"Microfilm to Replace Books." *Connecticut Libraries*, 15, 1 (January 1973), 28.

Miller, George. "The Magical Number Seven, Plus or Minus Two: Some Limits on Our Capacity for Processing Information." *Psychological Review*, 63 (1956), 81–97.

Miller, Richard E. "The Tradition of Reference Service in the Liberal Arts College Library." *RQ*, 25, 4 (Summer 1986), 460–67.

Miller, William, and Bonnie Gratch. "Making Connections: Computerized Reference Services and People." *Library Trends*, 37, 4 (Spring 1989), 387–401.

Milstead, Jessica. *Subject Access Systems: Alternatives in Design*. Orlando, Fla.: Academic Press, 1984.
"It is well-known that most seekers after information will prefer easily available information of lesser quality to that which is more difficult to reach, even though it may be of higher quality, at least in satisfying the need of the moment. . . . Naturally there is a tendency, if access to the original [rather than a surrogate] will be difficult, to rationalize that it is probably of limited value anyway, and hence not worth the trouble of pursuit" (p. 192).
"The effect of each part of the index system on the other parts of the system has been examined. Without this approach it is all too easy to cause severe harm to one part of a system by 'improving' another without careful examination of the impact of the improvement" (p. 193).

Mooers, Calvin N. "Mooers' Law, or Why Some Retrieval Systems Are Used and Others Are Not." *American Documentation*, 11, 3 (July 1960), ii.
"MOOERS' LAW: An information retrieval system will tend *not* to be used whenever it is more painful and troublesome for a customer to have information than for him not to have it."

Morton, Herbert S., et al. *Writings on Scholarly Communication: An Annotated Bibliography of Books and Articles on Publishing, Libraries, Scholarly Research, and Related Issues*. Lanham, Md.: University Press of America, 1988.
"The Committee on Scientific Information of the Royal Society, London, conducted a three-year survey of scientific information systems. It surveyed biologists, physicists, physical scientists, biochemists, and chemists. Of those solicited, 63 percent responded. By a wide margin the surveyed scientists favored journals printed from camera-ready copy and disapproved electronic journals" (p. 48).

National Enquiry into Scholarly Communication. *Scholarly Communication: The Report of the National Enquiry.* Baltimore: Johns Hopkins University Press, 1979.

O'Reilly, Charles A. "Variations in Decision Makers' Use of Information Sources: The Impact of Quality and Accessibility of Information." *Academy of Management Journal,* 25, 4 (December 1982), 756–71.
"The finding that it is accessibility, rather than quality, that is most related to reported frequency of use can be explained in several ways. . . . [A] more accessible source is more likely to be used than an inaccessible one, even if the quality of the source used is lower than another known by the decision maker to be available. . . . O'Reilly and Anderson (1979) offer several other explanations for the dominance of accessibility over quality as a determinant of information source use" (p. 767).

O'Reilly, C. A., and J. C. Anderson. "Organizational Communication and Decision Making: Laboratory Results Versus Actual Organizational Settings." Paper presented at the 24th International Meeting of the Institute of Management Sciences, Honolulu, 1979.

Paisley, William J. "Information Needs and Uses." *Annual Review of Information Science and Technology,* 3 (1968), 1–30.
Notes the reality of the human frailties and the irrational behavior involved in information seeking: "The Allen-Gerstberger findings [1968] closely parallel those of Rosenberg [1967]. Accessibility and ease of use are stronger correlates of channel use than is technical quality. When each of the other factors is partialled out, accessibility retains its predictive power best. . . . The most interesting finding of the Allen-Gerstberger study is that information 'acceptances' . . . are significantly related to perceived technical quality of a channel but not to accessibility or ease of use. There is a curious filtering process, then: engineers *use* channels in proportion to accessibility and ease of use, but they *accept* ideas from those channels in proportion to technical quality. The authors point to the apparent irrationality of a search strategy based on the least-effort principle when the most acceptable information is also the most effortful to collect" (p. 9). Elsewhere, in referring to biologists, Paisley remarks: "Failure to take full advantage of [an information] service is consistent with an 'information-gathering apathy' often noted among scientists and technologists" (p. 18).

Parker, Edwin B., and William J. Paisley. "Research for Psychologists at the Interface of the Scientist and His Information System." *American Psychologist,* 21, 11 (November 1966), 1060–71.
"The system we are trying to make efficient will have to contend with a

good deal of apparent irrationality and inefficiency on the part of scientists. . . . The task of psychological research in this context is to test the behavioral assumptions of system designers'' (p. 1069).

Pastine, Maureen. ''Bibliographic Instruction in the Humanities.'' In *Bibliographic Instruction: The Second Generation,* edited by Constance A. Mellon, 169–79. Littleton, Colo.: Libraries Unlimited, 1987.
''Retrospective materials, literary texts, and bibliographies are often considered by faculty and librarians to be of great importance, yet they are rarely used. Instead, poets, philosophers, artists, musicians, novelists, and other humanists have relied on their own files and their colleagues to provide needed literature citations. . . . For many, the library is the last place one goes to get information'' (p. 173).
''From the little research available, it is readily apparent that doctoral-level students in the humanities are woefully unprepared to conduct research in their own disciplines . . .'' (p. 174).

Pearson, S. W. ''Measurement of Computer Use Satisfaction.'' Ph.D. diss., Arizona State University, 1977. NTIS AD A-046-549.

Peischl, T. M., and M. Montgomery. ''Back to the Warehouse, or Some Implications on End User Searching in Libraries.''In *National Online Meeting Proceedings, 1986,* edited by M. E. Williams and T. H. Hogan, 347–52. Medford, N.J.: Learned Information, 1986.
Cited by Miller and Gratch (1989): ''Peischel and Montgomery (1986) . . . conclude that, for most types of users, the responsibility for quality research rests with the library, because infrequent or disinterested users do not perform effective searches.''

Poole, Herbert. *Theories of the Middle Range.* Norwood, N.J.: Ablex, 1985.

Popkin, Samuel L. *The Reasoning Voter: Communication and Persuasion in Presidential Campaigns.* Chicago: University of Chicago Press, 1991.

Putting Knowledge to Use: A Distillation of Literature Regarding Knowledge Transfer and Change. Los Angeles: Human Interaction Research Institute, 1976.
Citing Herner and Herner (1967) on information seeking: ''Time and effort consumption discourages the use of certain means'' (p. 35).
''[The technologist seeking information] is inclined to fall back on the standard manuals and textbooks with which he is already familiar'' (p. 53).
''[R]esearch workers depend heavily on . . . 'accidental' acquisition of useful information, 'inefficient' and 'informal' information seeking, etc.'' (p. 54).
''[S]tudies show research centers and other agencies are not always

effective in seeing that such information reaches the consumer, or that it does so in attention-arresting form'' (p. 74).

"Putting a Library in a Shoebox." *Popular Science,* 186, 3 (March 1965), 77.

Rayward, W. Boyd. "Librarianship and Information Research: Together or Apart?" In *The Study of Information: Interdisciplinary Messages,* edited by Fritz Machlup and Una Mansfield, 399–405. New York: John Wiley & Sons, 1983.

"Real Future Is Seen for Ultramicrofiche." *Library News Bulletin* (Washington State University), 35 (October 1968), 288.

Retrospective Conversion: Report of a Meeting Sponsored by the Council on Library Resources. July 16–18, 1984, Wayzata, Minnesota. Compiled and edited by Dorothy Gregor. Washington, D.C.: Council on Library Resources, 1984.

Rider, Fremont. *The Scholar and the Future of the Research Library: A Problem and Its Solution.* New York: Hadham Press, 1944.

Rogers, Everett M., and F. Floyd Shoemaker. *Communication of Innovations.* New York: Free Press, 1971.

Rosenberg, Victor. "The Application of Psychometric Techniques to Determine the Attitudes of Individuals Toward Information Seeking." Lehigh University, 1966. Grants AF-AFOSR-724-66 and NSF-GE-2569 (AD 637 713).

————. "Factors Affecting the Preference of Industrial Personnel for Information Gathering Methods." *Information Storage and Retrieval,* 3, 3 (July 1967), 119–27.

Roszak, Theodore. *The Cult of Information.* New York: Pantheon Books, 1986.

Rowan, Hobart. "Are American Business Leaders Doing Their Job?" *Washington Post,* November 11, 1986, A21.
"[Richard] Darman [of the Reagan Treasury] is in complete accord with Sony's Akio Morita, who recently said that 'the remarkable thing about management is that a manager can go on for years making mistakes that nobody is aware of.' "

Rowland, J. F. B. "The Scientist's View of His Information System." *The Journal of Documentation,* 38 (March 1982), 38–42.

Rudd, Joel, and Mary Jo Rudd. "Coping with Information Load: User Strategies and Implications for Librarians." *College & Research Libraries,* 47, 4 (July 1986), 315–22.
"Anecdotal evidence is widely available indicating that both students and faculty . . . avoid overload largely by either avoiding the library

or, once in the library, spending little time in the information search and
giving up quickly'' (p. 319).

Russo, J. Edward, Gene Krieser, and Sally Miyashita. "An Effective Display
of Unit Price Information." *Journal of Marketing,* 39 (April 1975), 11–
19.

Sage, Andrew P. "Behavioral and Organizational Considerations in the Design
of Information Systems and Processes for Planning and Decision Support." *IEEE Transactions on Systems, Man, and Cybernetics,* 11, 9
(1981), 640–78.
"Among the cognitive biases that have been identified [associated with
judgment and choice] are several which affect information formulation
or acquisitions, information analysis, and interpretation. Among these
biases, which are not independent, are the following . . . 2) Availability [citing Tversky and Kahneman, 1974 and 1981]—The decisionmaker
uses only easily available information and ignores not easily available
sources of significant information'' (p. 647).
"The rational actor model is often accepted as a normative model of how
decisions should be made, at least in a substantive or "as if" fashion. It is
often observed that the model is not an accurate description of actual
unaided choicemaking behavior'' (p. 650).

Salasin, John, and Toby Cedar. "Person-to-Person Communication in an
Applied-Research Service Delivery Setting." *Journal of the American
Society for Information Science,* 36, 2 (March 1985), 103–115.
"These findings suggest that information transfer might be improved by
making it easier for those seeking information to contact someone who
has expertise in the specific area(s) in which information is needed'' (p.
113).

Schneiderman, Ben. *Software Psychology: Human Factors in Computer and
Information Systems.* Cambridge, Mass.: Winthrop Publishers, 1980.

Senzig, Donna. "Library Catalogs for Library Users." *RQ,* 24, 1 (Fall 1984),
37–42.
"[F]requently people just don't take the time to look in a second catalog
if the first catalog has failed them. If the first catalog has something
listed, they often will not check a second catalog to see if it has additional
listings or a better listing'' (p. 37).

Sewell, Winifred, and Sandra Teitelbaum. "Observations of End-User Online
Searching Behavior over Eleven Years." *Journal of the American Society for Information Science,* 37 (July 1986), 234–45.

Simon, Herbert A. "A Behavioral Model of Rational Choice." *Quarterly Journal of Economics,* 69, 1 (February 1955), 99–118.

———. "Rational Choice and the Structure of the Environment." *Psychological Review,* 63, 2 (March 1956), 129–38.
"The principal positive implication of the model is that we should be skeptical in postulating for humans, or other organisms, elaborate mechanisms for choosing among diverse needs" (p. 137). He refers to such action as the tendency to "satisfice" rather than to "optimize" (p. 129).

———. *Administrative Behavior.* 2d ed. New York: Macmillan, 1957.
Cited by Ronald Taylor (1975) on "satisficing": "In satisficing, the decision maker sets a moderate standard, then searches for alternatives until he finds one that achieves this level. As soon as a satisfactory alternative is found, he terminates his search and chooses that alternative" (p. 75).

Slater, M. "Types of Use and User in Industrial Libraries: Some Impressions." *Journal of Documentation,* 19, 1 (March 1963), 12–18.
"But these libraries lacked comfort and visual appeal, and were sometimes also understaffed. It would seem that there are still some firms which imagine that providing a collection of books is the equivalent of providing an information service.
"Even the geographical location of a library seems to affect the volume and type of use. If a library is situated in an inaccessible place . . . it is at a mechanical disadvantage. It will probably have less custom than an identical library in a more convenient site, and the custom it does get may be of the wrong type" (p. 13).

Slovic, Paul. "Choice Between Equally Valued Alternatives." *Journal of Experimental Psychology: Human Perception and Performance,* 1, 3 (August 1975), 280–87.
"In other words, reliance on easily justifiable aspects to the neglect of other important factors could lead one to reject alternatives whose overall utilities (assessed outside the choice context) are superior to those of the chosen alternative" (p. 287).

Smith, Eldred. *The Librarian, the Scholar, and the Future of the Research Library.* New York: Greenwood Press, 1990.

Soper, Mary Ellen. "Characteristics and Use of Personal Collections." *Library Quarterly,* 46, 4 (October 1976), 397–415.
"A thesis by Rosenberg in 1966 revealed that research workers preferred information-gathering methods which they estimated were easier to use, rather than those methods they judged would provide the greatest amount of information" (p. 398).

Stam, Dierdre Corcoran. "The Information-Seeking Practices of Art Historians in Museums and Colleges in the United States." Ph.D. diss., Columbia University, 1984. *DAI* 45/10A, p. 3020.

From the abstract: "[T]hey maintain only weakly connected 'invisible colleges.'" "Almost all art historians, particularly in colleges, report extensive dependence upon their personal libraries." And: "In their pursuit of authoritative information, art historians begin most often with colleagues and experts. They also consult footnotes and the bibliographies of familiar monographs. Only late in the search do they consult bibliographic tools and librarians" (p. 3020).

Standera, O. L. "Electronic Publishing: Some Notes on Reader Response and Costs." *Scholarly Publishing,* 16 (July 1985), 291–305.
This study compares the responses of seventy-one faculty members at the University of British Columbia on the acceptance of the same journal in three different formats: paper, microfiche, and electronic. Only 5 percent accepted the last without reservations. The most important criterion was "ease of browsing," and the conventional print format was given the highest rating among the three formats in an overwhelming preference.

Steel, Walter. "Microimagery: Solution to the Information Explosion." *Intellect,* 102 (January 1974), 213–14.

Stenstrom, Patricia, and Ruth B. McBride. "Serial Use of Social Science Faculty: A Survey." *College & Research Libraries,* 40, 5 (September 1979), 426–31.

Stoan, Stephen K. "Research and Library Skills: An Analysis and Interpretation." *College & Research Libraries,* 45 (March 1984), 99–109.

Swanson, Don R. "On Improving Communication Among Scientists." *Bulletin of the Atomic Scientists,* 22, 2 (February 1966), 8–12.

Tagliacozzo, Renata. "Consumers of New Information Technology: Survey of Utilization of MEDLINE." *Journal of the American Society for Information Science,* 26, 5 (September–October 1975), 294–304.
"Of the many reasons which could have induced our users to request a MEDLINE search, the wish to save the time and effort needed to assemble a bibliography by traditional methods was predominant" (p. 298; 82 percent of respondents—845 out of 1,026 questionnaires—offered this reason).

Tagliacozzo, Renata, and Manfred Kochen. "Information-Seeking Behavior of Catalog Users." *Information Storage and Retrieval,* 6, 5 (December 1970), 363–81.
"It was rather surprising to discover that almost half the users who failed in their first attempt gave up the search" (p. 375).
"The majority of users generated only one or two query terms per search" (p. 375).
"The perseverance of the searchers who look for a specific document

does not seem to be very high: in the population that we studied, more than half of the searchers who failed in their first attempt to locate a book gave up the search'' (p. 380).

Taylor, R. S. "Question Negotiation and Information Seeking in Libraries." *College & Research Libraries*, 29, 3 (May 1968), 178–94.
"The system that is best able to display itself in a useful and functional way for the inquirer will be the most effective. Like information itself, the system that provides ease of access, specifically physical convenience, will be more effective than those concerned only with the quality of the scheme of subject organization" (p. 193).

Taylor, Ronald N. "Age and Experience as Determinants of Managerial Information Processing and Decision Making Performance." *Academy of Management Journal*, 18, 1 (March 1975), 74–81.
Cited by O'Reilly (1982): "Workers who have been in a job longer . . . may develop habitual preferences for certain information sources" (p. 759).

Truelson, Stanley D., Jr. "The Totally Organized Reference Collection." *Medical Library Association Bulletin*, 50 (1962), 184–87.

Tversky, Amos, and Daniel Kahneman. "Judgment Under Uncertainty: Heuristics and Biases." *Science*, September 27, 1974, 1124–31.
"*Biases* [in judgment] *due to the retrievability of instances*. When the size of a class is judged by the availability of its instances, a class whose instances are easily retrieved will appear more numerous than a class of equal frequency whose instances are less retrievable" (p. 1127).

———. "The Framing of Decisions and the Psychology of Choice." *Science*, January 30, 1981, 453–58.
"*Summary*. The psychological principles that govern the perception of decision problems and the evaluation of probabilities and outcomes produce predictable shifts of preference when the same problem is framed in different ways. . . . The effects of frames on preference are compared to the effects of perspective on perceptual appearance. The dependence of preferences on the formulation of decision problems is a significant concern for the theory of rational choice. . . . The frame that a decision-maker adopts is controlled partly by the formulation of the problem and partly by the norms, habits, and personal characteristics of the decision-maker" (p. 453).

Uytterschaut, L. "Literature Searching Methods in Social Science Research: A Pilot Inquiry." *American Behavioral Scientist*, 9, 9 (May 1966), 14–26.
"On only two checkpoints did it seem possible to trace with assurance the overall picture of a documentary processing in literature research: at its outset and at its final projection. Between these two stages, an inscru-

table mixture of subject experience and intuition has been used to get from one end to the other, obviously without any afterthought about documentary strategy'' (p. 26).

Van Arsdale, William O., and Anne T. Ostrye. "InfoTrac: A Second Opinion." *American Libraries,* 17, 7 (July/August 1986), 514–15.

These authors note an essential point: that improving ease of access can have damaging effects on the quality of research if severely incomplete sources are the only ones that are made easier to use. Although they are concerned specifically with the commercial InfoTrac system, their comments apply to other systems as well: "The concept of introducing an attractive and easy-to-use, but limited, searching tool into the undergraduate environment must be seriously addressed. Students may be eager to use the automated system, but they appear to have dropped efforts at more traditional searching and assumed that their electronic search will suffice. Our reference staff encouraged many students to pursue their research in other, more comprehensive sources, but few students did so. Typically, the undergraduate user prints out whatever results from the search term . . . and thinks the topic has been fully researched. The system encourages little or no judgment on the part of the student to select or use the information provided, an unfortunate consequence of most automated systems. . . . The popularity of [the automated system] is the reason given most frequently by other libraries for subscribing. User enthusiasm was also evident during our trial use. Does a library provide a service primarily because it is popular? As one of our reference librarians quipped, 'The fact that students would like us to write their term papers is no reason to provide the service.'

"Librarians frequently have to make tough decisions based on their knowledge of library purpose, technology, bibliography, and competing demands for limited resources. Popularity should seldom be the principal consideration" (p. 515).

Vaughn, W. S., Jr., and Anne Schumacher Mavor. "Behavioral Characteristics of Men in the Performance of Some Decision-Making Task Components." *Ergonomics,* 15, 3 (May 1972), 267–77.

"On the whole, the picture that emerges of man's performance in making decisions is essentially a documentation of Yntema and Torgerson's (1961) simplification hypothesis. He is slow to initiate action and conservative in his estimates of highly probable situations; and when he does act or accept a diagnosis, he is reluctant to change an established plan or a situational estimate when the available data indicate that he should. . . . He is not particularly inventive and tends to adopt the first solution he develops. He finds it difficult to use more than one criterion at a time in evaluation actions and tends only to identify criteria that reflect favorably on the action he is developing. . . . Some key tasks, central to most decision-making models, are not performed at all (e.g., the comparative evaluation of multiple alternatives, or the evaluation of a single action alternative against multiple possible states)'' (p. 274). Earlier, the authors note that ''empirical processes used by real-life decision-makers may be surprisingly simple'' (p. 270).

Veaner, Allen B. ''Encyclopedia in Your Waistcoat Pocket.'' *MICRODOC*, 10, 4 (1971), 104–6.

Vigo-Cepeda, Luisa. ''Patterns of Use of Assigned Learning Resources and Satisfaction Derived. . . .'' Ph.D. diss., University of Michigan, 1977. *DAI* 38/11A, 6375-76.
From the abstract: ''In fact, students reported using their personal collections and going to the bookstores to purchase new materials more frequently than using the libraries and their research collections'' (p. 6376).

Weiss, Carol. ''Closing the Catalog: Impact on Reference Services.'' In *Closing the Catalog: Proceedings of the 1978 and 1979 Library and Information Technology Association Institute*, edited by D. Kaye Gapen and Bonnie Juergens. Phoenix: Oryx Press, 1980.
''It is the responsibility of the public service staff to attempt to assess as objectively as possible what the users' real needs are, how they can be met, and what the priorities are'' (p. 99).
''Most people do not persevere in catalog searches. More than 50 percent will look up only one entry and then stop, regardless of whether or not they have found what they are looking for. Most subject searches are attempted under a single subject heading'' (p. 100).
''As a result, we tried to design a new system with human frailties in mind. Our primary goal, if most users were to stop searching after one lookup, was to make it possible for the majority to find what they wanted in the first place they looked'' (p. 100).

Werner, D. J. ''A Study of the Information-Seeking Behavior of Medical Researchers.'' Master's thesis, Northwestern University, 1965.
Cited by Gerstberger and Allen (1968) as concluding that ''the behavior of the users studied appears to be influenced by the perception of the ease with which an information channel might be used'' (p. 272).

Wilberly, Stephen E., and Robert Allen Dougherty. ''Users' Persistence in Scanning Lists of References.'' *College & Research Libraries*, 49, 2 (March 1988), 149–56.
''It is important for those who design and service information systems to realize that much, perhaps most, information seeking is discretionary

[rather than compulsory]. Because of this, users often have little or no reason to persist in using systems that are 'unfriendly'" (p. 150).

Yntema, D. B., and W. S. Torgerson. "Man-Computer Cooperation in Decisions Requiring Common Sense." *IRE Transactions on Human Factors in Electronics*, HFE-2, 1 (March 1961), 20–26.

"We would not be surprised to find that people tend to use rather simple procedures in making even the most important decisions" (p. 26).

Zipf, George Kingsley. *Human Behavior and the Principle of Least Effort*. Cambridge, Mass.: Addison-Wesley, 1949.

Index

A classes, 45–46, 126
Abstracts, 61, 63, 64, 216n.1
Actual-Practice model, 14, 75–90, 152, 155, 168, 181, 217n.1
Administrative priorities, 146
Afro-Americans, 22, 33–37, 42, 71, 81, 83
Almanacs, 58, 59, 64
Alphabet, 141–43
Alphabetical adjacency of narrower terms in *LSCH*, 36–37, 122
Animal sounds, 117
Anonymous Letters, 37–38
Artificial intelligence, 144–46
Aspects of a subject, 21–22, 31–37. *See also* Scattering of sources
 and Actual-Practice model, 75, 81, 84, 86, 152
 and bibliographies, 49
 grouped in catalog, 33, 125, 143
 linkage of tracing and class number, 40, 125
 listed, 21
 and Methods model, 160, 163, 168, 171
Atlases, 59, 63, 64
Author arrangement, 16, 26
Authority control, 26–29, 75, 113

Barataria, 17
Bibliographic Index, 54, 165
Bibliographic instruction. *See also* Lists of sources; Point-of-use instruction
 and Actual-Practice model, 76, 231

and index-Zs, 52–53
and Methods model, 158, 167, 174, 177, 185
natural language/*LCSH* distinction, 43, 155
not asking for help, 6, 13, 168
and Subject model, 9–10, 13–14, 42, 52, 57, 63, 67, 153, 155, 177, 228
and Type-of-Literature model, 52, 57–58, 63, 67, 69, 74, 153, 155, 174, 177
Bibliographies. *See also* Index-Zs
 alternate class numbers, 218n.3
 arranged by type of literature, 63–64, 66, 172
 arrangement of index-Zs, 193–200
 component of Traditional Library Science model, 45–56, 76, 109
 different from computer lists, 5, 7, 100, 124, 152, 182
 in Methods model, 165–66
 in review articles, 61–62
 separated from monographs, 5, 22, 35–36, 46–47, 76, 81–82, 84, 89, 152
 as type of literature themselves, 58, 59, 84, 124
Bibliographische Berichte, 54, 165
Billington, James, 145, 188
Black Women Novelists, 22
Blended families, 72–73
Browsing, 23, 49, 72, 88–89, 90, 95. *See also* Classification; Depth of access

243

Capital punishment, 29, 128
"Car 90," 119–20
Catalogs (as type of literature), 59, 86
Chapters of books, 123. *See also* Depth
of access
Chen, Ching-chih, 63–64, 70
Chronologies, 58, 59, 63
Citation searching, 10, 55, 71, 88–89,
100, 155
contrasted to *LCSH* and key word
searching, 146–47
in Methods model, 163–65
Classification. *See also* Depth of access;
Library of Congress Classification
and Actual-Practice model, 75
and Computer Workstation model,
114–15
limitations, 20–23, 43, 105, 110, 178
in Methods model, 170–71, 179
predictability of its features, 123–27
provides access to full texts, 44, 118–
20
in Traditional Library Science model,
15–24, 42–43
and Type-of-Literature model, 62,
69
Clocks and watches, 31–32, 42, 81
Closure, 158, 177
Coates, Eric, 18
Computer databases, 59–60, 64, 67–69,
72–73, 100–101. *See also* Paper
sources vs. computers
in Methods model, 168–70
Computer terminals, physical arrangement of, 56, 168–70
Computer Workstation model, 103–12,
113–50, 140
compared to Traditional Library Science model, 53, 55, 140–48
privileging certain formats, 154
problems, 131–40, 147, 153–54
Concealed propositions, 113–15, 147,
153, 189–90
Concordances, 60
Copyright fees, 18, 24, 60, 126, 131–34,
141, 153, 186, 190, 218n.1
Corpus Reformatorum, 17
Cost factors in digitizing libraries, 134–
37, 153
Cross-disciplinary/cross-format appearances of subjects, 14. *See also* As-

pects of a subject; Scattering of
sources
in the class scheme, 22, 43
in directories, 13
in encyclopedias, 12–13
in indexes, 10–12, 86–88, 124, 158–
60, 168
and Methods model, 163, 164, 168,
171, 176
Cross-references
and Actual-Practice model, 81, 84–85,
86
in *LCSH,* 26, 30, 37, 43, 84–85, 86,
120, 121, 122
not in bookstacks, 21, 31, 42–43, 49,
81, 143, 152
not in index-Zs, 52
not in key word sources, 72–73, 90.
See also Key word access
through tracings, 37–39, 122
The Cult of Information, 145–46
Cutter, Charles Ammi, 18
Czechoslovakia, 20

Departmentalization of knowledge, 18–19
Depth of access
in Computer Workstation model, 24,
107–9, 113–15, 127, 130–31, 140–
41, 215n.2
to full texts in class scheme, 15–18,
24, 44, 49, 75, 118–20, 121, 123,
125–26, 129–31, 153–54, 186
in Subject model, 9, 57
Dewey Decimal Classification, 15, 20,
24, 46–47
Dictionaries, 58, 60, 61, 63
Directories, 13, 58, 60, 63, 64
Divine right of kings, 79–81
Document types. *See* Types of literature
Documentation movement, 103–4, 189–
90
"Don't ask for help" dictum, 6, 13, 168

Ease of access. *See* Principle of Least Ef-
fort
Electronic publishing in libraries, 188
Encyclopedias, 10, 12–13, 46, 58, 60,
61, 62, 63
ERIC thesaurus, 143–44

First Stop, 12, 165

Footnote chasing, 75, 76, 86, 88–89, 90, 95, 152. *See also* Actual-Practice model; Principle of Least Effort
Foreign language works
in class scheme, 126
findable through *LCSH*, 29, 85–86, 117–18, 122, 142–44
in Methods model, 157
overlooked, 127, 140, 189
Forgery, 37–40
Form subdivisions
and bibliographies, 54, 153
listing of, 201–14
and Methods model, 172, 175
and other subdivisions, 71, 83
and types of literature, 65–67, 71, 153, 172
Format of information, 73, 223, 226
Franklin, Benjamin, 50–51
Free-floating subdivisions, 53, 65–66, 83–84, 123
Full-text access. *See* Depth of access

General works (A classes), 46, 126
Government documents, 11, 44, 55, 64, 86, 87, 109, 124, 156, 163–64
Guide to Published Library Catalogs, 54, 165
Guide to Reference Books, 63, 70
Guides to the literature, 60, 63

Hamlet, 28
Handbooks, 61
Harvard, 19
Hazlitt, William, 21–22
Height arrangement of volumes, 16, 25
Highways, 115–16
Human nature, 132–33
Hypermedia connections, 110

Idea of a University, The, 182
Importance of some reference sources, 55, 156, 179
Index to classification scheme. See *Library of Congress Subject Headings*
Indexes to journal articles
in Computer Workstation model, 109
in Methods model, 158–65
overlooked by researchers, 23, 86–88, 152

shelved in A and Z classes, 45–46, 53–55
as type of literature, 58, 61, 63–64, 71
Index-Zs, 49–55, 69, 89, 155. *See also* Bibliographies
arrangement of, 193–200
Information Access Corporation, 161
International Group of Scientific, Technical, and Medical Publishers, 218n.1
International Publishers Association, 218n.1
Invisible college. *See* People sources

Journal articles. *See* Indexes to journal articles

Key word access, 4–5, 7, 12, 75
in Computer Workstation model, 107–9, 113–14
false drops, 6, 90, 115
in indexes of bibliographies, 7
in Methods model, 163–65, 169, 177
not a system, 89–90, 127
paper vs. computer formats, 72–73
problem of synonyms, 29, 33, 78, 90, 121–22
replacing *LCSH*, 113–14, 126–27, 141, 143, 146–47, 186
unlike controlled-vocabulary sources, 55, 71, 89–90, 100, 177

Laziness, 92, 98, 100. *See also* Principle of Least Effort
LCSH. See *Library of Congress Subject Headings*
Least Effort Principle. *See* Principle of Least Effort
Leeks, 31–32
Librarianship
contrasted to information science, 98, 155, 186–87, 190
duties of, 45, 56, 98–101, 113, 183–88, 190–91, 228, 229, 234, 240, 241
mistakes in, 146–47, 188–90
Library of Congress available online, 103, 105, 106, 114, 133–34, 137, 139
Library of Congress Classification, 15, 22, 45–46, 115, 121. *See also* Classification; Depth of access

Library of Congress Subject Headings.
See also Cross-references; Form
subdivisions; Precoordination of subject terms; Predictability; Serendipity; Specific entry; Tracings;
Uniform heading; Vocabulary control
and Computer Workstation model,
107, 113–14, 115–18, 120, 144–46
contrasted to key word/citation searching, 146–47
contrasted to thesauri, 143–44
for finding bibliographies, 54
as index to classification scheme, 25,
30–37, 39–40, 42, 75, 81, 86, 120,
125, 141–44, 147, 186, 215n.1
in journal indexes, 86–88, 116–17,
124, 160–62
kinds of subdivisions, 70–71, 82–84,
123
in Methods model, 160–63, 172, 175,
177
overlooked in Actual-Practice model,
75–90
solves synonym problems, 29–30, 37,
78, 121–22
in tracings, 37–40, 122
for types of literature, 64–69, 74, 123–
24, 172
Library Science model. *See* Traditional
Library Science model
Library without walls. *See* Virtual
library
Limiting sets, 85, 126
Lincoln, Abraham, 17
Lists of sources. *See also* Bibliographies
become outdated, 14, 22, 64
in Subject model, 9, 14, 57, 71, 151,
154
for types of literature, 63–64, 74

Machlup, Fritz, 19
Manuals, 61, 64
Marxist view of human nature, 132–34
Metal-working machinery, 31–32
Methods of searching, 55, 71, 89–90,
100–101, 146–47
benefits of model, 176–77, 181–83
components of model, 156–72
and librarians, 183–88
objections, 177–79

principles, 157–58, 160, 165, 171–72
relation to Type-of-Literature model,
71, 73, 172–76
Microforms, 44, 45, 55, 104–5, 133–34,
140, 156. *See also* Nonbook formats
in Methods model, 163, 166
Minimal level cataloging, 145
Models of research. *See also names of
individual models*
conceptual, vii, 3–4, 6–7, 15, 22, 24,
40, 42, 59, 73, 91, 156, 173–74
physical, 3, 7, 15, 22, 40, 42, 55–56,
73–74, 91, 100–101, 156–58, 173–
74
problems with existing models, 151–56
Modern Researcher, The, 79–80, 218n.2
Multidisciplinary range of subjects. *See*
Cross-disciplinary/cross-format appearances of subjects
Museum of Comparative Zoology, 19

Narrower terms. *See* Specific entry
National bibliography (Z1201–4980), 47,
50, 51, 124, 193
National Research Council, 137–38
Newman, Cardinal, 182
Newsletters, 61, 62
Nonbook formats
in bibliographies, 45, 49, 55,
124
in Computer Workstation model, 109,
154, 219n.1
Documentation movement, 103
in Methods model, 176
outside class scheme and catalog, 23,
44, 151
Novgorod, 118

OCR (optical character recognition) scanning, 134–36

Paper sources vs. computers
bibliographies, 5, 51, 82, 186
Computer Workstation, 106–11, 113–
15, 129–40
indexes, 72–73, 186
references, 99, 232
People sources. *See also* Directories
in Actual-Practice model, 76, 88, 89,
90, 95, 152
in Methods model, 166–68

Personal bibliography (Z8000s), 47, 50, 51, 124, 200
Physical size arrangement, 16
Point-of-use instruction, 162–70, 176
Postcoordination of subject terms, 117–18, 124, 129, 143, 189
Precoordination of subject terms, 117–18, 140–47, 172, 189. *See also* Form subdivisions; Subdivisions of headings
index to class scheme, 118, 120, 125, 141–43
recognition of search options, 117, 122–23, 128–29
Predictability, 121–27
in arranging bibliographies, 50–52
in categorizations, 26, 120, 143
lacking in key words, 89–90, 127, 147, 186
in Methods model, 181
in specific entry, 77
in types of literature, 57–59, 62, 64, 67, 74
Preservation
electronic formats, 15, 127, 137–39, 154, 186, 188, 190
microfilm, 134
reference list, 148–50
Primary literature, 60, 70
Principle of Least Effort, 42, 69, 76, 156, 163, 190
annotated bibliography, 221–42
and Computer Workstation model, 103, 106
and librarians' duties, 92, 98–101, 184
literature review, 91–101
and Methods model, 175
Privileging formats, 154, 219n.1
Psychological overload, 139–40, 176
Published bibliographies. *See* Bibliographies

Qaddafi, Muammar, 26–28

Raster scanning, 134–35
Recognition. *See* Precoordination of subject terms; Serendipity
Reference questions, 70, 71, 173–75
Relabelling books, 216n.3
Related-record searching, 55, 88–89, 155, 169–70, 216n.4

Relations of the USSR, 116
Research Guides, 64
Research questions, 70, 71, 173–75
Review articles, 61, 64, 68
Risley, 119
Roszak, Theodore, 145–46
Royalties. *See* Copyright fees

Sable, Martin, 64, 70
Satisficing, 93, 182, 190, 226, 237. *See also* Principle of Least Effort
Scattering of sources, 5–6, 16. *See also* Aspects of a subject; Cross-disciplinary/cross-format appearances of subjects; Key word access; Nonbook formats
in the catalog, 26, 29–30, 33, 37, 125
in the classification scheme, 20–23, 31–37, 42, 49, 51, 75, 81–86, 143, 151–52, 162, 164, 167
in directories, 13
in encyclopedias, 12–13
in indexes, 10–12, 87–88, 124, 158–60, 176
School discipline, 82, 218n.3
Scientific and Technical Information Sources, 63
Secondary literature, 60–61, 70
Serendipity, 127–29
in the classification scheme, 15, 118–20, 125–26, 130, 186
in *LCSH*, 117, 120, 126, 128–29, 143, 147, 186
in printed indexes, 72–73
Shelf-arrangement. *See* Classification
Shipwrecks, 31–32
Social status of librarians, 155, 188, 220n.2
Soviet Union, 116
Specific entry, 76–78, 80–81, 90, 122. *See also* Alphabetical adjacency of narrower terms in *LCSH*
Standards for transporting data, 138
Subdivisions of headings, 53, 70–71, 78, 82–84, 117–18, 120. *See also* Form subdivisions; *Library of Congress Subject Headings;* Precoordination of subject terms
Subject bibliography (Z5000–7999), 47, 50, 51–55, 124, 193–200

Subject/Discipline model, 9–14, 42, 52, 75
contrasted to Type-of-Literature model, 57, 59, 62–63, 67
correspondence to classification scheme, 15, 22, 23–24, 42, 55, 73, 151
limitations, 151, 154–55
and Methods model, 71, 156, 171, 177
Subject expertise, 9, 13, 42, 57, 120, 143, 155, 173, 190

Television graphics, 21
Tertiary literature, 61, 70
Thesauri compared to *LCSH*, 143–44
Tracings, 37–40, 78–79, 115, 120–22
link to classification scheme, 40, 125
Traditional Library Science model. *See also* Bibliographies; Classification; Vocabulary control
adequacy/inadequacy, 40–44, 53, 55–56, 104–10, 151, 154–55
bibliography/index component (Class Z), 45–56, 69–70
classification scheme component, 15–24, 42, 55, 62, 69, 73, 75, 120
compared to Computer Workstation model, 53, 55, 140–48
having three components, 24, 55, 69-70, 75, 104
vocabulary-controlled catalog component, 25–44, 69–71, 81, 120

Traveling saleswomen, 17–18
Treatises, 60, 61, 62, 64
Types of literature, 14, 42, 57–74, 123–24, 155. *See also* Form subdivisions
arrangement principle within bibliographies, 63–64, 172
document types in journals, 67–69, 72
as physical model, 69, 73–74, 173
for reference questions, 70–71, 172–75
relation to Methods model, 73, 172–75, 177

Uniform heading, 29–30, 76–77, 90, 121–22, 128
Uniform title, 28–29
Union lists, 62

Venice, 85
Virtual library, 103–6, 110, 131–40, 153, 178, 188
Vocabulary control, 25–44, 64, 107, 113–14. See also *Library of Congress Subject Headings*
in journal indexes, 161–62
lacking in index-Zs, 52
overlooked in Actual-Practice model, 75–90

Whistler, Anna, 118–19
Wilson indexes, 161, 178

Yearbooks, 62, 64

Z classes, 46–55, 193–200